C000144382

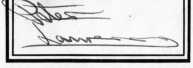

LONDON, 1990

B210 © APCo

The lower deck
of the Royal Navy
1900–39

Lional Yexley (James Woods), 1860–1933

ANTHONY CAREW

The lower deck
of the Royal Navy
1900–39

The Invergordon mutiny
in perspective

MANCHESTER
UNIVERSITY PRESS

Copyright © A. B. Carew 1981

Published by
Manchester University Press
Oxford Road, Manchester M13 9PL

British Library cataloguing in publication data

Carew, Anthony
  The lower deck of the Royal Navy.
  1. Great Britain. *Royal Navy* – History – 20th
  century 2. Great Britain. *Royal Navy* – Sea life
  I. Title
  359.1   VB258.5.G7

  ISBN 0–7190–0841–7

Photoset in Plantin by
Northern Phototypesetting Company
Bolton
Printed in Great Britain by
Redwood Burn Limited
Trowbridge, Wiltshire

Contents

Illustrations

Acknowledgements

Any writer of history is bound to be indebted to many people. I owe a particular debt to one man, without whose help this book could not have been written. Indeed, in a sense this is *his* history. Commander Harry Pursey, RN, was actively involved in some of the developments the book records, and after retiring from the Navy in 1936 he set about collecting the material for a social history of the lower deck during his period of service. It was only through access to this material and with his constant help and encouragement that I was even able to make a start on a history of the lower-deck reform movement.

Born in Sidmouth, Devon, in 1891, the son of a former naval rating and the grandson of a Royal Marine, Harry Pursey was educated at the Royal Hospital School, Greenwich, the Navy's orphanage, and joined the service in 1907 as a boy seaman. His first ship was the old 'wooden wall' training ship *Impregnable* at Devonport and his first commission was spent in the Mediterranean in the battleship *Ocean*. He qualified as a seaman torpedoman and then served for two years in the new battlecruiser *Indefatigable* attached to the Home Fleet. There he became actively involved in the lower-deck movement and helped to found the Royal Naval Seamen's Benefit Society, of which he became president in 1913. At this time he was also close to Lionel Yexley, the leading figure in the reform movement.

During the early part of the Great War Pursey served on board the light cruiser *Adventure* on the Dover patrol and then, as a torpedo instructor, was drafted to the new battleship *Revenge* and took part in the battle of Jutland. He was promoted to petty officer in 1916, then to warrant officer, and was recommended for a commission. As torpedo officer on the light cruiser *Forward* in the Aegean Squadron he was landed in the Greek islands to evacuate stores and bombs and was mentioned in dispatches. At the end of 1917 he was promoted to the commissioned rank of mate.

After the war Pursey saw considerable overseas service in the *Ark Royal* in the Black Sea and the Persian Gulf. In 1922 he was promoted to lieutenant and served in the Anti-submarine Flotilla and later as minelaying officer of the Atlantic Fleet destroyer flotillas, before seeing further service in the Mediterranean. Promoted to lieutenant-commander in 1928, he served for some time as the commander of the minesweeper *Dunoon* before being drafted to the aircraft carrier *Eagle* in the Mediterranean once more. This commission was cut short in 1930 by a recall to the Admiralty for special duty with a committee appointed by the First Lord, A. V. Alexander, to inquire into the system of commissions from the ranks. He greatly influenced the work of the committee, under whose subsequent recommendations officers commissioned from the lower deck received, for the first time, the same rank, pay, training and (theoretically) the same opportunities as cadet-entry officers.

Pursey's last ship was the battlecruiser *Hood*, then the largest warship in the world. In two and a half years as training officer and commander's assistant he travelled to the West Indies and French North Africa as well as being present during the mutiny at Invergordon in 1931.

On leaving the service Harry Pursey became a freelance journalist, writing as naval correspondent for a number of national and provincial newspapers. In 1937 he went to Spain and campaigned actively in British political circles for the breaking of the blockade imposed on Bilbao by the Nationalist forces. Later, as the Nationalist army gained control of the coastal towns, he helped organise the evacuation of some 60,000 Basque and Republican refugees. In the absence of a British consul in Santander he took on the functions of one himself before eventually escaping with a small party in a motorboat in August 1937.

During World War II he was a lecturer for the Ministry of Information and Army Welfare. It was in these years after leaving the Navy that Pursey began amassing his private collection of lower-deck ephemera, including the papers of his old colleague Lionel Yexley, Stephen Reynolds, the Devonshire fisherman and writer on naval affairs, and Lieutenant H. D. Capper, former leader of the Warrant Officers' Society. He wrote three important articles for *Brassey's Naval Annual* in the late 1930s which were meant as a skeleton for a

future social history of the lower deck. However, that history was
never written. In 1945 Harry Pursey stood for Parliament in Hull
East and became the first ex-lower-deck naval officer to sit in the
House of Commons as a Labour MP. He held his seat for twenty-five
years before standing down in 1970 at the age of seventy-nine. In
retirement he spent his whole time until his death in December 1980
assisting the steady stream of social and naval historians who sought
his help. I was one of them, and in return can do no more than dedicate
this history to his memory.

Well over a hundred former naval officers and ratings have also
helped with information. Some of them had distinguished careers, a
few achieved notoriety, but most remain obscure, no more than an
entry in a dusty ledger in the Admiralty basement. There is not room
here to list all their names, but some gave particular assistance and
must be mentioned. They appear not in order of seniority or
importance but in alphabetical order as befits a history of a movement
which aimed in part at democratising the Navy. Grateful thanks are
extended to CPO Telegraphist C. Beecroft, CPO F. J. Brooks, CPO F.
W. P. Brown, AB John Bush, Rear-Admiral R. Cobb, AB Fred
Copeman, CPO J. G. Cox, AB George Day, Commander Charles
Drage, Lieutenant-Commander M. J. W. Ellingworth, AB Len Fagg,
ERA Lewis Hanbidge, Commissioned Gunner George Hill, CPO
Stephen Hill, Commander Frederick Hodgson, Wing Commander G.
W. Jordan, Stoker B. Jowett, Chief Writer J. E. Kinnear,
Commissioned ERA F. C. Love, Captain W. R. Michell, Admiral of
the Fleet the late Earl Mountbatten of Burma, Chief Yeoman Roland
Purvis, Commander R. H. S. Rodger and AB Len Wincott.

My good friend Walter Kendall was the person who first awakened
my interest in the subject of radicalism in the Navy and convinced me
that a history of the reform movement was feasible. He and Pam
Kendall were also responsible for my introduction to Harry Pursey.
Most of the research was done with the aid of a Social Science
Research Council grant and a research fellowship at Sussex
University, where Asa Briggs encouraged the project and Keith
Middlemas gave me much valuable advice. Stephen Yeo and Bryan
Ranft both read the text in an earlier form and made helpful
comments. My parents, Catherine and A. J. Carew, undertook the
tedious work of transcribing taped interviews; Marjorie Abrahams
made my periods of research in London much more pleasant than they
would otherwise have been, and Christine Theobold typed successive

drafts with great diligence. Finally, my thanks to Vera and Edith Marsh, who sat through endless hours of lower-deck discussion with amazing forbearance.

Various people and institutions have generously made papers available to me. I wish to thank Mrs J. Nutting for access to the Beatty papers; Mrs Dorothy Pickering for access to the papers of Marine George Davis; the trustees of the Broadlands Archives for access to the Battenberg papers; Captain Stephen Roskill for access to his own Invergordon collection; C & T Publications Ltd for access to the papers of Sir Winston Churchill. I am also grateful for the permission of Her Majesty the Queen to make use of the naval papers of King George V. Finally, generous assistance was given by the staff of the Public Record Office, the Imperial War Museum, the National Maritime Museum, the Admiralty Library, the British Museum, the library of Churchill College, Cambridge, and the National Library of Scotland.

Introduction

[. . .] let the nation fully realise that no great measure of reform will ever be initiated by the Navy from within. It is a viciously conservative service, and had ever resisted progress. – Lionel Yexley, *Our Fighting Sea Men* (Stanley Paul, 1911)

For much of the first thirty years of this century lower-deck ratings in the Royal Navy conducted an important campaign to improve their service conditions. This book sets out to chronicle the development of that reform movement.

That naval conditions were such as to warrant a protracted campaign for reform is little known: still less known is the fact that ratings themselves organised to secure changes. Nevertheless between the 1890s, when at times nearly 100 men were deserting from the Navy each month because of the harshness of lower-deck life, and 1931, when upwards of 12,000 men of the Atlantic Fleet mutinied in protest over a drastic cut in pay, a long list of 'disabilities' provided a continuing focus for lower-deck organisation and agitation. Between these two dates the campaigning was not always even and consistent, and there were noticeable variations in its effectiveness. Broadly speaking, the movement grew in strength to reach a high point at the end of the Great War. Thereafter it declined, and in retrospect the years 1919–20 can be seen as the climacteric.

In 1917–18 sailors of the Russian Baltic Fleet and the German High Seas Fleet mutinied and in so doing helped spark off a train of events which led, in both cases, to revolution. No such development occurred in Britain, and it may even be that the absence of a revolt in the armed services was a key factor ensuring that the highly volatile political situation did not follow the pattern of Russia and Germany. How are these differences in national experiences to be explained?

Certainly there were dissimilarities in the circumstances of Russian and German sailors on the one hand and the lower deck of the Royal Navy on the other. In the former, for example, ratings were not volunteers, were subject to a much more autocratic system of command, and in the latter part of the war were suffering far worse conditions.[1] But it would be wrong to suggest that there was never any likelihood of British sailors rebelling too.

In fact there was considerable unrest in the Royal Navy in the final stages of the war and the immediate post-war period. What prevented it from boiling over, and hence made the crucial difference from the Russian and German navies, was that the Royal Navy allowed the ratings a controlled outlet for ventilating their grievances. Moreover, such improvements in conditions as had taken place in the previous decade or so were almost entirely the result of lower-deck representations. In other words, the system had a built-in safety valve which, however limited and unsatisfactory, gave ratings some hope of amelioration. In view of this it is ironic that just twelve years later, in a political climate far less troubled than that of 1919, the Royal Navy experienced a major shock in the form of the mutiny at Invergordon. How was it that the government and the naval authorities who had successfully negotiated a difficult and tense period of lower-deck unrest in 1918–20 blundered into a situation where men were forced to protest so dramatically in 1931?

The explanation is to be found in the long history of relations between the lower deck and the Admiralty during the early decades of the century, in the interplay of forces between an active campaign for reform and the naval authorities' attempts to accommodate themselves to it while maintaining control of the lower deck. That is the subject of the book. It is an attempt to account for the rise and subsequent decline of an organised movement which at times proved very influential but which ultimately failed to find a lasting role.

Consideration of this raises the wider question of collective organisation in disciplined, uniformed services, and here the Navy provides an interesting case study. While the Russian and German sailors of 1917–18 may have demonstrated in a dramatic way some of the wider implications of collective organisation by service personnel in a revolutionary situation, the protracted (and ultimately unsuccessful) attempts of British naval ratings to secure a mechanism for collective representation within the existing system highlight many of the difficulties of establishing such an arrangement in conditions of relative stability. What the lower-deck reform movement achieved between 1900 and the 1930s, and why it failed in the end, are matters of some significance, not only for an understanding of the period in question but also for the recently revived debate in various countries about the possibility of, and prospects for, trade unionism in the armed services.

HISTORICAL BACKGROUND

From the point of view of the lower deck the modern Navy dates only from 1853, when continuous service was introduced. Men now signed on for a ten-year period, with the prospect of a full twenty-year career and a pension ahead of them.[2] No longer would they be recruited for a single commission in a ship of their own choosing. However, the opportunity to revolutionise conditions presented by the creation of a full-time, professional body of continuous service ratings was not seized. Certain improvements followed, but in many important respects life on the lower deck remained much as it had always been.[3]

The lack of reform in conditions of service was emphasised all the more by rapid advances in naval technology. The Crimean war was the occasion of a sudden leap from the 120 gun wooden line-of-battle ship to the iron frigate carrying thirty guns and 1,000 tons of four-inch armour plating.[4] Steam power began to replace masts and sails; and major developments in weaponry began with the replacement of the smooth-bore muzzle-loading gun by the breech-loader, and later the arrival of the torpedo, the mine and the submarine. The foundation of the Royal United Service Institute in 1860 reflected this quickening interest in the technology of warfare.[5] True, naval conservatives fought a strong rearguard action against these developments, and progress was often delayed. But the revolution in *matériel* was undeniable, advances being registered even amidst the financial stringency of the Gladstone administrations, with the result that the pre-Dreadnought warships of the turn of the century bore no resemblance to the ships of the Navy on the eve of the Crimean war.

How then can we briefly sum up lower-deck life on the eve of the twentieth century? The late nineteenth-century Navy was in a state of general stagnation. No major sea battle had been fought since Trafalgar, and the absence of any obvious rival power bred an atmosphere of complacency. The service was hidebound by tradition, and it was often the less glorious side of tradition that most affected the lower deck.

In spite of occasional improvements in dietary, the basis of victualling bore more than a passing resemblance to the system in force in Nelson's day. Discipline was extremely harsh, and although flogging and capital punishment had ceased, day-to-day discipline was as arbitrary as it had been a century earlier.[6] The power of a captain on board his ship was all but absolute. Courts martial operated without regard to elementary principles of justice. Five years' penal servitude was a standard punishment for offences which in civilian courts would not have merited a prison sentence at all. The regime in naval prisons was intended to degrade rather than reform, and for trivial offences the Navy operated a range of humiliating summary punishments under which men were treated as children.

Basic pay remained static for over fifty years after 1853, and, although extra payments for particular ratings and skills were introduced from time to time, they were only doled out in pennies and halfpennies. The pensions which were supposed to compensate for low pay went only to men who had completed twenty-two years. There was none for the man invalided out before his time was up, nor for the dependants of those who died in the service.

During the nineteenth century the tradition of the 'tarpaulin' captain rising by merit alone had died out, and the prospects of promotion to the quarter deck were practically nil. In the eighty years after 1818 only two men of lower-deck origin were promoted to lieutenant, and then for gallantry, not as part of a normal career progression.[7] The Navy was frozen into rigid classes, and the gulf between quarter deck and lower deck was wider than it had ever been.

To a considerable extent the pattern of life on board ship was dictated by social considerations, not by the needs of efficiency. This, of course, affected the work the lower deck were expected to do. While the men were being taught special skills in navigation, signalling, gunnery, torpedoes and electricity, the most important thing was spit-and-polish. Everything was sacrificed to making the vessel look pretty.[8] Brasswork was polished, and iron bag racks, stanchions and even iron ring bolts on the decks were filed and burnished. Watertight doors were so worn with constant polishing that in some cases they no longer served their purpose.[9] And to prevent decks from being soiled and paintwork blistered during the quarterly heavy-gunnery practice it was not unusual for ammunition to be thrown overboard rather than fired; all this so that the ship might have the appearance of a yacht.[10] The mentality of some of those in command can be judged from the fact that, despite the calibre of the equipment at their disposal, mechanical instruction finally replaced mast and sail drill as the basis of seamen's training only in 1903, after a lengthy battle; even then boarding pikes were still being carried in ships.[11]

In this environment little thought was given to the interests of the men: the Navy accepted few responsibilities towards the lower deck. Their intellectual life was completely ignored. Once a boy joined a seagoing ship his formal education came to an end. No regular classes were provided, only the instruction a few officers gave voluntarily. Libraries were either non-existent or consisted of a few antiquated religious tracts.[12] Generally, men were not encouraged to read. Recreational needs were also neglected. At the home ports the Navy accepted no responsibility for the welfare of ratings on leave. No places were provided where they could relax in clean, congenial surroundings; they were simply turned loose and left to choose between the low pubs and brothels or the temperance missions.

If the domestic conditions of the service had hardly improved, the social environment from which it drew its recruits was undergoing far-reaching changes, especially in the closing decades of the century. The trade union movement was beginning to extend to the poorest grades of unskilled workers, and socialist ideas were gaining currency among the working class.[13] Traditionally the Navy had drawn its manpower from the dockyard towns and rural areas, but a larger proportion of men were now joining from the industrial districts where these developments were most advanced.[14] It was, therefore, inevitable that the new values should find an echo on the lower deck. The standard of living of common people was improving, and the argument no longer held that ratings would accept the degradation and squalor of lower-deck life because they knew no better. The sailors of the last decades of the nineteenth century were less prepared than their forbears to accept unquestioningly a way of life that had remained unchanged for so long: they were conscious that they too had civil rights and a dignity that demanded respect. It was among this generation of ratings that the movement to reform lower-deck conditions began. From the 1890s to the 1930s the movement strove with some success to improve the lot of the ordinary rating. In so doing it helped to drag the Navy into the twentieth century.

THE NATURE OF THE LOWER DECK

Before turning to the reform campaign itself it is necessary to look briefly at the lower deck to see what it consisted of. Naval ratings were not a homogeneous group. Theirs was a complex, stratified community – a collection of many distinct groups fragmented by branch, rank and informal status, and divided geographically into three port divisions. Men whose homes were in London, East Anglia and the North-east joined the Chatham Division; Portsmouth ratings came primarily from Hampshire, the Midlands and Scotland; while Devonport ships were manned largely by people from the West Country, Wales, Ireland and the North-west.

An initial analysis of the lower deck reveals half a dozen different functions: executive-military, engineer, artisan, medical, accountant and police. Within these functions there were further subdivisions into occupational groups, resulting in a score of different branches or classes of rating. The relative numerical strength of the more important ones is indicated by the following figures taken from one year, 1919:

Seamen	46,802	Armourers	938
Stokers	30,477	Electrical artificers	932
ERAs and mechanicians	5,042	Ships' stewards	697
Officers' stewards and cooks	4,598	Blacksmiths	391
		Joiners	311
Signalmen	4,476	Painters	266
Telegraphists	4,065	Plumbers	236
Cooks	1,994	Coopers	212
Sick-berth stewards	1,492	Carpenters' crews	163
Shipwrights	1,332	Sailmakers	101
Writers	952	Miscellaneous	1,262[15]

Two important groups not listed here are the Royal Marines – half sailors, half soldiers – and the warrant officers, one of the oldest ranks in the service, though becoming anomalous in this period and existing uneasily in the no-man's-land between lower and quarter deck. Each of the branches tended to be self-contained and inward-looking. The smaller ones in particular were often tight-knit, while the divisions *between* branches could be wide. One of the consequences was that it was always difficult for the reform movement to present a united front.

Seamen, the largest branch on the lower deck, joined the service as boys aged fifteen to sixteen and a half. They served for twelve years from the age of eighteen, and most were eligible to sign on again for a second period of ten years in order to complete time for pension. There was always a strong tendency for recruits to come from naval families in the home ports and neighbouring districts. Many others joined straight from orphanages, or perhaps industrial training ships, most seeking adventure but some simply escape from an unhappy home life. Most other branches of the service recruited personnel at a later age. This was certainly the case with engine-room artificers (ERAs) as well as the various grades of artisan tradesmen and the stokers. Such people would have had experience of industry and possibly of trade unionism before they joined up – a factor tending to encourage lower-deck organisation. For men with a trade union background, first contact with naval discipline could be a jarring experience. One lower-deck writer, Sidney Knock, records that many artisans were severely punished for refusing to perform tasks outside their specialisation and demanding to work at their trade.[16] Partly because of this disruptive influence, the Navy tended over a period of time to increase the percentage of ratings recruited as youths and trained by the service itself. But in the 1930s there were still some ordnance artificers, electricians, artisans, sick-berth stewards, armourers and accountant branch ratings who joined as men.[17]

In the course of the early decades of the century, with the service becoming more technical, it was frequently observed that the quality of the lower deck was improving in the sense that men were often better educated.[18] As a natural consequence they were more inclined to expect to be treated with dignity and to be aware that they had rights as well as responsibilities. The backcloth to much of the campaigning for reforms was precisely a tension between the quest on their part for respectability and a tendency for the Navy to treat them at times as children, at times as criminals, but rarely as responsible citizens in naval uniform.

Many read newspapers and journals, discussed issues that affected them and were conversant with contemporary affairs. In 1909 ratings in the *Albemarle*, for example, ran a Mutual Improvement and Debating Society and sponsored lectures on subjects ranging from Esperanto to socialism.[19] Sailors were often keen to better themselves, to improve their qualifications and to equip themselves for employment in Civvy Street. For this reason there was pressure for more education to be provided, and when it was not forthcoming some set about making their own arrangements for further education through correspondence courses. In the middle of the Great War it was estimated that some 280 warships had crew members enrolled in such courses, and so great was the interest that the International Corresponding School actually created a special department to deal with naval students.[20]

This new generation of ratings rejected the popular caricature of naval personnel. They resented the image of the jolly drunken sailor, especially when it was tied up with charity appeals to the public for help in the work of saving their souls. As George Crowe, former master-at-arms of HMS *Terrible*, wrote in 1903:

It is most difficult to impress the perhaps well-intentioned – but too often meddlesome – philanthropist, that the British man-of-warsmen of this age are not the socially forlorn type of humanity so vividly depicted in nautical novels, and that they view with deserved contempt and derision the 'naval slumming' and the contents of the many tons of childish literature with which ships are futilely flooded. [. . .] Bluejackets do not profess to be saints, neither can they be classed as special sinners. On board they are disciplined machines of war; on shore they are law-abiding citizens in the fullest sense of the term.[21]

Reversing the tradition of earlier years, growing numbers were marrying while in the service, and much of the pressure for better treatment from the Admiralty was prompted by a desire to see that naval wives were not made to suffer indignity and privation on account of being married to a rating. Until World War I the Navy did not even recognise their existence, appearing to operate on the old assumption that the sailor was simply a roving adventurer with a wife in every port. Until much later still, widows of ratings who died other than in battle received no pension, nor did the widows of naval pensioners. Issues such as these were to become major causes of resentment and discontent. By 1912 it was estimated that about ten per cent of junior ratings were married and fully two-thirds of all petty officers had a wife and family to support.[22] It was predominantly among such men – staid, respectable hands, most of them career sailors who had signed on a second time with a view to completing twenty-two years for a pension – that the reform movement developed. It is primarily on them, the natural leaders of the lower deck, that our study concentrates.

Officers have observed manifestations of socialistic doctrines among the inferior men for some time. [. . .] Of course their methods are dangerous and must be dealt with drastically, and it's far better to allow the officers to deal with their own men promptly, than that the men should imagine that such acts can be delayed for reference to a higher authority! – Vice-Admiral Sir Francis Bridgeman, Second Sea Lord, letter to Reginald McKenna, First Lord of the Admiralty, 17 January 1910.

More than once I have heard fathers say to their sons [. . .] 'You won't be able to speak to them in the Navy like you've spoken to me before now. You mustn't even speak up for yourself when you're put upon and in the right. Just you mind that. You'll be a marked man if you do. The way to get on in the Navy is to lie low, whatever happens, and jog along quiet, and take what comes, glad that it isn't no worse.' – Stephen Reynolds, *Seems So!* (1911), pp. 224–5.

During my boyhood and adolescence, and subsequently in the Army, I conformed. The world in which I was brought up demanded that. Yet in the kingdom of my mind I walked alone. – Lord Wigg, *George Wigg* (1972), p. 13.

ONE

The origins of the reform movement

The Navy is a Conservative Service; it will accept reform as an act of grace when agitation has made it impossible to stand longer against it, but to alter things – no matter how much the alteration may be needed – without agitation is against its tenets [. . .]. – *The Fleet,* February 1910

Dockies, brickies and navvies on shore have their unions to look after their affairs. There can be no unions or strikes in the British Navy, but there might easily be common and constitutional action among fleetmen to place their grievances before the public in a way which would arouse sufficient interest, sympathy and help for the worst of them to be redressed. – *The Bluejacket,* July 1900

FIRST BEGINNINGS

The reform movement was based on the campaigns of the lower-deck press and organised around a number of lower-deck death benefit societies formed in the late nineteenth and early twentieth centuries. The first organisation in the field was the Naval Warrant Officers' Friendly Society, originally formed in Devonport in 1792 and reconstituted in 1877.[1] It was followed by the RN Artificer Engineer and Engine-Room Artificers' Club and Benevolent Fund, founded in 1872.[2] In the course of the 1880s death benefit societies were set up by executive petty officers, firemen, chief and leading stokers, chief petty officers and writers,[3] while the following decade saw the creation of similar organisations catering for plumbers, coopers, shipwrights and domestics.[4] This brought the total number of lower-deck organisations around the turn of the century to twelve.[5]

The death benefit societies came into being because the widows of ratings not killed in action, received no pension. Consequently the men themselves had to provide what the State denied, some form of insurance so that their dead messmates could be buried decently and their dependants helped over the initial period of bereavement. But besides their official benefit functions the societies had other interests, the most important being to campaign for a redress of disabilities and to advance the claims of their members.

The chosen method of pressing for reform was to issue petitions or memorials to the Admiralty or to Parliament through the medium of civilians or MPs. The practice of petitioning was deeply rooted. In 1654 a council of war on board HMS *Swiftsure*, consisting of two admirals and seventeen captains, convened to consider a petition from the seamen of the fleet, resolved unanimously that it was lawful for the seamen to present their grievances in this way and that the latter should be forwarded to the Protector.[6] It was only after the Admiralty had failed to deal with the men's petition in 1796 that the Spithead mutiny of the following year occurred. And in 1858 the Warrant Officers' Society presented a petition containing proposals for improving conditions to the Royal Commission on Naval Manning, actually appearing and giving evidence in support of its submission.[7] As Commander C. N. Robinson, the naval writer, noted, 'The student of naval history cannot fail to be struck with the circumstance that every increase of pay or privilege was brought about by petitions.'[8]

Officers, too, employed the device to publicise their grievances, issuing petitions in the eighteenth century through the Amicable Naval Society. However, in 1860 the Admiralty moved to stop the practice. A petition signed by all the lieutenants of the Channel Fleet was answered with a circular letter which declared:

All combinations of persons belonging to the fleet [. . .] are prohibited. Individuals are not to combine, either by the appointment of committees or in any other manner, for the purpose of obtaining signatures to memorials, petitions or applications, nor are they collectively to sign any such document.[9]

The circular was subsequently incorporated into Queen's Regulations as Article 10.[10] Henceforth it was illegal to meet to discuss or take action on any collective grievance, and the maximum penalty for breaking the regulation was death.

It was under the shadow of this regulation that the emerging lower-deck societies of the late nineteenth century had to operate. Up to the 1880s the Warrant Officers' Society, which in the past had openly petitioned for improvements, employed a pensioned paymaster (no longer subject to naval discipline) to process its occasional 'Grievance

Circulars', later known as 'Earnest Appeals'.[11] The new societies too began to issue appeals from time to time, sometimes on issues that related to their branch only, and on other occasions working in concert with the warrant officers and naval dockyard employees.[12] In most cases pensioner members or outsiders would be deputed to contact sympathetic MPs and ask them to raise the matter with the Admiralty. An exception here was the Writers' Society, which shunned the hurly-burly of open agitation and, operating more as a Masonic lodge, relied on the influence it could exert among officers to bring the writers' case before the Admiralty.[13] Members of the engine-room artificers', plumbers', carpenters' and shipwrights' societies often still belonged to their respective trade union, and contact with MPs tended to be made by means of the union machinery. The Associated Shipwrights' Society petitioned the Admiralty in 1896 over the treatment of naval shipwrights as unskilled men and their relatively low pay. However, the Admiralty rejected the society's claim to speak for its members in the service.[14] A similar objection to trade union influence among ERAs was partly responsible for the Admiralty decision to train its own boy artificers from 1903 rather than rely on skilled men recruited from industry.[15]

The most vigorous of the early campaigns for reform was begun in 1890 by the Warrant Officers' Society under the leadership of Gunner Henry Capper. Its basic aim was to secure a regular channel of promotion to commissioned rank for warrant officers. Capper was attached to the Naval Ordnance Department at the Admiralty, and so was well placed to lead the lobbying of journalists and Members of Parliament. Over a nine-month period in 1890 he had some thirty letters published, mostly in the service press, and this prompted a number of leading articles on the subject of warrant officer promotions.[16] He drafted an Earnest Appeal in 1891 on behalf of the society, and arrangements were made for it to be brought before the House of Commons by Captain Price, the Tory MP for Devonport. However, Price's handling of the case in the Navy Estimates debate was inept, and it was evident that he carried little influence with his fellow Tories.[17]

The warrant officers concluded that a more fundamental approach was needed, and, in view of the fact that Devonport was a marginal constituency, they proposed to mobilise those among them who had the vote to unseat Price by supporting the local Liberal candidates at the next general election. In a letter to the *Naval and Military Record*

Capper, writing under a pseudonym, spoke of the need to distinguish between friends and foes and to capture all the naval constituencies in the seamen's interest.[18] At Portsmouth a meeting of representatives of most branches of the lower deck was convened to discuss the idea, but no agreement could be reached and it was left to each branch to act as it thought fit.[19] At Devonport it was reported that 138 warrant officers had pledged to support the Liberal candidates, but this was thought to be sufficient; in the August general election Price was defeated and Hudson Kearley and E. J. Morton were elected for the two-seat constituency.[20]

Yet, despite their efforts in Parliament, Morton and Kearley were no more successful than Price had been in securing concessions for the warrant officers, and the society began to cast around for other allies. In early 1893 a meeting of spokesmen from the societies representing warrant officers, stokers, painters and chief petty officers was held at the Speedwell Hotel in Portsmouth to discuss the idea of bringing all the societies into one federation.[21] In November 1893 Capper represented the Warrant Officers' Society at a meeting of the executive of Havelock Wilson's National Sailors' and Firemen's Union, one-third of whose members belonged to the naval reserve and therefore had a considerable interest in lower-deck conditions. The meeting adopted a resolution supporting the warrant officers' demands, and Wilson agreed to take up their case with the First Lord of the Admiralty. Capper subsequently proposed that the Warrant Officers' Society should contribute to the union's strike fund to cement the bond between the two organisations.[22] Five months later, in April 1894, he was in touch with the secretary of the London Trades Council and was proposing to his society that it should affiliate to that body.[23]

There is no evidence that these initiatives produced any results. Certainly the petitioning of the Admiralty and Parliament was largely ineffective. Throughout the 1890s the warrant officers failed to make any progress towards their primary objective – a path of promotion to the rank of lieutenant; time after time the chief petty officers failed in their effort to secure an increase in their members' pension, and in 1900 the Firemen's Society admitted that its petitioning had gone unrewarded.[24] The fact is that even within the service the societies were little known and carried little weight: membership was confined to a minority of petty officers; the grievances were aired in most cases by a small section of the lower deck; and the MPs who were expected to plead their case were rarely well informed about lower-deck matters.

LIONEL YEXLEY AND *THE BLUEJACKET*

What was lacking was the means by which the more general grievances could be publicised in the country at large to mobilise public opinion. Despite the fact that national newspapers devoted a good deal of space to naval matters, their interest in, or understanding of, lower-deck affairs was strictly limited, while the service press, run by officers, rarely paid any attention to the ratings and was scarcely better informed about their conditions than Fleet Street. Serving men were forbidden under Article 12 of Queen's Regulations to write to the press or communicate information about the service to outside bodies. Letters to newspapers might be published under a pen name, though apart from the warrant officers' efforts there was little of this. In general the appellation 'the Silent Service' was apt.

In 1888 a group of warrant officers associated with Capper had taken over a small magazine, *Our Gazette*, with a circulation of 500, which they published privately. In 1893 it became the monthly *Naval Warrant Officers' Journal*. Capper was the editor until 1894, and the Secretary to the Board of Admiralty let him know unofficially that as long as the paper was moderate in tone the strict terms of Article 12 would not be enforced against him.[25] The lower deck were not the only uniformed personnel who found it necessary to have their own journal to publicise their grievances. In 1893 a rank-and-file policemen's paper, *The Police Review*, was established, and the following year the editor, John Kempster, helped to form the Police and Citizens' Friendly Association to promote the reform of conditions.[26] However, a real campaigning lower-deck equivalent of *The Police Review* that spoke not just for a sectional interest such as the warrant officers, but for the entire lower deck, did not appear until 1898, when *The Bluejacket* was first published under the editorship of Lionel Yexley.

Yexley, whose real name was James Woods, was an ex-petty officer and was to play a dominant role in the reform movement during the next thirty years. Joining the Navy in 1879, he transferred to the coastguard service in 1890 and began to take an interest in coastguards' disabilities, narrowly escaping a court martial in 1895 for his part in organising a petition for better pay. Two years later, while still in the service, he accepted the editorship of *Hope: the*

Coastguard Gazette, a two-page advertising broadsheet which had printed a number of his letters and was owned by the small mail-order jewellery firm of J. N. Masters Ltd, of Rye.[27] It was then that he assumed the pen name Lionel Yexley. Realising the potential for a full-scale lower-deck paper, he purchased his discharge in 1898, forfeiting the pension he would shortly have been entitled to, and joined Masters as a clerk with responsibility for editing the paper. The following year he redesigned the *Gazette,* renamed it, and in October 1898 published the first edition of *The Bluejacket and Coastguard Gazette.*

From the start the newspaper's aim was clear: to give maximum publicity to the serious grievances that existed on the lower deck.

[. . .] injustices under which Bluejackets labour have been commited 'in a corner' long enough, and we want your support, so that in future they may have the 'full blaze of publicity'.[28]

It saw its role as radically different from that of the established service journals. They were the medium '[. . .] through which the officers speak to the men and tell them what to do', while *The Bluejacket* was a means by which '[. . .] bluejackets speak to their officers and the Admiralty and tell them what they want'.[29]

But its tone was, of necessity, moderate. Yexley's belief was that 'A moderately conducted bluejackets' paper, by and for bluejackets, is a necessary safety-valve for bluejackets' feelings, and we only tell our readers to trust us and stick to moderate methods [. . .]. These things [reforms] may not come as fast as either ourselves or our readers would like. But we must not [. . .] resort to other methods on that account.'[30] Moreover the paper went out of its way to stress that it had no complaint against officers as such; there was no hint of mutiny behind the grievances it aired.[31]

Such disclaimers were necessary, especially for a crusading journal. In criticising naval administration Yexley was running a grave risk. It was true that he was no longer subject to naval discipline and could not be threatened with the loss of his pension, but it was very much in the Admiralty's power to close the paper down. Indeed, in the early months of its existence Yexley claimed that strong representations were made to the Admiralty by retired officers belonging to the United Service Club and the Navy League to have it suppressed. In later years he learned that the Admiralty had considered what charges could be brought, but that since he was in possession of much evidence of corruption in the service it was judged unwise to draw attention to the matter.[32]

The Board of Admiralty were not the only people who would have been happier without the criticisms of *The Bluejacket*. Corruption may have been a result of lax administration at the higher levels, but there were many beneficiaries on the lower deck, particularly among naval police. In some cases ships' police took it upon themselves to prevent copies of the paper from coming on board.[33] Moreover a ship's commander was empowered at any time to invoke the regulations regarding trafficking and so prevent its sale on board. This was a common ploy to keep ships free from radical literature and was to be used in later years against *Reynolds's News* and the *Daily Herald*.

Despite its avowed moderation *The Bluejacket* was more hard-hitting than any other paper dealing with service matters, and its influence soon began to be felt. It campaigned effectively for improvements in the Navy's victualling arrangements, the system of punishments, promotion prospects and other issues. But it was not solely concerned with the narrow interests of the lower deck. As the voice of the career sailor *The Bluejacket* was also interested in the efficiency of the Navy as a fighting force, and it supported progressive officers who were struggling to revolutionise the service. It led the criticism of the Navy's inefficient gunnery, and pressed for the publication of gunnery returns. It was also among the first to draw attention to the fact that practice ammunition was being thrown overboard, something that no officer would ever admit. Yexley and *The Bluejacket* could therefore claim considerable credit for subsequent improvements in the accuracy of firing.[34]

The newspaper's radical bias soon increased the circulation. When Yexley took over the editorship it was under 2,000. By May 1899 5,000 copies were being distributed monthly.[35] The paper was sold on board ships in home waters wherever an agent could be found to place a bulk order. As with most small propaganda organs, some inflated claims were made. In November 1899 Yexley stated that the readership was at least 50,000,[36] and within a few months the figure had been raised to 70,000.[37] Readership was not the same as paid circulation, though he was correct in asserting that the *Bluejacket*'s influence extended beyond the immediate lower-deck audience. By the time he resigned the editorship in 1904 he claimed a circulation of 20,000.[38]

Yexley's style of campaigning eventually brought him into conflict with the paper's proprietor. Masters was a businessman whose main interest was in selling jewellery to sailors. Yexley found himself taking an editorial line against business methods that exploited ratings, objecting to some of Masters's own advertising and sales techniques. Towards the end of 1903 the two quarrelled, and at the beginning of 1904, for the second time in his life, Yexley quit a secure job to be free to work for naval reform.[39] This impetuosity and scrupulousness were characteristic of the man, and he gave little thought to his own material well-being. Even before then he had turned down the prospect of a rewarding position with F. T. Jane, the naval writer. Jane had parliamentary ambitions, wanted a permanent propaganda organ of his own and had expressed an interest in buying out *The Bluejacket* if Yexley was prepared to edit it. But Yexley was not willing to be anybody's paid political hack, and the idea fell through.[40]

THE LOWER DECK AND PARLIAMENT

There was no doubt that under Yexley *The Bluejacket* had given the reform movement a great stimulus. For the first time ever, frank public criticisms of long-standing injustices had been voiced. Men had been encouraged to write to the paper, and to see legitimate grievances aired gave them greater self-confidence.

Ratings now began to think of having their own representative in Parliament to take care of their interests. There was a touching faith in the efficacy of questions in the House of Commons. If only a question could be tabled, the solution to a problem or the settlement of a grievance would not be long in coming.[41] But few civilians were able to master the complexities of service conditions sufficiently to be able to argue the case for detailed reforms, and retired naval officers among MPs were often no better informed and sometimes even less sympathetic. As Admiral Fisher wrote to Yexley some years later: '[. . .] all these Admirals who talk and write (Sir Hedworth Meux and others) cannot point to *one single thing they have done for the Navy! Not one little thing!*'[42] Year after year Parliament debated the Navy Estimates with scarcely a reference to the lower deck. As Arnold White, the naval columnist, argued, 'The nation has no knowledge whatever of the public opinion of the bluejackets and marines of the Fleet.'[43]

The answer, some thought, was for the petty officers and men to elect their own candidate. But how? The vast majority had no residential qualification for voting in the naval ports: in 1905 it was estimated that the effective number of naval voters in Portsmouth was no more than 700.[44] Even householders were disfranchised if their ship happened to be away at the time, and it was widely believed on the lower deck that the Channel Squadron was deliberately sent to sea during general elections.[45] Some men harboured a vain hope that the Navy itself could be made an electoral constituency: if the ancient universities of Oxford and Cambridge could have their own parliamentary seats why not the Navy too? Others recognised that it was a question of either throwing their weight behind one of the main party candidates in the naval towns, or putting forward their own independent one.

The warrant officers had faced this problem in 1892 when they organised to help elect Kearley and Morton. Now their idea was that they and the petty officers, being virtually the only ranks with the vote, should select a suitable candidate and put him up at Portsmouth, where the naval and dockyard vote was strongest. The candidate himself need not be a sailor but should be someone closely connected with the Navy. On non-naval matters he would be free to vote as he pleased; the Navy, it was claimed, had no interest in 'politics'. Their proposal was that every warrant officer and petty officer should contribute 2s to the cost of the campaign, while ratings below this rank who could not be expected to afford as much would give aid in kind. The man the Warrant Officers' Society had in mind was F. T. Jane, who agreed to stand at the 1905 election provided his expenses were met.[46]

The growing self-confidence of the reform movement also manifested itself in other ways. Occasional public announcements of lower-deck society meetings began to appear in newspapers at the naval ports. In 1904 the ERAs' society began to publish its own magazine, *The Naval Engineering Review*. In 1900 the cause of lower-deck organisation had been supported at a by-election in Portsmouth, with the successful Liberal candidate, Thomas Bramsdon, expressing the view that it was '[. . .] disgraceful that men should not be allowed to combine in order to try to improve their pay and position'. And the opening years of the new century saw an increase in the number of lower-deck societies.[47]

THE LOWER-DECK SOCIETIES

To a large extent the early growth of lower-deck organisation came about as a result of the internal fragmentation of existing societies. Whereas most of them recruited members from within one branch, the Chief Petty Officers' Society included men from all sections of the service. However, having secured its long-standing aim of an increase in pension rates in 1903, the society no longer had a common objective. It divided, the Devonport and Chatham branches going one way and the Portsmouth branch choosing to remain independent. Out of this schism four entirely new societies were formed. By 1905 an Armourers' Society had come into existence; a Ships' Stewards' Death Benefit Society was formed in 1907; a society of ships' cooks also enjoyed a brief existence,[48] and by 1910 an Electricians' Burial and Invalid Relief Society was operating.[49]

By 1910 the total number was fourteen, but membership was still small and restricted to petty officers. The unstable nature of some of the societies and the secrecy surrounding the activities of others meant that membership figures were seldom announced. Some were registered under the Friendly Societies Act and published an annual return of members, but others preferred the protection that clandestine operations afforded.[50] The degree of organisation varied from branch to branch. Within twelve months of its foundation in 1877 the Writers' Society had over three-quarters of the branch in membership and remained a stronghold of lower-deck organisation thereafter.[51] With 870 members in 1906 the Executive Petty Officers' Society was probably the largest organisation of the day.[52] But among all junior ratings, and especially seamen and stokers – the two biggest branches by far – the penetration of the benefit societies was very limited. Altogether it seems unlikely that total membership in 1910 exceeded two or three thousand of the more than 100,000 ratings in the service.

The pattern of organisation in most of the societies was similar. There tended to be separate branches at Chatham, Portsmouth and Devonport. Corresponding representatives were appointed in ships to collect subscriptions from men at sea. Branches were often self-sufficient in matters of finance, the three ports linking forces only on basic grievances affecting the whole class.[53] Typical of many societies, the Portsmouth Chief Petty Officers' Society charged a monthly subscription of 8d and paid a £12 death benefit.[54] One branch would act as the head office until another volunteered. Most societies paid their secretary an honorarium of £2–£5 a year.

Inter-branch meetings were held only when necessary, and minutes were exchanged with branches at other ports. Naval pensioners played a prominent role in society affairs, usually acting as branch officers; indeed, it was often claimed with justification that the interests of pensioners and people in semi-permanent billets at home ports took precedence over those of the active-service ratings who constituted the bulk of the membership. Usually meetings were held in seamen's missions or public houses, and hotel landlords often served as trustees. The gatherings were conducted in the spirit of respectable working-class self-help organisations. The uplifting effect of membership was often stressed, and in 1906 a report of benefit society activities in Devonport commented: 'It is regrettable that this [. . .] is not more encouraged, and men allowed to "have ideas", and express them, for the interest of the naval Service, without being dubbed a "Sea Lawyer" [. . .].'[55]

The aims of the ERAs' society were: to give financial assistance to the nominees of deceased members, to promote the intellectual and moral condition of its members, and to disseminate scientific knowledge in connection with the engineering trade.[56] Other societies had broadly similar aims: to provide for the relief of widows, to organise social activities and encourage fellowship, and generally to promote the interests of the class. But how were the varied interests of the numerous different branches and ratings to be reconciled? With upwards of a score of different branches in the service the natural tendency of the lower deck was to divide rather than to unite over any given issue.

PETITIONS AND JOINT COMMITTEES

With Yexley's editorship of *The Bluejacket* at an end by the beginning of 1904, the task of advancing the cause of reform fell to the benefit societies. In November that year the first general petition was published. Entitled *The British Navy – Improvements Needed*, it was issued at Devonport on 3 November 1904, and purported to be a general statement by the lower-deck societies of ratings' disabilities. In fact it was the work of a chief writer, William Behenna, then secretary of the Chief Petty Officers' Society and vice-president of the Writers', and a handful of chief petty officer and petty officer colleagues at

Devonport. To cloak the involvement of active-service ratings in its preparation, it was issued from Cardiff by Wilson Tunley, a shipping clerk.[57] Copies were sent to MPs, naval officers known to be sympathetic, and the *Naval and Military Record*, where it was published in full. An accompanying editorial dubbed it a lower-deck 'Magna Charta', the name by which appeals were to be commonly known in subsequent years.[58]

The petition itself was a jumbled collection of twenty items, some of general interest, others relating to only one class. Important requests mingled with trivial ones, and several important issues were not included. Although low pay was a cause of growing dissatisfaction, there was no direct request for a general increase, nor was the grievance over victualling raised. From the point of view of mobilising support outside the service it was a far from clear statement of what ratings wanted. In the event the appeal had little impact. Only in the correspondence columns of the *Naval and Military Record* was there any detailed discussion, the main Portsmouth paper, *The Hampshire Telegraph and Naval Chronicle*, merely referring to it in a single paragraph two weeks later.[59]

But its significance lay not so much in its content as in the fact that it had been issued at all. As a general statement of disabilities the appeal left much to be desired, but its authors had attempted to bridge branch divisions, and this was a landmark. In future years, with wider participation of other sections of the lower deck in formulating its terms, the impact was likely to be greater, especially since the climate was becoming more favourable to reform. Admiral Sir John Fisher had become First Sea Lord in October 1904 and was known to be sympathetic towards the lower deck. In January 1906 a Liberal Government was returned, pledged to a programme of social change. Fred Jane, standing as an independent at Portsmouth, had fared badly and come bottom of the poll with only 1,859 votes. His election statement that he would confine his interests and votes to naval matters clearly did not appeal to civilian voters.[60] But at Chatham the lower deck had been largely instrumental in unseating the Tory Member in favour of the Labour candidate, J. Jenkins, a full-time official of the Shipwrights' Union. Lower-deck meetings and canvasses had been organised by George Crowe, master-at-arms at the barracks. Crowe had even addressed mass meetings inside the barracks during dinner time.[61]

The Chatham result had a profound effect on the lower deck. It was only the second time that the sailors' vote had been organised, and it taught them that they were not without some political muscle. Dockyard MPs who in the past had been largely able to ignore them now began to cultivate the service vote and were more willing to take up grievances.[62]

In February 1907 a revised edition of the 1904 appeal was prepared, and again it was issued through the medium of the civilian, Wilson Tunley. For the next seven years a new appeal was published annually. From 1908 the method of drafting the document began to be formalised, the task being undertaken by joint committees of the benefit societies at each of the three ports. Such committees had existed for some years as shadowy bodies, occasionally co-ordinating the societies' activities, though up to this point they had been of little consequence. However, their monthly meetings did provide a channel of communication between different classes of rating. The joint committees kept in touch through an exchange of minutes, and once a year from 1908 held an annual conference to draft the appeal. Since their concern was with the general questions that affected all classes of rating rather than death benefit matters, they tended to become the focal point of lower-deck politics. As such they were in clear breach of Article 11 of King's Regulations, and consequently their affairs were shrouded in secrecy. Only occasionally were they referred to in the naval press, and not until 1912 did regular reports of their activities begin to appear in *The Fleet*.

The weakness of the joint committees was the weakness of the death benefit societies: they were not wholly representative. They were dominated by chief petty officers and petty officers, and it was the representatives of the smaller but well organised classes of rating such as writers and stewards who gravitated to positions of leadership and tended to assume control. Furthermore the need for secrecy militated against free discussion of their activities. There was rarely any consideration of joint committee policies at society meetings. The programmes prepared on the men's behalf and contained in the annual appeals were never referred back to the societies for approval.[63] At times, as a precaution against leakages of information, the soceties were even discouraged from asking for minutes of joint committee proceedings.[64] The overall effect was that the committees tended to function as independent power bases.

The appeals drafted at the annual conferences reflected these weaknesses. Petty officers' interests were better looked after than

those of junior ratings, and disproportionate attention was paid to the
affairs of the non-seamen classes – writers, stewards, artisans and so
on. Moreover the lack of wider debate over the terms of the appeal
often resulted in an ill-thought-out document. As in 1904, important
demands were listed beside relatively trivial complaints, with no
indication of the priority attached to them. From year to year the
contents changed for no logical reason. A request would appear one
year and be omitted the next, only to re-emerge subsequently in a
different form. It was hardly an approach likely to result in the
requests being taken very seriously.

But, though never acknowledged, the lower-deck appeals were in
fact studied at the Admiralty. At times commanding officers would be
asked to furnish an opinion as to the desirability of a change proposed,
and over the years a number of concessions were granted, though
never on matters of great significance.[65]

THE FLEET

Far more effective from the point of view of the reform movement
were the efforts of Lionel Yexley and his new paper *The Fleet*, a
twopenny monthly, founded in May 1905 by Yexley in partnership
with Gerard Meynell, a director of the Westminster Press and a man
with a deep interest in lower-deck affairs. Meynell put up the money
and Yexley did the work, for the first few months drawing no salary.[66]
It was the first truly independent lower-deck paper. As distinct from
the benefit societies and the annual appeals, which spoke largely for
petty officers and senior hands, *The Fleet* declared, 'We recognise no
rank, no rating – we are "All Navy" with a leaning towards the
ordinary seaman, able seaman and stoker who must ever remain more
or less inarticulate in a disciplined Service.'[67] For the first time Yexley
was entirely free to attack the many evils he saw in the service. *The
Fleet* took over where *The Bluejacket* left off but, now that the climate
was propitious, the reforms came more freely. From the very first
edition, Yexley sent copies of the paper to the First Sea Lord, Jacky
Fisher, and in July 1905 *The Fleet* carried a personal message from
him wishing the new journal success.

In mid-1906, in the course of the campaign for victualling reforms,
Yexley made Fisher's personal acquaintance, and from that point on
the two became allies.[68] The connection was strengthened by the fact
that Esther Hallam Moorhouse, the naval historian and wife of

Yexley's partner, Meynell, was a member of Fisher's charmed circle of close friends. Having such an influential contact in high places was invaluable to Yexley, and the relationship continued to be a most important factor in the struggle for lower-deck reforms long after Fisher had retired.

As in the *Bluejacket* days, most naval officers regarded Yexley as a subversive influence and *The Fleet* as a scurrilous rag. Although he could be secure in the knowledge that he had a powerful ally, Yexley had to be careful not to antagonise them unduly. There was nothing to be gained by being 'anti-officer'; on the contrary, there was much to lose. His livelihood now depended on the paper's success, and commanding officers were still in a position to ban it. His legal position in criticising the administration of the service and communicating with ratings on service matters was doubtful, and in 1909 one *Fleet* correspondent whose identity was traced was arrested and punished.[69] Thus Yexley stressed that his campaigning was in no way to be taken as disloyal or as a criticism of naval officers generally. *The Fleet* was, he said, '[. . .] a literary bridge to span the gulf that discipline fixes between the ward-room and the mess-deck'.[70] The paper relied heavily on men writing in with their complaints, and he had to assure them that they would not be penalised. It was becoming more common for ratings to write to the press. In 1907 the *Naval Chronicle* was inviting articles from readers on naval subjects, offering to pay for them and guaranteeing anonymity.[71] But it could still be a hazardous business, and relatively few were prepared to be known as regular *Fleet* informants.

Despite competition from Yexley's old paper, *The Bluejacket*, now edited by one of his former colleagues, Tom Holman, *The Fleet* was able to build up a circulation of 12,000 within three months. Yexley claimed a doubling of the readership in the latter part of 1906 and a circulation three times that of any other service paper.[72] His aim was a paid circulation of 50,000, but although he boasted that 90 per cent of officers and men read it and that the overall readership was 200,000, it is doubtful if the circulation ever surpassed one-tenth of this.[73]

In the years after 1905 he systematically turned his attention to the chief disabilities of the lower deck, concentrating on the grievances most in need of redress, where his intelligence told him there was a reasonable chance of succeeding. Both in public and behind the scenes he pressed the case relentlessly. The overall effect of these individual campaigns was to create a climate in which expectations were raised, and although reforms were never abundant they came more freely than at any previous time. His strength as a journalist was that he had better sources of information than any other naval correspondent and was able to reduce to bare principles complex service matters that appeared incomprehensible to the civilian. Through his freelance writing in national and port newspapers, and questions which he occasionally arranged to have asked in Parliament, he sought to widen the campaign. Searching analyses of the problems would be published as pamphlets or long articles in *The Fleet Annual and Naval Yearbook*. He was much quoted in other publications, and in this way his views reached a bigger audience.

All the time he would be secretly using his influence at the Admiralty to win concessions. Through Fisher he was introduced in 1909 to the First Lord, Reginal McKenna, who asked him to submit proposals for lower-deck reform. Exploiting the connection with McKenna, he was able to gain access to naval establishments that would otherwise have been out of bounds.[74] The two met frequently in the next couple of years, always at the First Lord's suggestion, and during this period Yexley forwarded to McKenna and the Financial Secretary to the Admiralty, T. J. Macnamara, dozens of letters from ratings about their specific grievances.[75] It was, as Yexley said, the first time in history that the political head of the Navy had had a regular and direct contact with the thoughts and feelings of the lower deck.[76]

The Yexley–Fisher reforms

[. . .] it is the literal truth to say that quite one-third of an average able seaman's pay is spent at the canteen in supplying himself with decent food, which could and should be supplied to him as part of the contract entered into with him by HMG. – *Naval Warrant Officers' Journal*, September 1900

Why, on earth, should not a sailor have his uniform given to him by the state in the same way as the soldier, or the marine who is governed by the same department? – *Naval Warrant Officers' Journal*, August 1903

Lower-deck grievances are all traceable back to a few main causes. [. . .] the discipline has not adapted itself to the newer type of man; the system of punishments is harsh [. . .] too purely punitive, and behind the times as applied to the present-day Navy men. – Stephen Reynolds, *Daily Chronicle*, 17 July 1912

In the 1880s warrant officers and chief petty officers had lobbied for improvements in their promotion prospects and pensions. The first general campaigns in support of better conditions for all ratings were concerned with food, uniform regulations and, to a lesser extent, the Navy's system of punishments. They began at the turn of the century. The grievances over food and uniform affected the great mass of ratings directly and made for a most uncomfortable life. But there was another dimension to the problem – an economic one. The campaigns were an indirect attempt to ease the financial burden on the lower deck: in other words, for a disguised pay increase. The reform movement cut its teeth on them and began to develop what were to become standard methods of lobbying. In particular, this was the period in which Yexley forged his vital relationship with Fisher. Each of the issues needs to be looked at in turn.

THE PROBLEM OF FOOD

In the closing years of the nineteenth century discontent over victualling was growing, and by the turn of the century a serious situation had developed. The fact was that, barring a few additions to the standard ration, feeding arrangements had hardly changed since Nelson's time. The main complaints were that not enough was served up, there were too few mealtimes for a working man, the quality often left a great deal to be desired, there was not enough variety, cooking arrangements were primitive in the extreme, and the system was so inflexible that the same fare was served up day after day whether in the heat of the Persian Gulf or on winter patrol off Newfoundland.[1]

Of what did the diet consist? Two of the three official meals, breakfast and tea, were made up of nothing more than a pint of cocoa or tea without milk and a portion of dry bread or ship's biscuit without butter. The main meal of the day at noon was supposed to consist of 1 lb of meat and $\frac{1}{2}$ lb of vegetables per man. Where possible fresh meat was served, but otherwise – and this meant most of the time ships were at sea – the meat ration was salt pork every second day and salt beef or preserved meat alternately on the other days.

Officially there were only three meals. Cocoa was served at 5 a.m., dinner at noon and supper at 4.15 p.m.[2] The sailors were then supposed to wait nearly thirteen hours, with the likelihood of having to do heavy work in the course of the night watches. In practice two unofficial meals were taken: at 'stand easy' at 8.30 a.m., when they had their real breakfast, and again at 8 p.m. after 'stand by hammocks'. But they themselves had to provide both, and it was a heavy and much resented drain on their income.

Perhaps the worst aspect of the victualling system was the cooking arrangements.[3] Crews messed in groups of about twenty, and one of them would be responsible for preparing the day's rations. In the morning the dish for each mess was taken to the galley, where the ship's cooks, numbering no more than four in the largest battleships, were responsible for cooking it on equipment that was inadequate for half the numbers. Neither the men nor the cooks had any particular skill in preparing food.[4] The lower deck were therefore largely at the mercy of people who could, and often did, completely ruin a meal.

The patent inadequacies of the official victualling had resulted in the development over a long period of time of unofficial arrangements.

These were based on the 'savings' system, legalised after the Spithead mutiny, under which men were granted a cash allowance in lieu of rations not taken up, and ship canteens, which developed rapidly in the last quarter of the nineteenth century and provided an alternative supply where men could spend their savings.

Ship canteens assumed different forms. Some were run co-operatively, with the profits going to a ship's fund for the benefit of the crew. In other cases, and especially in the home depots, they were let out to firms of provisioners such as Lipton's or Miller's who ran them on a tenant basis. Still others were managed by 'bumboatmen' – small middlemen, often Maltese, who were not contractors themselves but simply arranged for a supply of provisions from recognised shore traders.[5] In theory the co-operative arrangement was the best, with an elected committee of ratings controlling the operation. But in practice, largely because of the hierarchical nature of the service and the tendency for a few senior hands to 'run the show', there was considerable scope for the misuse of funds. Tenants, on the other hand, and still more the bumboatmen, were often a law unto themselves, and while the lower deck were glad of any chance to supplement the official ration the lack of any close regulation led to exorbitant prices being charged.[6] The monthly cost to each man of goods bought collectively by the mess could range anywhere from 5s to 17s to be met out of an AB's pay of 1s 7d a day. Beyond this, if a man wanted something extra – a tin of sardines, jam, potted meat or cheese – he would have to buy it himself, and it was possible for an individual's outlay to be as much as 17s a month over and above his share of the collective mess bill. In the Mediterranean Fleet, where the bumboatmen held sway, it was normal to spend half one's meagre pay on supplementing the diet.[7]

Why were canteen prices so high? A major factor was blackmail and corruption. Tenant canteens had a regular supply of goods from the parent firms on shore. But co-operative ones had to buy their supplies where they could, and local traders were in the habit of bribing canteen managers for the right to supply low-quality goods at top prices.[8] In 1900 *The Bluejacket* reported that at one Portsmouth depot a local trader had offered £700 per annum to be allowed to supply the canteen.[9] Likewise, bumboatmen secured a foothold on warships by wholesale bribery of canteen committees and commanding officers. Boxes of oranges and flowers would be sent to the officers of ships bound for the Mediterranean in a bid to secure the right to operate the canteen. In 1906 Yexley came into possession of a letter from a naval officer's wife to a bumboatman indicating that she expected her furniture to be sent out to Malta free in return for a canteen tenancy.[10] The bribery also corrupted people lower down the scale, especially the ship's police, without whose consent nothing and no one was allowed on board: £120 down and backhand payments of £8 a month were a standard form of payment to masters-at-arms.[11] Once the bumboatman was safely ensconced the quality of the canteen food would fall and prices rise as he attempted to recoup the loss on the original bribe.[12]

Another root cause of inflated prices was the fact that captains expected the canteen to provide all sorts of stores and cleaning gear that the Navy should have supplied officially. Oilskins had to be bought out of canteen profits. Oil, cleaning rags, paint, brick dust, emery boards and so on for use in keeping the vessel smart were all expected to come from the canteen free of charge. To meet the expense the price of normal goods had to be raised.[13]

THE RICE COMMITTEE

The scandal of naval victualling, both official and unofficial, became the subject of Lionel Yexley's first major campaign when he established *The Bluejacket*. Throughout 1899–1900 it was his self-appointed task to keep the food question stirred with 'the long pole of the press'.[14] Many letters to the editor testified to the men's growing resentment, and *The Bluejacket* warned that

[. . .] the dissatisfaction is so general as to constitute a real menace to the well-being of the Service. [. . .] Even the bluejacket of today, disgusted with the contempt with which all his protestations are treated, might be tempted to forget his duty to the State by resorting to open violence.[15]

A round robin was drawn up by a number of petty officers, requesting improvements in the official ration; it was published in the June 1899 edition of *The Bluejacket*. They asked for bread to be included, the quality of various foodstuffs improved, an extra official meal at 7.30 p.m., and free issue of knives, forks, spoons and basins.[16] *The Bluejacket*'s lead was soon taken up. The socialist *Clarion* published a series of articles; the muckraking journal *Truth* began to carry stories of victualling corruption; the inadequacy of naval rations was raised by Havelock Wilson in the 1899 Navy Estimates debate, and among the service press the *United Service Gazette* called for a parliamentary committee.[17]

Helping to underline the ratings' case were disclosures that soldiers at the front in the Boer war did better than the men of the fleet. The unfavourable comparison with the army was brought home forcibly by complaints about the food served to soldiers on troopships to South Africa. Sir James Ferguson, a former Secretary of State for War, asked in Parliament whether casks of salt beef dated 1893 had been used for the troops on the *Kildonan Castle*. The government admitted the fact; the beef in question had been taken from HMS *Ramilles*, though there was nothing unusual about its age.[18] For the sailors the implication was clear and damning: what was unsuitable for Tommy Atkins in wartime was good enough for the lower deck at any time, and beef that had been in pickle seven years was not exceptional.

There was an outcry by MPs for a public inquiry, and at this point Yexley found an ally in Hudson Kearley, Liberal MP for Devonport.[19] Kearley was briefed by Yexley and during the debate on the Navy Estimates in March 1900 flatly announced in the Commons that he had information regarding underhand dealings in naval canteens and that sailors were being fleeced and exploited.[20] His statement forced the government's hand, and within a week the decision had been taken to appoint a departmental committee of inquiry.[21] Meanwhile, in the summer of 1900, James Douglas of the *Daily Leader* wrote a series of articles about naval victualling under the heading 'HMS Starvation' which kept up the pressure on the Admiralty.[22]

The committee was formally appointed under Vice-Admiral Rice in May 1900. It was a triumph for the reformers, but not an unqualified one. The Admiralty failed to comprehend the interrelation between the official and unofficial victualling systems, and the committee was debarred from examining closely the question of savings or from recommending any major changes in the canteen system, such as bringing it under closer government control.[23] With a general election imminent, *The Bluejacket* advised all sailors in home service to press their MPs for immediate reform, and the Admiralty was warned that if it had set up the committee as a delaying tactic it was making a fatal error.[24]

The Rice committee reported in 1901, but its terms of reference had prevented it from tackling the root of the problem. Two new official meals were recommended at 'stand easy' and in the evening at 7.30. Otherwise its positive proposals were of no great consequence, doing little more than introduce a few additional items such as jam, coffee and condensed milk.[25] These became part of the ration in 1903. The committee defended the quality of the food and claimed that there was no dissatisfaction, despite official figures showing that 92 per cent of the vegetables, 63 per cent of the salt pork, 66 per cent of the salt beef, 79 per cent of the suet, 90 per cent of the preserved potatoes and 94 per cent of the biscuit issued was refused in favour of savings.[26] It expressed the view that mess bills ought to be no higher than 4s a month and anything above this could only be the result of bad management and extravagance on the part of the men. Much canteen expenditure was thought to be unnecessary, and the report complacently concluded that '[. . .] the standard of living in the Fleet can only be regarded, judged by the corresponding standard on shore, as unnecessarily high'.[27]

When put to the test the committee's recommendations quickly proved inadequate, and loud criticisms of the new arrangements were soon coming from the lower deck.[28] There was still a lack of variety and, once the novelty of the new delicacies had worn off, the men tired of the deadly monotony of preserved meat and jam, jam and preserved meat, day after day, week after week. They protested at the quality of the jam, and in 1906 the Admiralty condemned as useless 270,000 lb that had been bought in the aftermath of the Rice report.[29]

With the evident failure of the Rice recommendations Yexley began systematically to collect information about the precise working of the victualling system. He set about obtaining mess accounts from scores of ships, examined canteen income and expenditure in great detail and for the first time was able to piece together a composite picture of the financing of naval victualling. By 1905 he was ready to resume his press campaign.

The climate was now more auspicious. Interest had been aroused. Oswyn Murray, later to become Secretary to the Board of Admiralty, had been appointed Assistant Director of Victualling and was soon to show himself favourably disposed to reform. In October 1904 the first loyal appeal from the lower-deck societies asked for better messing and cooking facilities and an official ration of bread. And in March 1905 the Admiralty received the report of a departmental committee on naval cooking which recommended a major increase in the number of ships' cooks, more rigorous training and better galley appliances.[30] By 1908 the reforms were well under way.

Meanwhile the problem with official victualling continued to be the lack of variety, the inefficiency and wastefulness of the Victualling Department, and the general disregard of the comforts of the men by many of the officers responsible for running the system. A prime example involved mess utensils. These were issued free for the first time only in 1903 and since then commanders in many ships had insisted that knives and forks be cleaned and laid out for inspection each day. On HMS *Dreadnought* the rule was that cutlery had to be set out in a pattern for Sunday inspection. It was to be ranged around the salt and pepper pots, handles towards the pots and one inch away, knives and forks in rotation, all properly cleaned and burnished.[31] The result was that men simply refused to use the cutlery and handed it back to the paymaster.[32]

There was no longer any grumbling about the size of the rations. Indeed, it was sometimes too much, and since food not eaten on one day was not allowed to be kept it had to be thrown overboard.[33] The inflexibility of the victualling system was best seen in the way certain rations were compulsory so as to turn the stores over and keep supplies in reasonable condition. Sailors were expected to take up a certain amount of preserved meat and biscuit each week, otherwise they were allowed only half savings. But in spite of this penalty these items were still refused. In fact the only way a regular turnover of stores was effected was by the unofficial destruction of a certain quantity each week, and the lower deck were paying heavily in the form of reduced savings in order to support this wasteful arrangement.[34] Month by month in 1905–06 *The Fleet* drew the attention of the public to these practices.

THE LOGIN COMMITTEE

By now Yexley had formulated his ideas for a root-and-branch reform of naval victualling. He believed that the task of feeding the fleet should be officially divided between the Victualling Department and the canteens; in other words, the integral part played by the canteens in the domestic economy of the service would be formally recognised. Whereas the official ration was valued at 10*d* a day, he wanted this reduced to a standard ration worth 6*d*. A further 4*d* a day would be paid as a messing allowance, to be spent at the canteen at the individual's discretion.[35] At the same time, Yexley wanted savings to be abolished. All they did, he maintained, was hide the shortcomings of the official ration and keep discontent within bounds.[36] He also

Fisher and Churchill at the launch of HMS *Centurion*, 18 November 1911

proposed close Admiralty regulation of canteens by an Inspectorate. This body would be responsible for awarding tenancies based on firm contracts that would specify prices and quality and would include penalty clauses. Any dispute would ultimately be referred to an Inspector of Canteens, who would have power to annul contracts.

His monthly articles in *The Fleet* were published as a booklet, *Naval Canteens – Use and Abuse,* in November 1905. Five thousand copies were distributed to the press, MPs and naval officers.[37] Meanwhile, standing as an independent at Portsmouth in the 1905 election, Fred Jane campaigned on a platform which included the reform of victualling.[38] On 30 April 1906 Yexley arranged for Gibson Bowles, MP, to raise the question of canteen irregularities in the House of Commons. The government spokesman blandly replied that it was not a matter for the Admiralty and that no information was available.[39] But Yexley was not now without support within the Admiralty itself. Earlier in the year Oswyn Murray as Director of Victualling had invited him to the Admiralty to discuss his allegations. After Bowles had raised the matter in Parliament, he wrote to Yexley:

[. . .] please go on criticising us to the full for it does us good. Above all, let the men know through *The Fleet* that if only they show a strong desire for reform they are certain in these days to carry the Board of Admiralty with them.[40]

It was a clear invitation to keep up the pressure. Yexley spent hours with Gibson Bowles explaining the intricacies of the canteen system, and on 24 May 1906 the MP returned to the subject in detail, challenged the victualling vote in the Commons and forced the government to agree to a committee of inquiry.[41] Yexley published his specific proposals in a leaflet, *Suggested Solution to the Canteen and Victualling Troubles of the Navy.* Copies went to MPs, naval officers and sailors, who were requested to send back their comments.[42]

By now the tide was running with the reformers. The naval correspondent of *The Times* supported *The Fleet*'s proposals,[43] and it was about this point that Yexley won over his most influential convert, the First Sea Lord, Jacky Fisher. Fisher asked Yexley to meet him at his home.[44] He wanted further background information about charges of corruption in naval canteens. At first he was sceptical of feeling at canteens having to supply free paint and cleaning gear. In fifty years' service he had failed to realise that such a tax on the men's pocket was bound to lead to resentment. Were they not as proud of their ship's appearance as the officers? The conversation became strained when the former petty officer answered bluntly that by insisting on such free supplies a captain was handing over his crew bound hand and foot to the bumboatmen to be robbed. Yexley's reminiscences provide a vivid description of Fisher's reaction. 'He did not reply, he just stiffened; his eyes opened until they became as round as saucers, and they looked at me with a kind of fixed glare. I could only liken him to one of the great cats at the zoo who give the impression of being about to spring.' The First Sea Lord called the meeting to an abrupt halt, but not before he had invited Yexley back the following week to resume their talk. This time he was more receptive as Yexley described the labyrinthine network of corruption that linked the canteen committees, bumboatmen, ship's police, victualling staff and officers. In the end he was convinced, and Yexley was satisfied that from here on he had an ally.[45]

The committee of inquiry was appointed in July 1906 under the chairmanship of Rear-Admiral Spencer Login. During the autumn it heard evidence from many sources, including sixty-four ratings elected at mass meetings of the lower deck.[46] The report, presented in January 1907, accepted the basic point, missed by Rice six years earlier, that cooking, canteens and official victualling were all part of the same problem.[47] *The Fleet*'s proposal for a standard ration worth 6*d* and a 4*d* messing allowance was accepted entirely. Official rations were to be pared down to a minimum and, to introduce some flexibility, men would be allowed to buy additional supplies from the paymaster at the old savings price. Wherever rations were being issued the committee wanted to see paymasters more in evidence as a deterrent to illicit practices.[48] Finally it recommended that an experiment in centralised catering be started on HMS *Dreadnought*, with a system of general messing.

On the subject of canteens *The Fleet*'s scheme was accepted almost *in toto*. There was to be an inspectorate of canteens responsible for overseeing contracts. The Admiralty would maintain a list of approved contractors with details of their prices. There would be a standard form of agreement that all tenants would have to sign, and rents would no longer be negotiable but fixed in relation to the size of the crew. On only a few points did Login disagree with Yexley's prescription, most noticeably over the question of responsibility for awarding tenancies. The committee preferred to leave this matter to commanding officers rather than the canteen inspectorate. But even here Yexley was subsequently seen to be right, and in October 1909 the Admiralty itself took over the allocation of canteen tenancies, so denying commanding officers the right to award contracts as a form of personal patronage.[49]

The government announced its decision to accept the report in June 1907, and over the next nine months the changes were formally introduced.[50] The new system was far from perfect, but it went as far as most men at the time thought it possible to go. Indeed, the victualling reforms of 1907 probably marked the biggest single improvement in the quality of service life ever made up to then. Apart from being better fed, the lower deck made substantial financial gains. Where they had been paying out at least three or four shillings a month in mess bills, they now found themselves in surplus at the end of the month, with as much as 5s 9d per head from unspent messing allowances. On this basis it was estimated that the reforms were equivalent to a pay rise of 3d a day – and that in an occupation which had seen no general increase since the introduction of continuous service fifty years before.[51]

All in all, it was an impressive vindication of Yexley's seven-year campaign. Almost single-handed he had been responsible for arousing public awareness and getting the Login inquiry set up. It was his criticisms that the committee had had to address itself to, it was largely his evidence that it had had to weigh, and it was to his specific proposals that it was compelled to turn once his analysis was seen to be accurate. From first to last he imposed his views on the committee without ever appearing before it.

THE UNIFORM ISSUE

When the Admiralty's new victualling regulations were issued in 1907, *The Fleet* commented sardonically, 'For the first time in the history of the Navy the proper feeding of the British Blue is to be considered as of more importance than mustering his kit.'[52] Kitbag mustering had become a veritable fetish, and in the early years of the century ranked only behind the food question among the men's grievances. The problem stemmed from the way in which clothing regulations had developed.

Since the introduction of an official uniform in 1857 the men had had to buy it out of their own pocket. It was perhaps a curious requirement in an armed service, but they regarded it as normal:

uniform was looked on as their own personal property. Over the years, however, more and more items had been added, things they were compelled to buy but in practice had little use for. At the same time necessities such as oilskins and seaboots were not compulsory yet still had to be purchased. During the 1890s regulations grew lengthier and began to be enforced in meticulous detail. This was the beginning of the heyday of kitbag mustering, when 'pocket drill' took precedence over military training and the 'uniform strategists', as the lower deck called those responsible, were in their element.

From being a relatively simple affair the official uniform had become cumbersome and costly, and the regulations were enforced in the worst tradition of service red tape. For example, they specified the contents of the sailor's 'housewife', his sewing kit, and at the peak of the craze the inspecting officer might go as far as to count the number of buttons and needles and measure the length of spare tape to see that they conformed to the rules. Rather than risk punishment, men kept the housewife rolled up for musters only and had a second kit, a 'jewing bag', for general use.[53] Whenever they returned to home depot after a posting they were immediately subject to kitbag musters which might last a couple of days and cost them dear because of the new items of uniform they were forced to buy. Most preferred to tip the clothing corporals instead, and in this way there emerged enormous scope for blackmail and corruption.

The first public criticism was made by *The Bluejacket* in May 1900. By early 1904 Commodore Login at Portsmouth barracks was beginning to attack some of the more obvious forms of corruption, and had insisted upon officer supervision of kit musters and clothing issues and closer regulation of the ship's police. This had the effect of drawing attention to illicit practices at the other depots.[54] In March 1904 allegations of corruption in clothing mustering were made by the *Naval and Military Record*, and the *Illustrated Daily Mirror* received a flood of letters confirming the practice.[55] The following month *Truth* announced the existence of definite and specific evidence of corruption at one at least of the naval depots and challenged the Admiralty to institute an investigation.[56]

Then in June 1904 Yexley returned to the subject with an outspoken attack in the magazine *Nineteenth Century*. On their first day back in depot, he announced, men were being asked to pay for several articles of clothing costing anything from £3 to £4. The result was that they were indebted to the Crown and drew no pay at all for several weeks.

At present the friction is acute. Five hundred men desert annually from Chatham Barracks alone, the majority of whom are driven from the Service by the harassing to which they are subjected over trivial matters connected with their uniform, and the summary punishments from the same cause throughout the Navy are innumerable.[57]

The article made a considerable impact. Then in October 1904 the first lower-deck loyal appeal included a request for a free kit. The call was supported editorially by the *Naval Chronicle*,[58] and public interest was now sufficient to force the Admiralty to act: early in 1905 a review committee was set up under Captain Stopford to look into the uniform question.[59]

As long as the regulations were permissive and clothing was regarded as a man's private property the question of who paid for it was not a big issue. But now that the Admiralty's policy was forcing up the cost to the rating the lower deck felt that the kit should be provided free.[60] The expense was already considerable: the complete uniform was worth over £9, and it cost on average £3 a year to maintain, or between 3*d* and 5*d* a day, depending on the owner's rank. 'Free uniform should follow compulsory uniform,' *The Fleet* pointed out, just as free schooling followed compulsory schooling.[61]

Yexley continued his campaign in *The Fleet*, and the lower-deck response in the form of letters to the editor kept the issue on the boil throughout the second half of 1905. Failing the introduction of a free kit or, better still, an upkeep allowance, *The Fleet* advocated a drastic reduction in the size of the kit: such unserviceable garb as the white working rig and the purely ceremonial items should be discarded and the total value reduced to no more than £3 10*s*.[62]

The Admiralty now came to realise that the men would probably be satisfied by a reduction in the size, and therefore cost, of the existing kit. In 1906 a number of changes began to be announced, with such things as serge frocks and drill frocks abolished, and monkey jackets, check shirts with collar attached and the 'housewife' made optional. Altogether the cost was reduced from £9 5*s* to £6 5*s*.[63]

This was a welcome change, yet it did not fully satisfy many ratings for whom a free kit was the only real solution. Yexley decided that the only thing to do was to build up a groundswell of popular support for the proposal. '[. . .] Governments and Admiralties rarely introduce reforms of a financial nature from any consideration of justice,' he wrote; 'clamour and clamour alone will wrest concessions [. . .].'[64] In

Parliament the government was pressed to introduce a free kit.[65] Throughout 1907 Yexley contributed a series of background articles to *The Fleet* on the clothing question, entitled 'Naval Uniform, Past, Present and Future'. If the army and the Marines could provide a free uniform, he asked, why not the Navy too? The old argument that sailors were paid more, in compensation, no longer held as a comparison between naval and Marine pay showed. In 1908 his book *The Inner Life of the Navy* also dealt at length with the issue and advocated sweeping reforms, while from 1907 onwards the lower-deck societies associated with the loyal appeals continued to request a free kit. The pressure seemed to be bearing fruit, with some further concessions in 1907–08. Oilskins, sea boots and stokehold boots were to be borne in ships' stores for issue on loan as required. The 'privilege' of a free kit on entry was extended to ship's steward boys and boy writers, and free cap ribbons were to be issued on joining a ship.[66]

During the last months of Fisher's term as First Sea Lord changes also began to be introduced designed to inject some flexibility in the enforcement of the regulations. Yexley had been in contact with Fisher as early as 1905 over the uniform grievance,[67] and though the First Sea Lord was entirely sympathetic to the principle that the cost to the ratings should be kept as low as possible, the financial stringency imposed on the Navy in subsequent years ruled out the concession of a free kit. However, he was equally out of sympathy with the 'bandbox sailor' mentality, with its excessive attention to meticulous detail in matters of clothing. Thus by 1910, the year of his departure from the Admiralty, the 'tape-measure fetish' of the 'uniform strategist' was more or less on its way out, and shortly afterwards new regulations laid down that general smartness was to be considered of more importance than a minute adherence to detail and exact measurements.[68]

The question of who should bear the cost of the King's uniform continued to be a major issue in subsequent years and an increasingly serious one for the lower deck as rising prices pushed the cost from £6 5s in 1907 to £8 in 1913.[69] The fledgeling Australian and Canadian navies, manned largely by men of the Royal Navy, now issued free uniforms, and by 1913 a demand for a 'free maintained kit' was to head the list of requests in the annual loyal appeal. But in the government the call fell on deaf ears. The men of the Royal Navy therefore went to war in 1914 with the singular distinction of being the only fighting force of any country expected to pay for and maintain their own uniform. It would take three years of wartime conditions and an ever increasing clamour for relief before an officially maintained kit was secured and the grievance finally eradicated in 1917.

CORPORAL PUNISHMENT

The pattern and principles of naval discipline in the early twentieth century were rooted in the distant traditions of the service. A series of Naval Discipline Acts dating from the 1860s remained the basis of discipline throughout the period under review.[70] The effect was that acts and omissions which in civil life were mere breaches of contract or petty offences became subject to severe penalties.[71] Much of the arbitrary day-to-day discipline harked back to the time of Nelson and the martinet Admiral St Vincent.

At the turn of the century the Naval Discipline Act still retained the death penalty as the ultimate sanction for a dozen offences. Technically it provided for flogging by up to forty-eight strokes of the cat – still listed among the recognised punishments in King's Regulations in 1939.[72] In practice flogging had been *suspended* as a punishment in 1881 (not abolished, as in the army), but if it was no longer used the Admiralty clung to it as a deterrent.[73] All ships carried a cat as a reminder of what might be: the Admiralty retained the right to sanction its use without parliamentary approval, and flogging continued as a recognised punishment in naval prisons.[74]

Boy seamen could be birched or caned, and youths up to the age of eighteen could also be birched, although in civilian life the upper age limit was sixteen. In 1901–02 241 birchings and 8,000 canings were carried out.[75] The maximum number of strokes with the cane was twelve. The cane itself was 3 ft 6 in. long, as thick as a man's thumb, and had waxed twine at either end to prevent it from splitting. The punishment was usually awarded for minor offences such as smoking under the age of eighteen. Birching was reserved for more serious ones and was carried out in public in front of all boys of the ship. The birch used was twice as heavy as a police birch and had previously been soaked in brine.[76] Up to twenty-four strokes were permitted, and they were inflicted on the bare skin. If the maximum number of strokes was given, half would be administered by one man and half by another. Whereas the cane bruised, the birch cut.[77] As *The Fleet* noted, birching in the service was 'a disgusting and brutal affair'.[78]

It was against the corporal punishment of boys that the earliest reform campaigns were organised, the lead being taken around the turn of the century by the Humanitarian League. In Parliament the league found a passionate supporter in the Irish MP Swift MacNeill, who bombarded the government with questions. In the early 1900s mounting pressure for reform built up as instances of punishment were increasingly reported in the press, beginning with a case in 1899 on board the battleship *Majestic* in which a boy had committed suicide to avoid flogging.[79]

In 1902 the Society for the Reform of School Discipline protested to the Admiralty that flogging of all kinds had been abolished in the navies of all civilised countries as well as in the British army.[80] In 1904 the campaign was intensified. *Reynolds's Newspaper* ran a competition for the best short essay describing flogging by birch or cane.[81] The Humanitarian League proposed to plaster walls in the naval towns with pictures showing a naval birching, and ostentatiously challenged the Admiralty to allow photographs to be taken for the purpose.[82] Meanwhile suspicions that the authorities were deliberately hiding the truth about the extent and nature of corporal punishments were fortified when it was learned in Parliament that figures were no longer being recorded, allegedly because of the expense.[83] All the time instances of severe punishment continued to be reported in the press. In the summer of 1904 Parliament was told that boys on board the training ships were being caned for being unable to swim.[84] In August a boy seaman from the battleship *Formidable*, charged with stealing and ordered to report to the commander, committed suicide.[85]

By early 1906, with the advent of a Liberal government, the climate was favourable for a final push by the abolitionists. In February Swift MacNeill moved an amendment to the King's Speech calling for the urgent abolition of flogging. The government appeared to appreciate that concessions could no longer be delayed and it was announced that birching would be suspended for a twelve-month trial period and that henceforth caning would be allowed only on the captain's orders.[86] Pressing home their advantage, the reformers raised the question of why boy seamen who had committed no offence were compelled to witness corporal punishment, and secured a commitment to terminate the practice.[87] The suspension of birching for most offences proved to be permanent, and this, coupled with the tighter controls on the use of the cane, represented a major step forward.

COURTS MARTIAL

Courts martial were empowered to try all offences against the Naval Discipline Act, and in the early years of the century there was concern among ratings about the way these bodies worked. It was an old saying in the Navy that courts martial did not try, they only punished: extenuating circumstances had no place in naval law and procedure.[88] They also disregarded some elementary principles of justice. In 1900 sailors charged with an offence were not allowed to give evidence in their own defence. A solicitor could appear only as a 'prisoner's friend', with no right to address the court or cross-examine witnesses. All he was entitled to do was suggest questions for the prisoner himself to ask. There was no right of appeal against a decision, and sentences took effect immediately, even before the case had been reviewed in the normal manner by the authorities. In these respects the Navy lagged far behind practice not only in civilian courts but in the army and the Royal Marines.[89] Only in the first decade of the century, in the face of lower-deck pressure, did the Admiralty allow prisoners to give evidence and permit the prisoner's friend to cross-examine his client.[90]

On the lower deck there were now some who favoured doing away with courts martial in peacetime and having servicemen tried in civilian courts.[91] Between 1908 and 1911 the protracted legal action in which George Archer-Shee, a naval cadet dismissed from the service after being accused of theft, challenged the Admiralty ruling in the courts and finally secured compensation had a profound influence on the lower deck's attitude towards naval justice. What this case demonstrated was that there was one law for the officers and another for the men, and that whereas there was no chance of a rating ever being able to appeal in the civil courts against a miscarriage of justice a member of the officer class with enough wealth and influence could do just that.[92] More and more men looked outside the service for help in securing justice, and before World War I it was becoming the practice for some lower-deck societies to engage a lawyer to defend any of their members tried by court martial.[93] If the lawyer was impeded from conducting the defence effectively in the court, at least it was possible in some cases for him to secure an annulment on the grounds that the members of the court martial, themselves inexpert in matters of law, had disregarded some of the basic legal niceties.

At the turn of the century a large number of courts martial were held every year. Between 1892 and 1902 the incidence of disciplinary offences tried in this way nearly doubled, from 2·63 to 4·77 per 1,000 men.[94] Heavy sentences were handed down, yet the amount of 'crime' as the term was understood by civilians was quite small. In 1902 there were no fewer than 321 courts martial, 327 of the offenders tried being accused of crimes against superior authority.[95] The defendants in such cases were accused of striking, using threatening language to, doing violence to, or behaving with contempt towards a superior officer, but in almost every instance the superior concerned was only a petty officer or Marine NCO. Many of the striking offences occurred not in the execution of duty but as a result of personal arguments. For such an offence a rating could in theory be sentenced to death, but in practice the penalty was up to two years' imprisonment.

With the lower-deck press ready to publicise each and every abuse in naval discipline and the public in general beginning to cast a critical eye on the Navy's judicial procedures, the Admiralty began to modify its attitude to 'crime'. From 1902 there was a steady reduction in the number of courts martial, and especially in the number of striking and related offences. Officers investigating a case were now more prone to take into account the circumstances of the offence.[96] In 1909 there were 106 courts martial, one-third the number of seven years earlier, and the incidents involving striking had fallen by almost two-thirds.[97]

There had previously been a tendency for sentences to be excessive; so much was clear from the number that were reduced or annulled on review.[98] During the Fisher era this began to change. In 1907 the Admiralty issued a confidential circular calling attention to the unnecessary severity of the sentences. The result was at once apparent in a steady decrease in the length of prison terms. By 1912 four out of five court-martial sentences were for less than twelve months' imprisonment, whereas in 1870 only one-fifth of the ratings sentenced got less than one year.[99] The reduction in the number of men court-martialled for particular offences over the decade 1902–12 can be seen from the following table.[100] The difference was almost entirely due to a change of mentality at the Admiralty rather than to a different pattern of behaviour on the part of ratings.

Punishment inflicted for:	1902	1912
Striking, or attempting to strike	172	86
Threatening language	33	6
Disobedience	50	5
Behaving with contempt	72	5
Drunkenness	20	5
Desertion	26	4
Total	373	111
Number borne	104,724	119,903

NAVAL PRISONS

A great many of those court-martialled would end up in prison. At any given time, naval ratings serving prison sentences could be numbered in the hundreds – at Lewes prison alone there were always over 100 inmates – and the routine was arduous. Men sentenced to hard labour spent the first month in solitary confinement, and for two weeks they slept without a mattress. They were put to work at the treadwheel or capstan, or were made to break stones. For seven hours a day during the first month they picked two pounds of oakum and for two stretches of an hour and a half each day they were required to do shot drill, without doubt the hardest punishment of all: a heavy shot had to be shifted from one spot to another and back again.[101] The repetitive stooping and picking up was said to induce an excruciating pain in the loins. While doing the punishment they were dressed in a coarse canvas suit, and when they began to perspire the constant rubbing of the canvas scored the skin off their loins and could cause an irritating skin disease.[102]

In 1909, after much questioning in Parliament, the First Lord, Reginald McKenna, finally introduced changes which brought the Navy into line with the army.[103] They constituted a major reform in prison routine. The aim of the new system was to abolish the stigma of imprisonment by eliminating the degrading conditions associated with naval prisons. With the exception of Bodmin, these establishments were to be closed in 1911 and replaced by new detention quarters. Henceforth offenders would no longer be known as 'prisoners' but as 'men under detention'. They would wear uniform rather than prison clothes, would be confined in a room, not a cell, and would be supervised by petty officers. Instead of picking oakum and doing shot drill, they were to do a mixture of physical training, service drill and industrial work, the drill being designed to strengthen them physically. As the Parliamentary Secretary to the Admiralty explained, 'We mean to make punishment deterrent – severely deterrent [. . .] but not degrading.'[104]

The opening decade of the century thus witnessed the first concerted demands for the reform of a number of conditions of service, and by 1910 some notable victories had been won. Victualling had been substantially improved, some of the heat had been taken out of the vexed question of uniform regulations, and the worst excesses of the system of punishments for what the Navy regarded as serious offences had been checked. All this was the direct result of vocal protest and energetic agitation by individuals. In these years the pattern of campaigning that was to characterise the reform movement was established. The annual loyal appeal of the lower-deck societies had been launched, and though it was issued anonymously and never contained more than a bald list of grievances it did serve to focus the attention of the lower deck on some important and general complaints. In parallel, though conducted quite independently and with considerably more effect, were Lionel Yexley's campaigns in *The Fleet* which, for the first time ever, succeeded in carrying interest in the question of reform beyond the confines of the service. It was largely through Yexley's tub-thumping style that the press generally was alerted to conditions on the lower deck and began to report such matters, a welcome development which, in turn, encouraged the men to protest even more vigorously.

At all times the reform movement relied on the sympathetic support of people outside the service to help mobilise public opinion, and here MPs such as Swift McNeill, Gibson Bowles and Hudson Kearley and journalists like Arnold White and James Douglas were invaluable allies. But without doubt the most vital support was that from within the Admiralty itself – from Oswyn Murray, J. T. Macnamara and Jacky Fisher. It was Yexley's good fortune to attract Murray's attention when the latter was first appointed Assistant Director of Victualling, and they maintained a reasonably close relationship for the next twenty years, during which time Murray graduated to Assistant Secretary to the Admiralty and finally Permanent Secretary. He encouraged Yexley's public criticism in order to strengthen his own hand within the department, and it was from this time that Yexley's special relationship with the Admiralty dated.

Most important of all for the future success of the reform campaign was the relationship that developed between Yexley and Fisher. They first made contact when *The Fleet* was founded in 1905. In the next four years, with regular prodding from Yexley, Fisher presided over the changes discussed here, and towards the end of his term of office he was in regular communication with Yexley. Six months before leaving the Admiralty he confided, '[. . .] what has passed unobserved is what I am most happy about during my years at the Admiralty in what has been done for the Lower Deck, and I was looking forward to still more.'[105] But during his period as First Sea Lord – the early years of the Dreadnought race – there were no large funds for spending on lower-deck reforms, and much remained to be done after his departure. In his final weeks at the Admiralty he was busy drafting plans for several important reforms: a general revision of the system of discipline, an increase in pay for all ratings, and better promotion prospects for the lower deck, including advancement to commissioned rank. He communicated this to Yexley, but told him that it was to be treated confidentially and not taken as a manifesto for the lower deck. His successor, Sir Arthur Wilson, however, was not a reformer and Fisher had no illusions about the fate of his proposals. He warned Yexley that Wilson could not be expected to display the same enthusiasm, and in sending a list of some of his proposals to the First Lord, McKenna, he noted despondently, 'This is a copy of paper I gave to Wilson. He told Bridgeman [Second Sea Lord] he didn't want it. It will be his loss – no one else's.'[106] Fisher's unfinished programme would provide the main focus of the next phase of events.

The Yexley–Fisher–Churchill reforms

The British public must wake up to the fact that the POs and men of the Navy are almost universally dissatisfied [. . .] with the old fashioned methods of maintaining discipline [. . .].

The whole system of unofficial punishments is bad and mischievous and we are no longer doubtful that the system prevails almost universally in the fleet. – *Naval and Military Record*, 8 November 1911

We expect our bluejackets to take part of their wages in the coin of flattery. It never seems to occur to us that they require other coin, transmutable into food and clothing for wives and families, or, if it does, we take no effective steps to see that their requirements are met. – Gerard Fiennes, *Pall Mall Gazette*, 11 November 1912

[. . .] the Naval Service is the most antiquated, not only in this kingdom, but in the civilised world, in the matter of promotion. It is beyond the power of any man, however capable, however ambitious, ever to reach the rank of officer. The deep blue sea would seem to be the grave of the democratic spirit, and at the close of the Nineteenth Century snobbery sails supreme on British waters. – *Constabulary Gazette*, 14 October 1899

If the most brutal forms of punishment had been abolished by 1910, the humiliations and annoyance associated with the Navy's summary punishments were still felt for some time afterwards. By the end of the first decade of the century unrest on this count was increasing rapidly. It became the subject of Yexley's next major campaign, and as a result of his efforts a substantial measure of reform was achieved in 1912. That same year historic improvements were also made in the scale of pay and the prospects for promotion from the lower deck. On each of these three issues Yexley was assisted by Fisher, now in retirement. But whereas before there had been no driving force at the head of the Admiralty with enough commitment to force improvements through, there was now such a person in the shape of Winston Churchill, the new First Lord. It was this trio of Yexley, Fisher and Churchill, working in close co-operation, who were finally responsible for bringing to an end the dark age of naval discipline, for the first general pay rise for sixty years, and for opening up what was intended to be a real path of promotion from the lower deck to commissioned rank for young men of ability.

SUMMARY PUNISHMENTS

The Navy granted commanding officers sweeping powers to punish their men without trial. They could sentence them to be dismissed with disgrace; imprisoned for up to three months; reduced to the ranks; placed in solitary confinement for up to two weeks; stopped from going on leave; stopped from receiving rum; stopped smoking; stopped pay and allowances; given extra work, or stood in the corner like naughty boys. The sort of offences for which such punishments were often awarded included drunkenness, leave-breaking, negligent performance of duty, gambling, being improperly dressed and using profane language.

But much of the summary punishment was also awarded for offences the service manufactured. The *King's Regulations and Admiralty Instructions* (with 900 pages and 2,000 clauses) laid down comprehensive rules of conduct for officers and men, yet many captains also adopted an additional list of unofficial regulations. These were contained in *A Battleship Commander's Order Book*, a compilation of the various ship routines in force in three battleships of the Mediterranean Fleet in the late 1890s.[1] The manual was geared to achieving a high degree of smartness as an end in itself and, although it had no official standing, was widely referred to and enforced.

The book consisted of 303 pages closely packed with regulations covering every conceivable situation, and sailors were confronted with a seemingly unending list of dos and don'ts of the most trivial type. They were not to go over the lower booms with their trousers turned up; they were not to lean on the forecastle rails; towels and soap were to be kept in their white hat covers; cap ribbons were to be worn with the *S* of *Royal Sovereign* over the nose; kettle lids were not to be used for kneeling on – and so it went on for page after page.

Men who fell foul of these regulations were invariably subjected to what the service called '10A', a universally detested punishment.[2] Anyone awarded 10A was required to turn out an hour before the hands were called in the morning. He had to drink his cocoa on an exposed part of the upper deck under the watch of a ship's corporal. Breakfast and dinner would be eaten on the upper deck under supervision, and from 12.30 p.m. until the end of the dinner hour and again from 8.30 p.m. until 10 p.m. he would be made to stand facing the bulkhead, like a child in disgrace. The punishment might last up to fourteen days, and during this whole period his rum would be stopped and he would not be allowed to smoke.

While 10A was a terror for junior ratings, what petty officers feared most as a summary punishment was disrating.[3] In the army disrating could take place only after a court martial, but the Navy did not even give a man the right to apply for a court martial, and the Admiralty steadfastly refused to make it a matter for a formal trial.[4] Yet it was a serious punishment, liable to have far-reaching financial implications, since it could affect pension as well as current rate of pay. A man who held the rank of petty officer on going to pension received double the standard rate for the time he had held that rating. If, however, he was disrated and was unable to pick up his rate again the extra pension was lost, and this might all be due to a captain's whim.[5] Yet despite the severity of the punishment the number of men reduced to the ranks was high, ranging from 850 to 900 in 1907–08.[6] With approximately one in twelve petty officers being punished in this way each year, men could never be sure from one day to the next that some incident would not lead to their downfall.

On a day-to-day basis the system of discipline depended on how the individual captain exercised his far-reaching powers.[7] In fact where summary punishments were concerned there was no such thing as universal naval discipline, only the discipline of this or that ship.[8] Ratings never knew quite where they stood: as the lower deck would say, 'Another ship, another navy.'

Many of the common offences were committed in frustration at the perversity of the regulations. Until they began to be reformed the clothing rules were one of the most important causes of punishment. Frequent leave-breaking was more often than not the result of a failure to grant liberty in a consistent manner throughout the service. Likewise offences against gambling regulations stemmed from the fact that, whereas some commanding officers permitted card-playing, others assumed that if men were playing cards they must be gambling and deserved to be punished accordingly. But for whatever offence, in every single year from 1902 to 1911 more summary punishments were awarded than there were actually men on the lower deck. Every petty officer and rating had a better than even chance of being punished at least once a year.[9]

Nowhere was the mentality of officialdom better demonstrated than in its attitude to men who tried to find out what their legal rights were under this regime. The rules were often obscure and there was no copy of King's Regulations available for inspection.[10] To discover what they said a man would have to ask at the ship's office. There he would probably be told to get the captain's permission. This was the surest way of being branded a sea lawyer. Anyone bold enough to persist would be taken before the captain by the master-at-arms, more as a defaulter than as a genuine seeker after information.[11] As *The Fleet* commented:

> Of the discipline of intelligence which inspires men with a common object and so blends them into one coherent and cohesive whole there is no trace; we have instead a routine of stupidity and a discipline of the bath brick and brightwork rag whose only cohesive force is 10A.[12]

THE CAMPAIGN OF PUBLICITY

For a number of years the lower-deck press, and even occasionally the establishment service press, had protested about aspects of summary discipline.[13] As early as 1900 *The Bluejacket* had called for the abolition of ship's police, whose presence on board did nothing to further proper discipline.[14] From 1904 onwards the loyal appeals demanded the introduction of courts martial before disrating. They also criticised the arbitrary practice of stopping a man's leave when he was charged with an offence, and the arrangement whereby a sailor convicted in the civil courts could be punished again by the Navy for bringing the uniform into disrepute.[15] Occasional concessions were granted.[16] Automatic stoppage of leave was abolished in 1909. The same year the King's Regulations were amended with a view to discouraging hasty punishments. In future the investigation of a minor offence was not to be held until a day after it had been committed.[17] And in 1910 the rules on disrating were modified so that in cases involving petty officers the evidence would be taken down in writing and the sentence reviewed by the Admiralty.[18] But neither of the two last concessions made any appreciable difference as far as the lower deck were concerned.

In 1909 Yexley turned to the subject in an article, 'Naval Summary

Punishment and other Things', in *The Fleet Annual*. He analysed the statistics and pointed to the significant fact that Marines in barracks were punished far less than seamen and Marines on board ship. Whereas more than one punishment per man was awarded, on average, each year in ships, the rate for Marines in barracks was only about a fifth of this.[19] The reason lay almost entirely in the sensible pattern of discipline in barracks, where the atmosphere was more relaxed and there was a noticeable lack of inspection and parades. This permissive regime had not led to any lowering of standards, nor had it in any way impaired the Marines' fighting capability. Yet when they were drafted to sea they were subject to the same petty regulations as bluejackets and tormented by the pinpricks of pseudo-discipline.[20] The article also remarked a tendency for punishments to go unrecorded, and suggested that the number might be double the recorded ones. They were assuming 'sinister proportions' and 'threatening the wellbeing of the whole service'.[21] And on this point Yexley was supported by the lower-deck loyal appeal, which in 1909 called for an end to unauthorised punishments.

In the 1911 *Fleet Annual* he resumed this theme. The situation was growing more serious. 'The Navy,' he wrote, 'is reeking with discontent, which grows day by day, and which if not fairly met must end in explosion.'[22] The same year he published a comprehensive review of naval discipline in the book *Our Fighting Sea Men*. This was to have the greatest influence of all in the campaign for reform. It was an eloquent plea for a more enlightened system of discipline based on a recognition that the latter-day rating was a man of some education who did not need to be driven by punishment. The existing petty discipline was liable to turn otherwise decent individuals into sulky, habitual offenders.[23] The vast difference in the number of punishments awarded from ship to ship indicated that something was fundamentally wrong with the system. It all came back to the unbridled power of the captain.[24]

Yexley argued for stricter control of the way punishments were awarded. Too often the verdict was agreed between the commander and the master-at-arms, the judge and the prosecutor, even before any hearing took place.[25] He called too for a change in the forms of punishment. At one extreme the penalties were petty, serving only to antagonise the men. At the other they could be excessively severe. This was especially so in the case of cell punishments, yet in 1908 no fewer than 7,695 had been awarded, one for every fifteen men in the service.[26] Some sentences were followed by automatic, consequential punishments, often of a financial nature, and this could make it very difficult for a man to redeem himself. He became trapped in a pit from which it was hard to escape. Many simply resigned themselves to the fact that the Navy had a down on them and lived for the day when they could get out. For all the more serious summary offences Yexley proposed the establishment of ship courts martial, in effect a return to the practice of Cromwell's navy, in which members of the lower deck would be allowed to serve on the courts in a system of judgement by peers.[27]

The book was widely commented on in the press. During its preparation Yexley had been in close contact with Admiral Fisher, and the former First Sea Lord was largely responsible for some of the reviews.[28] A vigorous discussion followed in the columns of *The Observer, Vanity Fair*, and *Pall Mall Gazette* and the *Army and Navy Gazette*.[29] In the *English Review* Stephen Reynolds joined the debate with a strongly worded article, 'Navy Discontents', supporting Yexley's stand.[30] On the other hand the *Naval and Military Record* dismissed Yexley's argument as sensationalism, though it was later forced to reconsider after a flood of readers' letters substantiating the criticisms of naval conditions.[31] As the *Record* subsequently conceded, '[...] the numerous letters we have received point to such a widespread dissatisfaction with the conditions of pay and service as cannot have been known to the public, or even to the officers of the Navy'.[32]

CHURCHILL AND THE BROCK COMMITTEE

Our Fighting Sea Men was published in autumn 1911. In October Winston Churchill was moved from the Home Office, where he had recently presided over the reform of prison conditions, to become First Lord of the Admiralty.[33] The change was almost to guarantee the successful conclusion of the campaign for disciplinary reform. Fisher and Churchill had been close for a number of years. With his friend and admirer now the political head of the Navy, Fisher became the *éminence grise* at the Admiralty, or, as his biographer put it, the 'uncrowned First Sea Lord'.[34] In these circumstances Yexley was certain of the First Lord's ear, and on 1 December he met Churchill, who assured him of his general support.[35] Yexley now forwarded to the new First Lord letters of complaint received from the lower deck, particularly on the question of disrating.[36] Within three weeks at his new post Churchill asked Captain Troubridge, the Naval Secretary, to outline proposals for the reform of discipline.[37] Then in February 1912 a departmental committee of inquiry was set up under the chairmanship of Rear-Admiral Federic Brock to look into the whole issue of summary punishments.[38]

The Brock committee heard evidence from over ninety officer and men. The evidence of the officers was particularly revealing.   nost all agreed that unless the captain had the power of summary disrating authority in the service would collapse, and some senior officers expressed views that would not have been out of place in the mid-nineteenth century. Captain Fremantle of the battleship *Dreadnought* voiced the feelings of this school when he told the committee, 'I do not consider that much is wrong with the discipline of the service at the present day [. . .]. The situation is certainly not one which calls for any drastic revision in the Regulations [. . .].'[39]

It was among this group of officers that the idea of courts martial for petty officers faced with disrating was most strenuously resisted. The suggestion was 'nothing but Socialism, trade unionism and everything else', declared Captain Leveson of the battlecruiser *Indefatigable*: as it was, there was not half as much disrating as was necessary.[40] Some officers, like Captain Vaughan Lee of the battleship *Collingwood*, also expressed strong opposition to any relaxation of the punishment of men confined. Prisoners were so well treated in the new detention quarters, he complained, that they came back looking as though they had been on holiday. They did not look thin enough. By contrast, ratings looked very broken down at the end of fourteen days' in the cells, and for this reason he was a great believer in cells.[41]

Likewise it was Captains Vaughan Lee and Leveson who spoke out most strongly for those who believed in the value of 10A and making the rating stand facing the paintwork. Under questioning Leveson admitted that it was like putting a child in a corner, but then, the rating was a child: '. . . men must learn to stand still; soldiers were better sentries than sailors because sailors would not stand still. Sailors were simply childish men, and must be treated as children.' When he was finally pressed to suggest an alternative punishment he replied directly, 'You will have to put them in a sort of cage.'[42]

Brock had no sympathy with the views of the 'drive and punish' school, but neither did he approve of the reform campaign, and much of his questioning of lower-deck witnesses was aimed at securing an admission that Yexley and *The Fleet* were at the back of the unrest. 'Do the men agree with him [Yexley]?' 'Do they read *The Fleet*?' 'Does he [Yexley] upset people?' 'Does he put ideas into their heads? 'Is there much socialism in the Navy?' 'What about the activities of the lower-deck societies?' he pressed the witnesses.[43]

Finally the committee invited Yexley to the Admiralty to give evidence. There was little love lost between him and Brock: the chairman referred to him as an agitator, and Yexley later described the atmosphere in the committee room as rather frigid.[44] He was grilled exhaustively on his writings, but he stood his ground. Indeed, he warned the committee that, if anything, the unrest in the service was more serious than he had ever described.[45]

The report that was submitted to Churchill in 1912 represented a cautious step along the road towards a reform of discipline. In positive vein Brock proposed a thoroughgoing revision of 10A, abolishing the practice of standing on the quarter deck and eating meals under the watch of a sentry, and substituting extra work and drill. Leave arrangements were to be simplified, all but the worst offenders being allowed to land at least once a month. Leave-breaking was to be punished by a combination of fines and stoppage of leave, but this would completely purge the offence: there were to be no consequential punishments. Nor was there to be any general ban on the playing of cards. Officers below the rank of commander would no longer be allowed to award heavy punishment without the approval of superiors. And, to reassure men of their rights, it was proposed to place an extra copy of King's Regulations on board for their perusal.[46]

In other respects the committee lined up alongside the traditionalists. There was a proposal to increase the use of the cane as a punishment for boy seamen. Cell punishment was to be retained along the existing lines and was not to be made more like detention, with its emphasis on rehabilitation. The ship's police were not to be abolished as many people had urged, and, finally, the committee could find no sufficient reason for recommending courts martial for petty officers faced with disrating.[47]

Brock's report probably went as far as most naval officers were willing to go, and some sections of the Admiralty evidently thought it had given the ratings too much. But as far as Churchill was concerned the proposals did not go nearly far enough, and from the moment the report landed on his desk he took personal control of the situation, making his views plain to his Admiralty colleagues. He expressed

reservations about any increase in the use of the cane. Three of the Sea
Lords agreed with Brock that petty officers should not have the right
to a court martial before being disrated, but Churchill was not at all
impressed with their arguments. 'The treatment of this question does
not appear to me to be adequate,' he wrote. 'The position of the PO
ought to be safeguarded in the same degree [. . .] as that of NCOs in the
Army. [. . .] Every PO must have the right to trial by Court Martial
before being disrated [. . .].' On the question of cells he was equally
forthright:

Cells punishment on board ship is more severe and less beneficial than
detention [. . .]. Cells should never be used in harbour for longer periods than
three days. [. . .] Detention is beneficial. Cells are injurious. Let a scheme be
prepared to carry out this system.[48]

By mid-August 1912 he had secured agreement within the Board of
Admiralty on many of the committee's recommendations, and on 7
September the famous circular letter No. 32 was issued, incorporating
the Brock proposals on 10A, leave, consequential punishments and
card-playing, and also placing restrictions on the power of the ship's
police.[49] Heralding the new regime, the *Daily Express* remarked:

We have treated you like naughty boys, while demanding from you the best
work of a man. In future we will treat you like self-respecting men. [. . .] it is
shameful to recall how badly they have been treated in the past.[50]

But Churchill had not finished yet. In accordance with his demand,
immediate arrangements were made that no one would serve more
than three days in cells if proper detention quarters were at hand.[51]
On 27 September another circular letter announced that at long last
captains' power to disrate would be circumscribed, and petty officers
would be entitled to opt for a court martial rather than summary
punishment.[52] Finally, in November, a confidential letter to
commanding officers set out guiding principles for the new
disciplinary system: it recognised the gulf between officers and men
and recommended a more relaxed, flexible shipboard routine.[53]
     Taken together, the changes marked the beginning of a new era.
Significantly, 1912 was the first year ever when the number of
summary punishments was less than the total number of lower-deck
ratings.[54] The circular letters of 1912 provided the framework for a
new, intelligent form of daily discipline based on twentieth-century
needs. But the success of the scheme could not be guaranteed by paper
regulations. It was a change in attitude that was needed, particularly

among naval officers, and for any noticeable shift here the men had to await the watershed of World War I.

LOWER-DECK COMMISSIONS

The avenue of promotion from the lower deck to commissioned rank which, up to the Napoleonic wars, had produced a number of 'tarpaulin' officers was almost completely closed in the course of the nineteenth century. The last man from the lower deck to be elevated in this way was John Kingcome, who was commissioned in 1818 and retired as Admiral of the Red Sir John Kingcome. In the course of the next eighty-four years only four men were commissioned from the ranks.[55]

From 1890 onwards the Warrant Officers' Society lobbied for regular commissions for its members, and in 1903 the campaign met with some success when 100 chief warrant officers were elevated to lieutenant.[56] Jacky Fisher, then Second Sea Lord, was responsible for this departure. Each year from 1904 the loyal appeals asked for the scheme to cover more branches and a larger number of men. It was a demand that Fisher sympathised with, and from 1905 he too pressed for more commissions for warrant officers. But, as he indicated to Yexley in 1909, he was having difficulty convincing his Admiralty colleagues, and it was only on the eve of his retirement that he was able to widen the scheme.[57]

The trouble was that it only benefited older men nearing the point of retirement, and they could not expect to be promoted beyond lieutenant. There was no opening for young, capable ratings to enter the wardroom and then rise to the highest command. This was Yexley's criticism, and in 1907 *The Fleet* had suggested a completely new arrangement under which young petty officers who were successful in a competitive examination would be raised to the rank of acting lieutenant and placed under close scrutiny for twelve months as potential officer material.[58] Here was the germ of the idea which eventually came to fruition in Churchill's 'mate' scheme of 1912.

In the summer of 1910 the whole issue of lower-deck promotion came to a head, following a suggestion in the House of Commons that schoolboys from poor families be granted scholarships to help them enter naval college as officer cadets.[59] The proponents of lower-deck promotions were quick to denounce the idea. Interviewed in the *Daily News*, Yexley seized the opportunity to point out that there had been

A SEA-CHANGE

("INTO SOMETHING RICH AND STRANGE").

FIRST LORD OF THE ADMIRALTY (at Earl's Court). "WELL, THINGS HAVE CHANGED SINCE YOUR TIME; BUT OUR LOWER DECK'S AS GOOD AS EVER."

SHADE OF SIR RICHARD GRENVILLE (of the "Revenge"). "YES; AND I HEAR THEY'RE UNDERPAID AS WELL AS EVER."

FIRST LORD. "AH! THAT'S ANOTHER CHANGE WE HOPE TO MAKE."

Churchill's promise of a pay increase for the lower deck in 1912; as seen by *Punch* no genuine lower-deck promotion for nearly a hundred years.[60] Meanwhile, conservatives in the service feared democratisation in any shape or form; the *Naval and Military Record* spelled out this view unequivocally:

> The British Navy has long obtained an ample supply of capable officers, and also a fair proportion of the most able Admirals and Captains in the world, without recruiting from the Democracy to any visible extent [. . .] we should view with grave apprehension any attempt to officer the fleet at all largely with men of humble birth.[61]

Similar sentiments were to be repeated a number of times from this quarter. 'It takes three generations to make a gentleman,' wrote one officer. 'The present naval officer is in every way quite suitable for the needs of the Service, and it is a good maxim to "let well alone".'[62] Indeed, the disdain for the lower deck demonstrated by some participants in this debate aroused strong feelings among ratings. An angry letter to *The Fleet* proclaimed, 'It is not birth we want in the Navy today, it is brains, and the tradesman's son with brains is worth a dozen dukes' sons with only their fathers' splendour behind them.'[63]

One of the points in the programme of reforms left by Fisher for his successor, Wilson, to deal with in 1910 was a system of promotion to enable ratings to climb to the highest ranks. In retirement Fisher kept up his prompting of Yexley and advised him of the obstruction at the Admiralty:

> You cannot in a democratic state go on drawing 99% at least of your officers from the Upper Ten! *It won't last and it ought not to last.* I have just had McKenna here on his second visit to me and he sees all this but no one to back him.[64]

Now he told Yexley that if he cared to draft a practical scheme for the advancement of capable young ratings he would push it for all he was worth.[65] The offer was accepted and Yexley promptly produced a comprehensive plan for lower-deck commissions which was first published in outline in the *Naval Chronicle* and *The Fleet* in the autumn of 1910 and then in full in *The Fleet Annual* in 1911.[66]

The main problem was to devise a means of ensuring that men who had risen from the lower deck would be on an equal footing, for purposes of subsequent promotion, with pukka officers of the same age who already had the benefit of several years' experience on the quarter deck. Yexley's solution was to select lower-deck candidates from among young leading seamen and petty officers who had passed the examination for warrant officer and were still under the age of twenty-six. They were to be promoted to the rank of acting warrant officer and would then join the sub-lieutenants for instruction and take the same examination. On being promoted to lieutenant, their seniority would be antedated in accordance with their examination marks and credits for their previous lower-deck service, thus cancelling the age advantage held by lieutenants who had entered as cadets. This way, at the age of twenty-seven to twenty-nine, they would be available for all the duties of a lieutenant.

As promised, Fisher took up the cause in earnest, all the time trying to win over McKenna, the First Lord. In early October 1911 he wrote to Yexley:

I keep on telling McKenna (I wrote him 8 sheets the other day!) that he will be wise to anticipate the irresistible coming agitation for greater recognition of the rank and file of the Navy and their legitimate aspirations.[67]

But there was no interest in the scheme at the Admiralty. Fisher was beginning to despair of the Liberals when in October 1911 he urged Yexley to forge an alliance with prominent members of the Navy League and through them have lower-deck grievances brought before Parliament from the Tory side of the House.[68] However, within two weeks McKenna was to be replaced by Churchill, the obstruction was to some extent removed and the situation was ripe for a renewed onslaught.

Within days of Churchill's appointment Fisher had travelled back from holiday in Switzerland to meet the new First Lord and urge on him his unfinished programme of personnel reforms, including lower-deck commissions. Churchill's arrival at his new post was followed by changes in the Board of Admiralty, and three of the four Sea Lords were replaced. Fisher urged him to seize the opportunity of the *interregnum* to make a speech announcing his intention to open up commissioned rank to the lower deck before the new Sea Lords settled down.

Fight *like hell* against increasing entry of cadets. The remedy is to promote more Bluejackets and Marines from Warrant Officers.
N.B. you will have fearful opposition but you will have a Mutiny at the Nore if you don't handle the Lower Deck grievances and the grievances of the 39/40ths of the population whose sons cannot enter as Naval Officers because of the expense.[69]

In December 1911 and January 1912 Yexley and Churchill had their first meetings. They talked at length about reforms in general and lower-deck commissions in particular. Yexley argued for his scheme for early promotions and elicited Churchill's broad support.[70]

Fisher and Yexley between them had completely won Churchill over to their viewpoint, but there was to be no easy progress along the path of reform. Churchill told Yexley of the opposition he was encountering from the Sea Lords.[71] Personnel matters were the responsibility of the Second Sea Lord, and Prince Louis of Battenberg had been newly appointed to this position. But Battenburg showed little enthusiasm for lower-deck commissions, and in the months following his appointment in December 1911 he made no effort to press for change. Within the Admiralty the running had to be made by Churchill. Taking Fisher's advice, he decided to announce his intentions in his speech on the Navy Estimates on 18 March 1912, but he only managed to force Battenberg to draft an outline of a scheme for commissions a matter of days beforehand, and the Sea Lords had not yet given their assent to it.[72] Reflecting Prince Louis's antipathy, the draft fell short of what Yexley and Churchill wanted. In particular there was to be no antedating of seniority. Nevertheless, with this as his brief, Churchill went ahead and enthusiastically announced to the House his ideas of promoting men from the lower deck on the basis of merit.[73] His aim was to establish the principle of lower-deck commissions, hoping to build on it later. The proposals were accepted by both sides of the House, and, surprised by the Tory support for the scheme, the Sea Lords had little option but to approve it at the next Board of Admiralty meeting.

Even so, when the detailed regulations governing the scheme were announced, regulations which were the responsibility of Battenberg's department, the original proposal had been watered down even further. Instead of successful candidates being promoted to lieutenant, they were to be given the rank of 'mate', thus interposing an intermediate rank in which men would have to serve for two to three years.[74] And with no antedating of seniority, those finally promoted to lieutenant at around the age of twenty-eight would be unable to advance beyond the rank of commander on the retired list.

Battenberg's son, Lord Mountbatten, has argued privately, and his biographer in print, that Prince Louis was responsible for the introduction of lower-deck commissions and that Churchill merely followed his lead.[75] There is no evidence to substantiate this view, indeed there can be little doubt that Battenberg was opposed to the idea of ranker officers advancing to higher commands. 'I do not think we can permit this,' he wrote. 'Taking them as a whole (there may be a few brilliant exceptions) they must be considered as a somewhat inferior article.'[76]

As Second Sea Lord Battenberg must be held responsible for the limitations of the 'mate' scheme, his emasculated version of the Yexley–Churchill proposal. Men promoted from the lower deck were to be treated as a group apart, and the social stigma of being designated offically as an 'ex-mate' was to pursue ranker officers throughout their wardroom careers until the rank was eliminated nineteen years later in 1932. The forces of reaction at the Admiralty had got their claws into the scheme from the start, and a barrier effectively preventing men from reaching the higher ranks had been erected at the outset. Consequently, relatively few men came forward as candidates for mate, and opponents of the scheme took this as a comforting sign that there was no interest in lower-deck commissions among ratings.[77]

Beyond this, the administration of the scheme was calculated to ensure that it was not a great success. There was no deliberate attempt to select as candidates only the younger ratings of definite merit who might be expected to go far. Men were deterred from applying by the practice of selecting only teetotalers and those who were single: the drinking habits of the lower deck and the prospect of unrefined lower-deck wives entering the social mileu of the wardroom were evidently not acceptable.[78] No orders were issued by the Admiralty urging commanders-in-chief to make sure the scheme succeeded, and little encouragement or advice was given by officers to men who showed interest in promotion. Small wonder that within a year an Admiralty committee reported that the system as constituted was not succeeding.[79]

Yet despite what can only be regarded as a deliberate attempt to sabotage the scheme within the Admiralty, it was not a total failure in the early years. By the end of the Great War 371 lower-deck ratings of the seaman branch, 161 ERAs and twelve Marines had been promoted to lieutenant.[80] An important breakthrough had been made, and, given the will on the part of officialdom, it could be improved on in years to come. The fact that the mate scheme in the inter-war years never amounted to more than a form of tokenism was entirely due to the fact that the Admiralty and the officer class in general did not possess that will. But in 1912 the arrangement appeared to be a bridgehead; and for its main architects, Yexley and Churchill, it represented a not inconsiderable achievement in the face of substantial opposition.

THE PAY OF THE LOWER DECK

In April 1853, with the introduction of continuous service, the basic pay of an able seaman was fixed at $1s$ $7d$. The rate of pension had been set at $\frac{1}{2}d$ per day per year of service back in 1831, and when continuous service was introduced the full period for which the pension was payable was twenty years, making a total amount of $10d$ per day. Neither the basic rate of pay nor pension was increased during the next sixty years. To earn more than this ratings had to have special qualifications in areas such as gunnery or torpedoes or up to three good conduct badges with an extra $1d$ per day each to the holder. While many men were able to supplement their income in this way, the problem was that so much of it was unsecured: they could lose their non-substantive rate, and likewise good conduct badges could be stripped away for a trivial offence.

After 1902, when soldiers over twenty were granted a 50 per cent increase, ratings' pay compared unfavourably with that of the army.[81] At the turn of the century it was also the case that the merchant service was paying seamen 50 per cent more than the Royal Navy.[82] The usual justification was that, unlike merchant seamen, matelots received a pension. But the basic pension was a miserable sum, at least one in three men left the Navy without any entitlement, and even for those who did draw it the pension could be a mixed blessing since it was common for employers to take on ex-naval ratings below the going wage on the grounds that their Navy pension would make up the difference.[83]

However, on the whole there was little complaining about levels of pay at the turn of the century. Occasionally it was suggested that rates might be higher. *The Bluejacket* argued that an able seaman should get $2s$ and attributed the stagnation in pay to the fact that sailors had no union to represent them, no parliamentary spokesman and, until quite recently, no paper of their own.[84] But for the most part men knew that they were economically more secure in the service than outside.

In 1905 the Admiralty appointed a committee under Captain Montague Browne to inquire into the qualifications for substantive and non-substantive pay. It was not concerned primarily with levels of pay but with differentials between junior ratings and petty officers, and its recommendations, which were implemented in 1907, benefited the former hardly at all. The substantive pay of an able seaman was increased by 1*d* a day, but this was cancelled out by the abolition of the 1*d* he received as a 'trained man'. Understandably it was viewed by the lower deck as a typical 'Admiralty rise' and caused considerable resentment.[85]

As the decade progressed concern about the level of pay became more apparent. From 1907 onwards the annual loyal appeal of the lower-deck societies called in general terms for an increase, though without specifying any precise figure. Uniting round a common pay policy was no easy matter. Each branch of the service had a separate scale of remuneration, and altogether there were no fewer than eighty-nine different rates for lower-deck ratings.[86] The difficulty was compounded by the fact that not all men had the same entitlement to payment for good conduct badges. At the same time a fall in living standards was becoming more widely felt as prices rose steadily between 1900 and 1912, reducing the value of pay by about 15 per cent.[87] The cost of rented accommodation in the naval towns became a particularly important problem as the Admiralty policy of concentrating the fleet in home waters led to a greater number of sailors marrying and setting up home.[88] And the constant movement of ships meant a great deal of travelling by train at their own expense if men wanted to spend their leave with their families.[89]

When the committee of dockyard Members of Parliament met the First Lord in July 1909 to discuss lower-deck issues they pressed him to introduce incremental payments for men with specified periods of service.[90] Lord Charles Beresford called for pay increases, and in *The Fleet* Yexley proposed progressive increments of 2*d* and 4*d* after three and five years' service.[91] Meanwhile the country was convulsed by a wave of strikes over pay and conditions, the average number of disputes in 1910–11 being almost double that for the previous seven years and the number of strikers higher than in all the other years since 1900 put together.[92] The success of much of the industrial action was not lost on the ratings. Policemen, postmen, firemen, railwaymen and dockyard labourers had all forged ahead of them. In the course of the dockers' and seamen's strikes of 1911 great play was made of the fact that wages had not been increased for twenty years.[93] Basic pay for able seamen had not changed in sixty years, and there was now a quickening in the pace of organisation.

When the lower-deck societies met in late 1911 to formulate next year's loyal appeal they included for the first time a specific demand for a 20 per cent increase for all ratings, averaging out at 4*d* a day for able seamen and 7*d* for petty officers.[94] Churchill's naval biographer has suggested that when the new First Lord arrived at the Admiralty the question of pay was the most urgent of all the lower-deck problems facing him.[95] He was under strong pressure from the movement to tackle the issue, and there was great disappointment when he failed to make any statement on it during the Navy Estimates debate in March 1912. Kinloch-Cooke, the Member of Parliament for Devonport, called for a Royal Commission on pay and pensions and was supported by 156 MPs.[96] In the spring and early summer demands in the press and Parliament for an increase in pay for sailors built up to a crescendo, the *Daily Chronicle, Daily Mail, Morning Post, Pall Mall Gazette, Weekly Dispatch, Naval Chronicle* and *Truth*, all lending their weight to the campaign.[97]

In May Yexley wrote to Churchill offering to put forward a detailed proposal for raising lower-deck pay and indicating that progressive increments sufficiently large to satisfy the main body of seamen and stokers could probably be introduced at a relatively small cost.[98] But Churchill was meeting with opposition from Lloyd George at the Treasury over his proposed expenditure on lower-deck reforms. Just before going on a Mediterranean tour in the Admiralty yacht with the Prime Minister, Asquith, he invited Fisher to join the party at Naples. His aim was to enlist Fisher's considerable influence in convincing the Prime Minister of the need for a pay increase. Fisher wrote from Naples to let Yexley know about the invitation, promising that he would urge the Prime Minister to consult him.[99] Later Fisher reported back to Yexley:

I had an opportunity in a tête-à-tête conversation with the Prime Minister at Naples to suggest to him to have an interview with you, as to the blue-jackets' pay etc., and he promised me he would send for you privately on his return to England, I told him he might rely on you as trustworthy and discreetly silent and thoroughly reliable in putting forward what was reasonable [. . .] .[100]

Meanwhile he kept up the pressure on Asquith, telling Churchill:

I propose unless you write to me the contrary to again speak to the Prime Minister next Thursday July 11th after Defence Committee about giving

£200,000 for the Bluejackets' pay or else, *believe me*, there will be a very nasty business in the autumn that will stagger the Empire![101]

THE YEXLEY SCHEME

In fact Asquith left the ball in Churchill's court, and on 22 July the First Lord told the House of Commons that he intended to increase lower-deck pay and that the details would be announced in the autumn. But the battle with the Treasury was only beginning. Churchill asked his department to prepare proposals on the assumption of having up to £500,000 to spend.[102] But as a fall-back he also asked Yexley to put forward his own scheme, to cost not more than £300,000.[103] If all the men were to be allowed was a few extra pennies, Yexley would know better than anyone how to distribute them to best advantage.

Yexley immediately arranged to meet the members of the Chatham lower-deck joint committee at his house in Ilford to sound them out on the minimum acceptable level of increase.[104] In dealing with the representatives of one port in this way he was undermining the already tenuous solidarity of the benefit societies behind the loyal appeal and the 20 per cent claim. However, he was able to elicit from them the fact that junior ratings would be satisfied with progressive increases of 2d after three years' service and a further 2d after six years, and a standardisation of the system of payment for good-conduct badges.

The entire scheme was contained in a thirty-page memorandum to Churchill in which he pointed out:

[. . .] what has been very forcibly born upon me is the fact that the present clamour is not so much for a RISE of pay as a re-arrangement of pay so as to enable men:– (*a*) to earn as much over their full period of 22 years as they did in a past decade (*b*) to make the various maximum rates for the various classes actual and not theoretical maximums.[105]

In October Churchill submitted his departmental scheme to the Cabinet. He proposed to increase pay at the lowest level by 4d after three years' service. His lengthy memorandum accurately reflected the urgency of the situation. He told his Cabinet colleagues:

[. . .] there is a deep and widespread sense of injustice and discontent throughout all ranks and ratings of the Navy. This discontent and the grievances which produce it are fanned and advertised in Parliament and the press. It is rendered more dangerous by every successful strike for higher wages which takes place on shore. It is rendered more legitimate by the social legislation upon which Parliament is engaged, and by the measures like the Minimum Wage Bill which secure to the coal-miner minimum rates of wages which, though spoken of in terms of biting contempt by the miners, are nearly double what the sailors can hope to obtain [. . .] .

The sailors have hitherto been restrained by their sense of discipline and loyalty, but we have no right to trade on this indefinitely. [. . .]

The reports of the German agents dwell continually upon the discontent of the sailors with the conditions of their pay, and there is no doubt that the German opinion on this point is as well founded as it is widespread.[106]

Still the Treasury continued to resist such expenditure. Churchill warned again: 'Unless this question is dealt with effectively [. . .] a continuance of the agitation, which is as dangerous as it is novel, is certain.'[107] Indeed, the Admiralty's failure to make the long-awaited announcement in the autumn led the men to fear a betrayal, and sections of the press and Members of Parliament renewed the pressure for a prompt settlement of the issue.[108] Churchill drafted a letter to Lloyd George warning him that the Sea Lords might resign over it and advising that in such an event he would go too.[109] But the letter was never sent, the Chancellor remained intransigent and Churchill had to revise his proposals downward.

This was the situation he had anticipated, and he was able to base his revised scheme on Yexley's proposals. Allowing himself slightly more than Yexley had had to work with, he returned to the Cabinet in mid-November with a compromise scheme for raising an able seaman's pay by 3d after six years. There was no question of this being adequate or satisfactory, he insisted. It was a palliative rather than a cure; it would not be the final settlement that he had hoped for and it would not bring naval pay up to par with civilian rates. Moreover, he added, 'it will not effectively terminate the movement to better [. . .] conditions which has been so strongly marked since the great and successful strikes of 1911.'[110]

The increase was approved by the Cabinet and announced in the House of Commons on 4 December 1912. In private correspondence with the King, Churchill made no attempt to disguise his disappointment at the size of the increase.[111] On the lower deck, feelings were mixed. The rise amounted to 15 per cent in the case of able seamen, although it applied only to those aged at least twenty-four with six years' service. By and large it was regarded as a payment on account, an instalment towards a full settlement that many hoped

would come the following year.[112] Nevertheless it was the first real
increase for decades and that alone marked it as an event of
considerable historical significance. It defused the situation, and for
that the Admiralty and the Liberal government were largely indebted
to Lionel Yexley and his close contacts among the lower deck.

MARRIAGE ALLOWANCES

The problem of low pay was felt most acutely by married ratings, of
whom there were a growing number now that more and more units
were based in home waters. The economic difficulties of married men
were an important contributing factor in the unrest of 1911–12.
Unmarried ratings could manage on the existing rates, but for a
married man with a family naval pay might mean starvation wages.
There was no naval equivalent of the army and Marine system under
which married men received 6d a day lodging money and rations for
themselves and their wives.[113] There were no married quarters, and
there were no arrangements for wives to follow husbands on foreign
postings. By 1912 there was a growing feeling on the lower deck that
the existence of wives ought to be recognised by the payment of a
marriage allowance.[114]

When Churchill announced in July 1912 his intention to raise
lower-deck pay he spoke of the particular hardship faced by married
ratings, but he made it clear that he approved of men marrying while
in the service.[115] The lower deck took this to mean that a marriage
allowance was about to be introduced. As Yexley pointed out to the
First Lord when submitting his proposals for a pay increase:

[...] in the majority of cases I found men carrying about with them
newspaper cuttings referring to that part of your speech; in the pay
proposals contained herein one has to frankly face the fact that they were put
forward on the assumption that they would be backed up with a marriage
allowance on similar lines to the Marines. On that point there was finality:
'Mr. Churchill has promised it,' and from that they would not budge.[116]

Churchill did subsequently include a scheme for a marriage allowance
of between 3d and 6d a day in his initial proposal to the Cabinet, but
the financial stringency of the Treasury forced him to abandon the
project amid great disappointment among the lower deck.[117]

In 1913, for the first time, the loyal appeal now carried a specific
request for a marriage allowance. The question was raised in the
Commons, and the pressure on the government intensified when the

new Australian navy, manned by British ratings, announced a scheme of allowances for its married men.[118] Within the Admiralty Churchill was still keen to treat the matter as a priority, and urged his officials to produce a viable scheme.[119] But by the spring of 1914 nothing had materialised. Churchill was again under pressure in the House to do something, and at last in May Yexley was asked to draft concrete proposals. As on the pay question in 1912, he consulted the Chatham joint committee, and the proposal they came up with involved a 9d per day allowance for men with six years' service, rising to 1s for ratings with twelve years', plus 1d per day for each child.[120] If the Admiralty happened to have £150,000 to £200,000 unspent by the end of the year, Yexley was informed, there would be some likelihood of the proposals being accepted.[121]

In fact the outbreak of war in August did what years of special pleading had failed to achieve, forcing the Admiralty to foreshorten its leisurely time scale for recognising the rating's wife. On 4 September Churchill secured Cabinet approval for the immediate introduction of what were termed 'separation allowances'.[122] Indeed, the government now demonstrated a generosity of spirit towards the lower deck that had never been seen in peacetime. The allowances were in some respects more generous even than the benefit societies had asked for, married men below the rank of petty officer being allowed 6s per week, plus 2s for the first two children and 1s for each subsequent child.[123]

The 1912 increase in basic rates that many men regarded as a payment on account was not augmented before the Great War. Only the separation allowances increased the standard of living, though for some of the recipients they were equivalent to a pay rise of nearly 50 per cent. Married men had never been better off, and again their debt was to Lionel Yexley and the work of the reform movement organised around the loyal appeal.

The reforms of 1911–12 were more than had been achieved in any previous period. Yet in view of the growing unrest in the Navy they were probably the minimum the Admiralty could have got away with. In some ways conditions on the lower deck had actually been deteriorating, and there was a clear need for a reversal of policy. This was certainly the case in the matter of summary discipline. But in other respects the lower deck simply seemed to be reflecting the general mood and movement of civilian society. These were turbulent years, and the democratic sentiment behind the campaign for lower-deck commissions, for example, reflected a growing challenge to elitist values outside the service – a trend which Fisher saw clearly. As Stephen Reynolds observed:

Democratic changes on land are beyond Admiralty control, yet they ricochet into the autocratically governed Navy, intensifying the contrast. It [the Navy] is no longer a thing apart, and the regulations designed to keep it so have partially broken down.[124]

Likewise the pressure for a pay increase would not, in all probability, have been as great as it was but for the labour unrest of 1910–12 and the advances resulting from trade union militancy.

If it is true that the Navy managed to come through this period of unrest by conceding only the minimum likely to be acceptable to the men, it is clear that the personal involvement of Yexley and Fisher and their fortunate relationship with Churchill were of enormous significance. All the major reforms of these years bore their personal stamp – in basic outline as well as in many final details. The nature of their relationship is therefore a matter of some interest. There is no doubt that in naval terms all three were radicals. However, it was not simply a commitment to lower-deck reform that bound them together: other trade-offs were involved.

In the case of Fisher and Yexley it was the First Sea Lord who really began to cultivate the relationship in 1909.[125] He had been embroiled in a conflict with Admiral Lord Charles Beresford over a range of naval policies for much of his period of office; no doubt Fisher saw Yexley as an ally and his journal as a potential weapon in the war of words that would continue. Beresford was planning to stand for Parliament at Portsmouth and was talked of as a possible First Lord if the Tories won the election.[126] As a result he was intent on wooing the lower-deck vote. To prevent his election if possible it was important for Fisher to secure the support of the most influential lower-deck journalist. He encouraged Yexley to stand against Beresford in the election, and even before he left the Admiralty was feeding him with information to reinforce his reform campaign.[127] Fisher suggested subject matter for articles in *The Fleet*, topics that were sometimes close to the heart of his battle with Beresford, and he was able to feel that the journal was available for him to use at any time. As Esther Hallam Moorhouse, the naval writer and wife of Yexley's co-director of *The Fleet*, Meynell, told Fisher, ' [. . .] his paper and my pen are always at your disposal, if in any way they can help you'.[128] In turn,

Yexley's success as a campaigning journalist depended on his being able to point to regular achievements, and it was largely with Fisher's help that his agitation got results. Fisher was thus in a sense broker between the Admiralty and Yexley; Yexley relied on him for his privileged position as an insider, and the success of his campaigning required that he remain on much the same wavelength as Fisher.

The relationship between Yexley and Churchill also worked to mutual advantage. As we shall see, from 1910 onwards Yexley entertained ambitions to become a Member of Parliament, and it was the connection with Churchill that offered him his best chance of being adopted as a Liberal candidate. At the same time it was to Churchill's advantage to be publicly identified with Yexley in matters of naval reform. With Beresford leading a demagogic campaign for change in the Navy from the Tory side — a campaign which occasionally included aspects of personnel reform as a popular vote-catcher — Churchill was happy to have Yexley rather than Beresford identified in the public mind as the person most responsible for the reform agitation. At all costs no credit for the Churchill reforms was to go to Beresford.[129] Beyond this, Churchill, with his populist style of leadership at the Admiralty, could only benefit politically from the enthusiastic coverage he received in *The Fleet*. Without doubt the most significant outcome of this three-cornered relationship was the situation in 1912 in which the Admiralty was able to propose a pay increase well short of the asking rate among the benefit societies and yet know, despite ominous rumblings from the service, that it would be accepted without trouble.

However, the centrality of Yexley's role and his personal contacts with Fisher and Churchill left the lower deck with no officially recognised machinery for pressing grievances. The societies with their annual appeals had been actively interested in the reform campaign, but they were unable to play more than a minor role beside Yexley and *The Fleet*. This fact did not go unnoticed, jealousy was aroused, and the relationship between a number of lower-deck society leaders and Yexley was soured in consequence, making it difficult for them to collaborate in future reform campaigns. How the Admiralty itself would react to the need for a more formal method of raising general service complaints remained to be seen.

FOUR

Naval unrest and lower-deck organisation

Ask the average naval officer what he thinks of it and he will pooh-pooh the idea of there being any unrest at all; he will point to his petty officers and the seemingly cheerful way they do their work and probably tell you that all this talk of unrest is the work of irresponsible agitators who don't know what they are saying. If one points to the various Appeals that emanate from the lower deck ratings as an outward and visible sign of the real feeling of the men, the same attitude is adopted – 'a few irresponsible agitators'. These officers are unconsciously adopting the same attitude that was adopted by the average naval officer prior to the great mutinies of 1797. – Lionel Yexley, *The Fleet Annual and Naval Year Book*, 1914

Food, uniform regulations, pay and discipline – all these were matters of great concern on the lower deck in the early twentieth century, and at times they contributed to the rumbling unrest in the Navy. Obvious signs of dissatisfaction with service conditions were to be seen in the growth of the lower-deck societies, the lower-deck press and in the vigorous agitation over such grievances. But there were other signs of unrest in this period too which are not as easy to interpret. These were the spontaneous reactions on the lower deck to felt grievances – sometimes acts of individual or collective indiscipline, sometimes attempts by large numbers of men to get out of the Navy. Here we are dealing with protest action in narrow terms, rarely having a positive content and unlikely to be consciously associated in the minds of those involved with any wider movements for reform. By its very nature this area is hard to probe. The symptoms were frequently that people were being punished for some act of retaliation in circumstances that were not always clear, and the Navy customarily drew a veil over its disciplinary proceedings, especially when there was any hint that what was at issue was a fundamental challenge to authority. (Appendix I sets out a list – by no means complete – of serious cases of indiscipline or collective refusals of duty in this period for which some evidence exists.) The records of courts martial are not open to inspection, so that details about mutinies are hard to come by, and in cases of desertion or discharge by purchase we do not know why ratings chose to quit the Navy. But it is a reasonable assumption that much of this behaviour was a protest against unacceptable features of service life and was conditioned by a general atmosphere in which it was becoming more common for ratings to question and reject the *status quo*. Certainly some observers in the naval hierarchy, the press and on the lower deck saw the occasional outbursts as symptomatic of growing indiscipline and deteriorating morale which resulted from the growth of the reform movement. And equally clear too was the fact that a general awareness on the part of Admiralty officials and politicians of growing dissatisfaction helped to speed up the reforms in 1911–12.

DESERTION AND DISCHARGE BY PURCHASE

Outright rebellion or mutiny carried such terrifying penalties – lengthy periods of imprisonment with hard labour or even death – that men could be driven a long way before they would risk inviting this sort of punishment. But in the early years of the century there were plenty of other signs that all was not well. The rate of desertion during the first decade was phenomenally high, and at times men were almost literally streaming away from their ships. Every year between 1,600 and 2,300 men attempted to escape from the service in this way.[1] Twenty years later the rate of desertion was little more than a tenth of this level.[2] In 1901–02 849 seamen and 879 stokers were lost, and in the following three years the Admiralty listed a total of 5,486 men as having 'run'.[3] When the six ships of the Second Cruiser Squadron, commanded by the popular Rear-Admiral Prince Louis of Battenberg, visited the United States and Canada in 1905 a total of 346 men jumped ship at the various ports of call. The largest single group of deserters, some sixty-eight, fled from Battenberg's own flagship, HMS *Drake*.[4] In the next two years a total of 1,896 men absconded.[5]

Another sign of dissatisfaction with conditions was the large number of men who took the first possible opportunity to secure their discharge. In 1900 34 per cent of sailors quit the Navy as soon as their first twelve years were up, while many others bought themselves out even earlier.[6] Altogether, in the period 1906–07, 1,070 men bought their discharge. Twenty years later the comparable figure was to be only one-fifth of this number.[7] Normally the Navy had little difficulty in finding replacements, but in 1912, before the major reforms of that year had been conceded, it was 1,300 men short of its target figure for recruiting.[8] In the course of the year 1,700 men took their discharge, 900 of them buying themselves out, while many more had their applications refused.[9] *The Fleet* was inundated with so many letters from men asking how to go about purchasing their discharge that Yexley had a form reply printed, and in evidence to the Brock committee he claimed that he was receiving inquiries at the rate of 500 a month.[10] The constant drain of trained men was a great loss to the service and an obvious cause of worry, so much so that the Admiralty was reluctant to disclose detailed information about the numbers who left after their first period, claiming that it was not in the national interest for the facts to be broadcast.[11]

'REGRETTABLE INCIDENTS'

There were other, more direct, indications of unrest. In spite of the harsh penalties reserved for acts of collective disobedience or refusal of duty, such offences occurred on one or more occasions in almost every year from 1900 to 1914 (see appendix). Undoubtedly more acts of mutiny took place than were ever recorded, all of them involving individual ships or establishments.[12]

The most important and widely reported outbreak in these early years occurred at Portsmouth barracks in November 1906. It followed a long period of unrest and came at a time when victualling and canteen corruption was at a peak, with clothing regulations causing considerable trouble and the ship's police running the establishment very much for their own benefit.

In the summer of 1906 a growing volume of complaints from the depot reached *The Fleet* and Yexley went down to make a first-hand investigation. He found considerable irritation among the men over the attitude to discipline of one or two officers.[13] In particular there was deep-seated resentment against Lieutenant Collard, who had been known to punish men illegally by making them kneel down before him. In November 1905 he had punished a stoker in this way, and it was widely believed on the lower deck that on that occasion he had ordered, 'Go down on your knee, you dirty dog, and learn your manners.'[14] Beyond this, there was discontent over the administration of canteen funds, and particularly over the fact that Commander Drury-Lowe had overriden a unanimous decision of the elected canteen committee on some matter of finance. Yexley arranged for a Tory MP, Carlyon Bellairs, to ask a question in the House of Commons, and he was preparing to raise the issue again in November when a mutiny took place in the barracks.[15]

The 'emeute' followed an episode in which Lieutenant Collard had again disciplined a group of stokers for disorderly behaviour by ordering them 'on the knee'. The disturbance extended over two evenings and involved stokers attempting to rush the barrack gates and force an entry into the officers' quarters, a mass petition to see the commodore and an incident in which hundreds of men, forced to assemble on the parade ground in the middle of the night, subjected the commander to catcalls and abuse. Rioting in the streets accompanied the eruption within the barracks, over 100 people were arrested and a strong detachment of Marines from Eastney barracks and ships in Portsmouth harbour was called in to restore order.[16] Eleven men were court-martialled on charges arising out of the disturbance and Edwin Moody, an alleged ringleader, was sentenced to five years' penal servitude. Lieutenant Collard was also court-martialled on a charge of giving improper commands; though found guilty on one count, he was only sentenced to be reprimanded.[17]

The commodore of the barracks later informed the Second Sea Lord privately that the depot had been like a volcano ready to erupt for twelve months previously, though he placed the immediate blame for the events on 'deserters from the Army, and Socialist vagabonds' and other 'riff raff we have as stokers'. But it was for Yexley that he reserved his most vitriolic comments:

There is a very dangerous man called Yexley, the editor of a paper named *The Fleet*. [. . .] I find he is raising mutiny and discontent as far as in him lies, and panders to the Lower Deck where his principal sale is. [. . .] the question in the House [i.e. by Bellairs] was prompted by this little reptile. He was a chief yeoman of signals in the Service, we have educated him and taught him long words [. . .] and now he spends his time fomenting trouble in an underhand way.[18]

Of course Yexley had no hand at all the mutiny but had merely reported the growing discontent. Some years later he told the Brock committee that something of the sort had long been on the cards because of the system of petty punishments that prevailed in the

barracks.[19] In fact the episode compelled the Admiralty to recognise
that conditions in naval depots generally needed investigating. A
committee was appointed for the purpose, and the *Naval Chronicle*
urged it to make a clean sweep by investigating the general grievances
over pay, food and conditions. Likewise in *The Fleet* one
correspondent observed:

> [. . .] it did not require the occurrence of the serious events at Portsmouth
> and elsewhere forcibly to demonstrate that throughout the Service there is a
> widespread feeling of discontent, or to show that beneath the surface there is
> much that calls imperatively for reform.
> [. . .] The food of the British sailor is still inadequate both in quality and in
> quantity, his pay is still a paltry pittance, [. . .] and his daily life is still passed
> under a discipline so severe that it often becomes unnecessarily harsh or even
> capriciously cruel.[20]

The cause of the mutiny thus lay beyond the fact that an improper
order had been given to a group of stokers. But what about the other
instances of insubordination in this period? Single-ship mutinies or
acts of collective indiscipline were always sparked off by some
condition peculiar to the ship. But mutinous behaviour, like industrial
action, was rarely the result of a single factor. Apart from the
immediate cause, there were usually a number of underlying
grievances, and here the same complaints tended to recur –
inadequate leave over a lengthy period; the ship's company being
driven too hard; aggravation over canteen administration; excessive
punishments, or some high-handed action on the part of an officer.
Indeed, the act of disobedience itself – perhaps involving the ditching
of a gun sight or some other valuable piece of equipment over the side
– was often specifically calculated to draw public attention to the
vessel in question, in the hope that it would lead to an investigation of
conditions on board. This was the pattern on the battleship *Majestic*
in 1899, the *Barfleur* and *Alexandra* in 1900, the *Magnificent* in 1901,
the *Ramillies* in 1903, the *Cornwallis* and the *Astraea* in 1904, and so
on in episode after episode.[21]

In cases like these the press was often hard put to obtain more than
cursory details of what had happened, especially if the ship was on a
foreign station. Sometimes captains would post a notice ordering men
not to discuss the ship's affairs when on shore, and the Admiralty was
usually very reticent about disclosing information relating to ship
disturbances.[22] In some instances only the stark phrasing of a
subsequent court-martial charge or a brief entry in a log remains as a

fragmentary record. However, in the years leading up to the Great War there was a tendency for 'regrettable incidents', as they were often referred to in the press, to occur with greater regularity, reflecting both the growing dissatisfaction of the lower deck with a whole range of service conditions and their increasing readiness to take protest action.

THE GROWTH OF LOWER-DECK ORGANISATION AND 'NAVAL UNIONISM'

During the first decade of the century reports of unrest had been mainly confined to the service press. Suddenly the national newspapers began to take an interest in what was happening. Not only were the abundant signs of discontent being reported but sections of the press realised for the first time that the lower deck were organising on account of it. The lower-deck societies were growing rapidly, and newspapers linked this to the signs of disaffection on board some vessels. Existing societies increased their membership and new ones proliferated. Blacksmiths, coopers, painters and plumbers, collectively one of the worst-paid groups in the Navy, established a Naval Artisans' Death Benefit Association in the first half of 1912, and during the same year new societies were formed by officers' stewards and sick-berth staff. The following year saw the beginning of organisation among telegraphists, carpenters, ships' police and cooks.[23] Until now the great weakness of the societies had been the exclusion of most of the junior ratings from their ranks. Their main concern had been to look after the interests of petty officers, and many of the loyal appeal requests were aimed at preserving and increasing the status of POs. But with the mushrooming of lower-deck organisation in 1912 there was also a tendency for the younger men to combine. The most significant development here was the establishment of separate societies for junior ratings in the seaman and stoker branches of the service. In the former case, able seamen had sought membership of the Executive Petty Officers' Society as early as 1910, but had been rebuffed. As a result, in 1912 a society catering specifically for able seamen was established at Devonport, and this became the Royal Naval Seamen's Benefit Society in 1913.[24] Within a few months a Stokers' Society had also been established as a sub-section of the Mechanicians' and Stoker Petty Officers' Society.[25] Still, membership of benefit societies was very much a minority interest and it was estimated that no more than 10 per cent of the lower deck belonged to them in 1913.[26]

Nevertheless for many people lower-deck organisation represented the biggest threat to the service. As the commodore of Chatham barracks told the Brock Committee:

I do not think that in the lower ranks there is worse discipline, but I consider that the danger comes from the various organisations, trade unions, that are creeping into every branch [. . .] .[27]

The previous year the Second Sea Lord, Vice-Admiral Bridgeman, had written to McKenna in the wake of a mass refusal of duty on board the *Leviathan*, flagship of the Fourth Cruiser Squadron:

I forgot if I told you that I had formed the opinion that the insubordination in 'Leviathan' was the outward manifestation of a deep laid scheme – resulting from the mischievous socialistic literature that our men are now flooded with; they are taught how to be insubordinate without breaking the law.[28]

In a similar vein in the press there was much exaggerated discussion about socialism in the Navy. Arnold White, one of Fisher's confidants, took up Admiral Bridgeman's line and argued that it was 'the canker of the Service'. Great play was made of the fact that socialist speakers regularly addressed men of the Home Fleet on the promenade at Weymouth.[29] In May 1912 sensational newspaper articles on naval trade unionism appeared, with gross overestimates of the amount of organisation on the lower deck.[30] The scare was accentuated by the fact that it followed only days after the gaoling of the militant union leader Tom Mann for publishing his *Don't Shoot* leaflet, aimed at troops called out to industrial disputes. A similarly exaggerated account of the tendency towards trade unionism in the Navy appeared in the *Daily Citizen* when the Seamen's Benefit Society at Devonport was formed.[31]

However, it was by no means all exaggeration. Astute observers of the lower deck detected a distinct radicalisation. As the writer-fisherman Stephen Reynolds argued in the *Daily Chronicle*:

[. . .] numbers of men, disappointed by all parties alike, have jumped from the old-time naval conservatism to political views considerably in advance of radicalism; and had the lower deck been in a position to offer a *quid pro quo* for the co-operation of the civilian trade unions, the general public would probably have had lower deck grievances forced upon its notice some time ago.[32]

No doubt the more militant among the ratings wanted the benefit societies to develop in the direction of trade unionism. An undercurrent of opinion even favoured the formation of one big union, an idea first put forward in the *Naval Chronicle* in 1910.[33] A few wanted the societies to copy trade union methods up to and even including the use of strike action. A lower-deck correspondent in the *Portsmouth Evening News* reflected this view in the middle of the 1912 reform campaign:

There is one thing left for the bluejackets to do, they must combine themselves with the trade union movement. Surely if the authorities refuse to recognise the right of men to live comfortably and decently, the men may reserve to themselves the right to withhold themselves when the nation's interests are at stake. [. . .] The Naval authorities are manufacturing 'rebels' by the score, who will make it their business to overthrow the system that now imposes such disgraceful burdens upon them.[34]

The longer the grievances went unresolved the greater was the appeal of proposals to amalgamate the societies and link up with the Labour movement.

Throughout 1912 the press dwelt on the unrest in the Navy. A naval officer writing in the *Weekly Dispatch* observed that 'Discontent is rife on the lower deck. [. . .]'; the *Daily Graphic* reported that men who were nearing the end of their service time were generally felt to be the lucky ones; the *Army and Navy Gazette* spoke of discontent having an adverse affect on efficiency afloat and recruiting ashore; and in the *English Review* Stephen Reynolds wrote of a growing sense of grievance, ' [. . .] smouldering discontent which might at any moment recently have burst into blaze, and which has, in fact, thrown off more sparks than the public is aware of'.[35] Meanwhile, in the House of Commons, the government was asked whether a Cabinet committee recently appointed to inquire into the causes of labour unrest would also be investigating the discontent among ratings.[36]

THE *LONDON* AND THE *ZEALANDIA*

Churchill's 1912 reforms helped to lower the temperature but the Admiralty could not legislate a similar change in the mentality of naval officers. This was much slower in coming, and in the meantime the old attitude to discipline still caused resentment. Disaffection on board individual ships continued to be reported, and one of these cases involving the battleship *London* produced a backlash, with a section of the naval establishment evidently feeling that a stand had to be taken against the reform movement if the fomentors of discontent were to be stopped. Considerable publicity was given to the unhappy state of affairs on the *London* in 1913 when *The Fleet* began to investigate unrest in the ship. Lower-deck complaints all centred on the harsh disciplinary methods of the newly appointed captain, Kemp.[37] *The Fleet's* disclosures about the *London* caused Captain Kemp to bring a libel suit against Yexley in May 1914, and the court case had all the hallmarks of a showdown. The six-day hearing was given great publicity. Many captains subscribed to Kemp's legal fees, while for Yexley several ratings from the *London* came forward and gave evidence. Men of all ranks attended the High Court proceedings in uniform, and heard counsel for the plaintiff argue that the case was not merely a libel action but raised the more serious question of how discipline was to be maintained.[38] Yexley lost, was ordered to pay £3,000 damages and costs and was subsequently declared bankrupt. But the fact that the Admiralty had not taken decisive measures to limit his campaigning within the service led conservative elements to keep up the counter-attack. The *United Service Magazine* argued that the Kemp *v.* Yexley case had shown the Admiralty to be soft on socialism, while the *Morning Post* depicted the trouble on the *London* as an instance of trade unionism against discipline.[39]

A similar polarisation of opinion ran through interpretations of what was potentially the most serious mutiny afloat before the Great War, on the battleship *Zealandia*. As on the *London*, the crew had quickly become disaffected on the appointment of a disciplinarian captain, Walter Cowan. In March 1914, as the culmination of a period of unrest, a large number of stokers refused to obey an order, a number of men were subsequently arrested and placed in cells, and this in turn prompted a further demonstration of collective defiance on the part of the stokers. Twelve men, seemingly chosen at random, were tried by court martial and eight of them sentenced to two years' imprisonment with hard labour. The manner in which the twelve had been arbitrarily selected as scapegoats angered the *Zealandia's* crew, who claimed that there had been no ringleaders and that the disobedience was general and entirely spontaneous. The Admiralty was forced to move quickly. It decided that a technical irregularity had occurred during the trial which prevented an effective defence. The sentences of the eight stokers were therefore annulled and the men transferred to other ships.[40]

What made the *Zealandia* affair potentially so much more serious than others was that it preceded by only a matter of days the mutiny at the Curragh. Indeed, the *Zealandia* was part of the battle squadron sent to Lamlash in anticipation of civil war in Ireland. The air was full of talk of mutiny and some naval officers sympathetic to the loyalist cause defended the notion that they had the right to refuse to fire on kith and kin.[41] In this climate, with rebellion among army officers being condoned in high places and some naval officers ready to join with them, incidents such as that on the *Zealandia* were seen by the lower deck as all the more defensible.

As far as the *Morning Post* was concerned the threat to order and discipline was grave. In June 1914 the paper declared, 'Matters have gone very far, so far in fact that in the test of war the discipline might conceivably fail. In the opinion of not a few naval officers it would fail.'[42] This was certainly overstating the case, but the establishment had cause for concern. The danger confronting it was analysed by Yexley in cool, reasoned fashion. He drew attention to the disturbing amount of unrest and the fact that the Navy had escaped mutinies on a dozen ships in half as many months.[43] The one thing that had so far prevented a general eruption was the poor organisation of the sailors and the divisions between the different branches of the service. But the lower deck were rapidly beginning to bridge those divisions and improve the level of organisation. Corresponding representatives of the benefit societies now spanned the fleet. The Chief Petty Officers' Society had no fewer than 100 sub-committees all round the world in 1913, and by spring 1914 the Seamen's Society had members on forty-four ships.[44] These representatives were beginning to compare notes when ashore and to discuss service conditions more openly, with a corresponding effect on the collective consciousness of the lower deck. In the past, disciplinary questions on any individual ship had been a closed book as far as the rest of the fleet was concerned. But increasingly information about such matters was being relayed throughout the fleet, and there was some doubt as to whether the Admiralty could successfully call on the men of other ships to quell a disturbance among their fellow ratings.[45] Certainly Yexley doubted whether seamen in the *Zealandia* could have been used against the stokers had the situation deteriorated, and there was also doubt about whether help would have been forthcoming from other ships in the squadron, as these were known to be disaffected too.[46]

Yexley drew no comfort from this analysis: he wanted to see the Navy reformed and made more efficient in consequence, not paralysed by a collapse of discipline. The danger he described was still rather remote, but it could not be totally dismissed, and it was in these circumstances, and just one month before the outbreak of the Great War, that *The Fleet* found itself calling for an inquiry into unrest in the Navy.[47]

LOWER-DECK PEACE IN WARTIME

In the early stages of the war the lower deck, like most other sections of the community, were caught up in the wave of enthusiasm that swept the country. *The Fleet* proclaimed that 'the magic of war' had wiped out all grievances, and Yexley announced a moratorium on any further discussion of ratings' disabilities.[48] Benefit societies met infrequently; some suspended their activities for the duration, and publication of the annual loyal appeal ceased. Moreover the isolation of the fleet at Rosyth and Scapa Flow, and the censorship of mail, prevented complaints reaching the press, and even *The Fleet* published no letters to the editor during the first year of war. In any event, for several months the lower deck were financially better off than before: separation allowances made a big difference, and allowances payable for children were doubled early in 1915.[49]

This happy state of affairs did not last for long. Pay, still 1s 8d a day at the lowest level, for able seamen with less than six years' service, was barely adequate at the start of the war, and no further increase was forthcoming. Separation allowances were the only cushion against the spiralling cost of living ashore and afloat, and in the course of 1915 they began to be outdistanced by the rise in prices. Yet for quite some time complaints were muted. Until the battle of Jutland in May 1916, when war-weariness began to set in, there was still a sense of idealism which pushed grievances into the background.

However, the strain of having to live on a constantly shrinking budget began to tell, and, despite regular assurances that all was well with the men, oblique references to the tensions that were building up occasionally surfaced in the press. There were a variety of complaints, all with an economic base. Anomalies persisted in the structure of pay and pensions, and as they became more pronounced discontent grew. Some 'Hostilities Only' (HO) ratings were being paid more than their active-service counterparts.[50] Reservists who had been called up received their naval pension on top of their pay, whereas men who reached pensionable age during the war were forced to stay in though not allowed to draw their pension. Some HO ratings were fortunate enough to be receiving full or half-pay from their civilian employer as well, while others, accustomed to earning good wages in Civvy Street, found it impossible to maintain their standard of living.[51] All round, the basic problem was inadequate pay, and the problem was intensified by the mounting cost of food in the naval canteens.[52]

By early 1917 discontent was growing and Yexley felt it necessary to give voice to some of the grievances. He raised the obvious question of pay, the inadequacy of separation allowances, and the system of hospital stoppages, a long-standing practice under which men who went sick had 10d a day stopped out of their pay (50 per cent for an able seaman on basic pay) after the first thirty days in hospital. The assumption that those on the sick list must be malingering had never been accepted by ratings and was even less acceptable in wartime.[53] In drawing attention to these matters Yexley was at pains to emphasise the change that had taken place in the mood of the lower deck. It was radically different from what it had been only twelve months earlier, and the Admiralty was advised to take note of the fact.[54]

At the home ports the joint committees of the lower-deck societies were revived in April 1917, and the petty officers' and warrant officers' societies were discussing the idea of amalgamating.[55] MPs were approached to take up the men's case. In the motion for the Easter adjournment James Hogge raised the main grievances, but the Financial Secretary to the Admiralty, Macnamara, held out little hope of concessions, and by implying that ratings were really not so badly off he managed only to increase their resentment. By now the question of inadequate pay was a constant topic of conversation on the lower deck.[56]

In July 1917 a conference of joint committee representatives and petty officers on leave from the Grand Fleet was held at the Union Jack Club in London to draft an appeal – the first since 1914.[57] It contained five requests: a rise in pay of 9d a day for able seamen and 1s for higher ratings; the abolition of hospital stoppages; the payment of pensions that had been withheld; the basic pension rate to be 11d a day rather than 10d; the entry of civilians as officers and higher ratings to be stopped, and opportunities given to active-service ratings to fill vacancies. The sharp tone of the appeal contrasted with the respectful petitioning of pre-war days. The points listed were 'to be immediately redressed', and it was pointed out that the wartime quiescence of the men had been misinterpreted by the authorities; it was not inspired by contentment, merely by loyalty.[58] The appeal was supported in the national press, and at the end of July the issues were discussed at length in the House of Commons, but again the Admiralty response was disappointing.[59]

Far from the lower deck regarding the Admiralty as 'the little fathers of the fleet', with the best interests of the men at heart, as Macnamara claimed, the Admiralty had now alienated the ratings.[60] Yexley contributed a series of articles to the *Daily Express* focusing on their conditions.[61] He was also in correspondence with Fisher again, urging him to exercise whatever influence he had to rectify the latest complaints. And forwarding Yexley's intelligence about lower-deck conditions to his close friend and former Civil Lord of the Admiralty, George Lambert, Fisher asked, 'Are we going to have another mutiny at the Nore?'[62]

Pressure on the Admiralty and the government came from another quarter, too. In the course of the summer a number of trade unions with members in the services had joined forces, through the General Federation of Trade Unions (GFTU), to press for increases in pay for soldiers and sailors. At the same time the government were alarmed to learn that a meeting to form a Soldiers' and Workmen's Committee had been held at the Brotherhood Church, Southgate, on 28 July 1917.[63] In early August the federation's General Secretary, W. A. Appleton, organised a meeting of members of both Houses of Parliament at the Commons to discuss the question of pay. Ben Tillett, the veteran leader of the dockers' union, and Admiral Beresford attended, and the meeting set up a standing body to pursue the campaign.[64] In the light of these events the Cabinet decided to establish a Committee on Soldiers' and Sailors' Pay under the chairmanship of the former First Lord of the Admiralty, Sir Edward Carson.[65]

By early September the Admiralty was considering a series of concessions designed to remove the discontent, and on 18 September the Cabinet approved the measures. Among other things, pay was to be adjusted so that the $3d$ a day progressive increase for able seamen would be paid after three years instead of six. Messing allowances were to be increased by $1\frac{1}{2}d$. Hospital stoppages were to be abolished, except in the case of men suffering from VD. The basic pension would be raised from $10d$ to $11d$ a day, and men retained in service after their pension date would receive the full amount. In view of the fact that clothing prices had risen by up to 30 per cent a kit upkeep allowance was also granted, at long last conceding the principle of a free kit.[66] The new conditions were to come into force on 1 October. But in typical Navy fashion not a word of this was communicated to the fleet, and a month later many men still had no official information about the concessions.

In the Grand Fleet the lower deck were growing impatient. From July to September the fleet lay at Rosyth. Leave was given, and for the first time since the outbreak of war large numbers of ratings were able to get together and discuss their predicament. Meetings were held in the shore canteen, and when the fleet sailed for Scapa Flow in mid-September discussions continued, with petty officers paying 'social visits' to their opposite numbers in other ships.[67] As a result of this activity the men of the Grand Fleet drafted a new petition to be handed in by every ship's company to their commanding officer in mid-October, before the opening of Parliament. It was an altogether more radical document than the appeal which had been prepared at the home ports in July, calling for a 50 per cent pay rise and a substantial increase in the messing allowance. The wording was also more uncompromising. The issues raised were 'demands', not requests. It spoke of the government's action provoking 'deepest resentment' and 'intensified discontent' among ratings, and in a threatening tone stated that immediate concessions were 'indispensably necessary for the continued efficiency of the fleet'. The petitioners could not contemplate the present injustices being upheld 'without serious national results'.[68] The ratings generally were unaware that the October concessions had been granted, and the submission of the Grand Fleet petition went ahead.[69]

The Admiralty now began to inquire into the nature of lower-deck organisation. Naval Intelligence, frequently out of its depth in these matters, believed that the National Union of Railwaymen, the Dockers' Union and the Engineers in ship repairing had been behind the development, and on their initiative an agreement had been reached with the lower-deck societies whereby the unions would support the ratings in any measures taken to obtain better pay. With some exceptions, senior officers in the fleet and home ports tended to treat the situation less seriously. In the Grand Fleet, Admiral Beatty was of the opinion that there was no serious discontent, and from Portsmouth the C-in-C, Admiral Colville, reported, 'The spirit of

Trade Unionism seems to be slowly permeating the different branches of the Service in the RN Barracks but, at present, with very little effect.' However, his assessment was quite at variance with that of senior officers attached to the gunnery and torpedo schools in his own port who saw around them discontent, dissatisfaction and general unrest. Vice-Admiral de Robeck, commanding the Second Battle Squadron at Scapa Flow, summarised the position best of all when he reported:

[. . .] the lower deck has lost confidence in the powers of the Board of Admiralty, and, as a result, have gravitated towards trades unionism. To what extent this actually exists I am not in a position to give reliable data. However, it does exist and to such an extent that the fact should not be neglected as if allowed to grow it will be impossible to eradicate.[70]

At the home ports and in the fleet there was a strong belief that outside agitators were behind the petitions. At Portsmouth Admiral Colville cited Yexley as someone whose activities 'might be suppressed with advantage'. At Scapa Flow Admiral Madden, commanding the First Battle Squadron, considered that the Grand Fleet petition was 'produced by a body who have as its head one Lionel Yexley and by them sent for distribution to the Fleet, where evidently they have agents'.[71] In fact Yexley was in no way connected with the preparation of the July appeal and was disturbed that it had been issued in wartime, although, as mentioned above, he did enlist Fisher's support to canvass for reforms.[72] Likewise the Grand Fleet petition in October was solely the work of men in the fleet. Still, Macnamara felt that the trouble-spots were the home ports, where ratings came into contact with dockyard workers, and therefore 'the depots are the centres to be watched' .

This view was almost certainly wrong. In fact at the end of 1917 men at home port enjoyed many more creature comforts than ratings in the fleet, and this was recognised by those fortunate enough to be serving in southern England. Given this situation, unrest was always more likely to develop among units in the fleet, but the source of trouble was not outside agitators, as Macnamara thought, but rather the influence of Hostilities Only ratings.[73]

Hostilities Only ratings, with their 'lubberly' ways, were at first treated as something of a joke. To the professional sailor the HO rating was 'Cuthbert',[74] and there was a tendency for the two groups

to remain separate. John Bush describes the position on the battleship
mess deck:

Broadside mess tables were suspended by two steel 'crowfoots'. In the Grand
Fleet messes the crowfoots halfway down the table marked the barrier
between the haves and the have nots. Towards the ship's side sat the senior
hands, the LS, a few old ABs recalled from pension. These people forever
argued about the Channel Fleet, Charlie Beresford and the training brigs in
which they first went to sea. Up the other end sat HO ABs who discussed
Leeds United and Newcastle and life in the coal pits.[75]

They also brought with them their union views. Many skilled men such
as blacksmiths, plumbers, coopers and painters joined as HO ratings
with the rank of able seaman, and were amazed to find that fitters,
boilermakers and others entered the service as petty officers with a
significantly higher rate of pay. This went against their union
principles, and was a major source of discontent.[76] Over the long
months and years of messing together the HO men taught active-
service ratings many of the values of civilian workmen. Their
influence was reflected in attitudes towards authority and pay. Within
the Admiralty it was noticed that there was an increasing tendency for
men to expect to be paid extra for work done. In this sense the basic
pay was seen as no more than a retainer. Allowing for a little
ideological bias, Admiral Madden came close to the point when he
attributed much of the discontent in the First Battle Squadron to the
fact that recently joined HO men were not as good as earlier recruits,
and were infecting the remainder of the ships' companies with
'socialistic ideas'.[77]

Some officers may have been inclined to underrate the sense of
grievance among those they commanded, but in dealing with the
ratings responsible for organising the Grand Fleet petition the
Admiralty was careful not to do anything provocative. Two recalled
pensioners, Petty Officer Walter Vale and Master-at-Arms James
Scrivens of the *Resolution*, were arrested and court-martialled for
combining to circulate letters contrary to Article 11 of King's
Regulations.[78] It was a serious charge carrying the stiffest penalties,
and the two might have expected to be dealt with severely in wartime;
court-martial sentences had become increasingly heavy in recent
years. Yet on being found guilty they were given only nominal
sentences, losing their long-service and good-conduct medals and
badges. The situation was clearly too delicate for the Admiralty to risk
antagonising the lower deck further.

When eventually the full details of the October concessions became known the lower deck were less than enthusiastic, even though a number of their requests had been met in full. Worst of all, there was no real increase in pay, and the messing allowance was still considered far too low.[79] On 2 October 1917 a deputation from the joint GFTU – Parliamentary committee saw the Prime Minister to complain about the inadequacy of the package and to urge the need for a real increase in pay.[80] The Admiralty was forced to take a second look at the lower-deck petition. The concessions had not been overgenerous, and the Second Sea Lord admitted that the revision of the pay structure meant very little except to the lower ratings.[81]

Yexley now wrote urgently to Macnamara. 'There are still quite a number of questions unanswered and my correspondents are clamouring.'[82] The very next day, 2 November, at a by-election in Salford North Ben Tillett, who had stood as an Independent and campaigned on a platform of higher pay and better treatment of soldiers and sailors, was swept to victory with a two-to-one majority over the coalition candidate.[83] The government needed no further warning. Before the end of the month the Cabinet had agreed to increase service pay.[84] There was to be a 2d a day increase for able seamen, rising to 5d for chief petty officers, and the measure was announced to the fleet on 4 December.[85] At the lowest level the pay of an able seaman was now 1s 10d. It was the first time since 1860 that the rate had really changed.

The men's patience had been severely tried, and it is arguable that only their basic loyalty, and the fact that it had been possible for them to ventilate grievances to some extent, had prevented a serious breakdown of discipline. There were those in the Admiralty who now suggested clamping down on the lower-deck societies. Subscribers to this view canvassed the idea of calling in Scotland Yard to undertake a thorough investigation of the nature and activities of the societies, especially with reference to Article 11 of King's Regulations. There was a genuine concern that, if left unchecked, they might become too powerful to be stopped at a later date. But wiser heads saw it differently. In the fleet Admiral Madden submitted that it would be a mistake to suppress discussion of grievances afloat, while the Fourth Sea Lord turned down Admiral Colville's suggestion that Yexley should be silenced.[86] Fortunately for the service these more cautious views prevailed. The December concession had again been the minimum necessary to take the heat out of the situation. How long the men would be satisfied with it remained to be seen.

The increasing signs of unrest and the development of collective lower-deck organisation during these years were undoubtedly related. The more numerous the cases of desertion and of men seeking to buy themselves out, the more justification there was for the reform campaign and the greater was the appeal of the benefit societies. Similarly, some, if not all, of the many instances of negative protest in the form of refusal of duty were prompted by the selfsame conditions that led a minority of ratings to combine and lobby for positive change. What was clear, however, was that the lower-deck societies were not *responsible* for any of the more dramatic forms of protest action in individual ships or establishments.

Yet this was something that the naval authorities were never quite sure about. There was a frequent tendency to suspect the benefit societies of conspiring to sow seeds of discontent. It was a reflection of the gulf between many Admiralty officials and naval officers on the one hand and the lower deck on the other. When the junior ratings in the seaman and stoker branches – hitherto the weak link in the chain of lower-deck organisation – began to join the benefit societies in 1912, giving rise to sensational stories in the press about the spread of trade unionism to the Navy, this merely reinforced the suspicions of the naval hierarchy. Senior officers were all too ready to equate lower-deck organisation with militant trade unionism, and trade unionism with socialism. From there it was but a short step to invoking the spectre of outside agitators. To some extent the reform movement benefited from this tendency to exaggerate and misrepresent the real nature of lower-deck organisation, at least in so far as Admiralty fears of widespread unrest helped to hasten changes.

In another respect the authorities' failure to see lower-deck organisation as it really was worked against peaceful and continuous reform. The tendency to equate benefit society organisation with the most militant form of syndicalism then current led in turn to a belief that the very basis of authority was under threat. Such thinking lay behind the suggestion from within the Admiralty in 1917 that the activities of the societies be restricted. Yet there was really no basis for the belief that the lower-deck societies, or even the fully fledged naval trade unionism desired by some men, were anti-service in conception. On the contrary, organisation was strongest among petty officers, men the contrary, organisation was strongest among petty officers, men whose commitment to the Navy in terms of number of years invested was greatest. For such people, what the benefit societies seemed to offer was a routine mechanism for channelling collective grievances in an orderly manner with greater prospects of a successful outcome than individual complainants could expect. It is true that the rapid growth of the societies between 1912 and the outbreak of war reflected to some extent the number of grievances outstanding: but it also reflected the recent successes of the reform movement. Many ratings joined the societies not in a negative spirt of confronting the Admiralty but because of the apparent achievements of their campaign to date. Had their lordships been able to accept wholeheartedly such a role for the benefit societies it might have reduced much of the tension of 1912 and would probably have avoided the build-up of resentment and militancy in 1917. But of course the Admiralty did not embrace the principle of collective organisation on the lower deck.

Yet, fortunately for the service, it did not in practice completely reject collective organisation. A relatively permissive line was taken towards the benefit societies, their practice of issuing loyal appeals was tolerated, and the contents of these documents were quietly studied. In effect this provided a safety valve, and the existence of an outlet for lower-deck pressure was the crucial factor distinguishing the Royal Navy from the German and Russian navies in 1917. At a critical time the Admiralty was prepared to listen, to show leniency to the organisers of the Grand Fleet appeal, and was astute enough to take Admiral Madden's advice. It had come close to losing the men's trust and confidence in 1917, and the government had retrieved the situation only at a late hour by a few *ad hoc* reforms. But continued reliance on *ad hoc*ery and the Admiralty's equivocal attitude to lower-deck organisation were to pose bigger problems still within a year.

'Direct representation'

[We ask] that Admiralty will recognise in the Lower Deck Societies a loyal body of devoted workers, whose only wish is to leave the Lower Deck a better and happier place for their influence. We ask that Article 11 of the King's Regulations be cancelled or amended to admit the legality of the Societies. It is observed that the Admiralty have recently recognised the right of Mercantile Marine Ratings serving under the Naval Discipline Act to belong to their unions. – Draft loyal appeal, Portsmouth, March 1918.

Portsmouth is very interested in Chatham's activities [. . .]. The question of employing a House of Commons Lobbyist has received very careful consideration at this Port [. . .] but political action is being deferred for the present. It is hoped to get straight in touch with the Admiralty, and so state our legitimate aspirations. Upon the success, or otherwise, of this depends out future action. – Minutes of Portsmouth Joint Committee meeting, 12 June 1918.

The grievance petitioning of 1917 was primarily concerned with low pay but it also raised, by implication, the question of the ratings' right to put forward collective requests for improvements in conditions, and this was perhaps the most fundamental issue of all for the reform movement. Significantly, Admiral Beatty's main concern on seeing the Grand Fleet petition in September 1917 was not over the actual points raised but with the fact that a lower-deck committee had drawn up such requests in contravention of King's Regulations. This was subversive of discipline.[1]

The establishment of some form of official machinery by which ratings' views on pay and conditions could be represented to the Admiralty was something the lower-deck societies had long hankered for. It grew out of a recognition dating back over ten years that the weakness of the annual appeals was that they had to be issued anonymously and lower-deck representatives could never appear in public and give evidence in support of their requests.[2] Yexley's lobbying had been very effective, but it was a product of his personal talents and influential contacts. It did not represent a long-term solution to the men's lack of democratic rights. There were two methods favoured by ratings by which they thought their views might be better represented to the Admiralty and the government. As we have seen, one was to have an MP who would act as a spokesman. The other was through a system of "direct representation" at the Admiralty.

PARLIAMENTARY REPRESENTATION

Fred Jane's bid for election to Parliament in 1905 had failed miserably and Jenkins, the Labour member for Chatham, who had been elected with lower-deck support, proved to be of little value to the ratings. However, interest in parliamentary representation did not end there: the question simply had to be thought through more carefully. On the urging of journals such as the *Pall Mall Gazette*, serious consideration was now given to electing a lower-deck candidate; but there were a number of difficulties.[3]

Without a change in the law it would be impossible for an active-service rating to stand. Compared with their officers, lower-deck men with political aspirations were at a great disadvantage. Together with their army counterparts, naval officers were the only State employees entitled to sit in Parliament, a right safeguarded by an Act of Queen Anne. Until the late nineteenth century they had even been allowed to hold their seat while on full pay, though by the end of the century it was understood that only officers on half-pay could be Members of Parliament. Even so, they could still move freely between the Commons and the Navy, resuming their service career when further employment opportunities presented themselves. Whenever Admiral Beresford was on half-pay the Tories would find a safe seat for him, and when a suitable posting came along he vacated it and went back to sea. But for ratings there was no chance of mixing work and politics.[4] In 1879 a naval officer, Captain Verney, had publicly advocated that a rating should stand for Parliament in Portsmouth and if elected be transferred to a quiet posting in the Royal Yacht. His argument was that a seaman should be given the same facilities as the Admiralty gave the commander of the Royal Yacht, at the time none other than Charles Beresford. Hardly surprisingly, his remarks were not well received at the Admiralty.[5]

If the lower deck were to proceed with the idea of having a parliamentary spokesman they would have to put up a pensioned rating as candidate. Even then there was the problem of bridging the divisions between men of different political persuasions. Party politics were never much discussed on the lower deck, but that did not mean that ratings were without political views.[6] Traditionally the service contained a substantial bloc of Tory supporters. On the other hand the 1906 result at Chatham showed that ratings could be induced to vote Labour. However, the post-1906 Labour MPs' record on lower-deck questions was not at all impressive. They were basically uninterested in sailors' affairs, and their habit of calling for reductions in naval spending simply appeared as a threat to the position of the men. In 1906, when Gibson Bowles, the Tory MP, had challenged the victualling vote and forced the government to establish an inquiry into the scandal of naval victualling, *The Fleet* noted that he spoke to a House empty of Labour members:

It was the story of a hundred thousand British workers who led hard, laborious lives to keep open the ocean highways, and whose cause was being pleaded to the empty benches of the workers' representatives.[7]

To avoid party conflict there was some support for an 'All Navy' candidate who would simply confine his attention to naval matters. Yet, as Jane's experience showed, this approach had little chance of success in any constituency where the lower deck did not constitute the overwhelming majority of electors. For it to work the lower deck would have to be counted as a single constituency with separate representation, just as the universities of Oxford and Cambridge had their own members of Parliament.[8]

In the January 1910 election Jenkins lost his Chatham seat and no lower-deck candidate stood at any of the home ports. Henry Capper offered to become the candidate of the warrant officers, but there was no support for this within their society.[9] Yexley considered standing at both the January and December general elections. In 1909 he had canvassed Fisher's support, but although the First Sea Lord urged him to allow his name to go forward he told Yexley that he could not, while still in office, publicly identify with his campaign. At length Yexley decided against the idea.[10] The most important feature of these 1910 elections from the naval point of view was the candidacy of Admiral Beresford at Portsmouth. Charlie B, as he was known, staged a vigorous, knockabout campaign, carefully designed to win the lower-deck vote. A lower-deck election committee was formed; meetings of naval ratings were organised with Beresford as the star speaker. Men attended in uniform and were encouraged to state their grievances publicly. In effect the gatherings turned into an open discussion of the latest loyal appeal.[11] Beresford was still on the active list, but no objection to all this was voiced by the Admiralty. The campaign was successful, but the important thing for the lower deck was not his election — Beresford in Parliament was of little more help than any of the other naval officer MPs. Its significance lay in the precedent it set for public meetings of ratings to discuss their grievances. Such meetings were in direct contravention of King's Regulations, but the general view was that if it was acceptable for a senior admiral to do it, it was acceptable for the men to do it too. The experience was a landmark for the movement and gave new weight to the idea of a lower-deck MP.

Meanwhile Yexley continued to harbour the idea of standing for Parliament. Winston Churchill, after putting out feelers in the Liberal Party, asked Fisher whether Yexley would stand against Beresford in Portsmouth. Yexley accepted and the Portsmouth Liberals adopted him as one of their candidates for the election, expected in 1915.[12] At Devonport at the same time the lower deck were confident of having a ship's steward, Nick Revington, adopted as a Liberal candidate too.[13] In the event the war set back the electoral timetable, but the issue was not forgotten, only deferred for a few years.

REPRESENTATION AT THE ADMIRALTY

Paralleling the interest in parliamentary representation was the idea that ratings should somehow have a direct voice at the Admiralty. In 1907 and 1909 a committee of dockyard MPs went to see the First Lord to lend their weight to certain requests contained in the annual appeal, but this was a second-best arrangement.[14] What the lower deck wanted was direct access to the Admiralty, and from 1909 onwards the appeals asked for this in one form or another. The request was inspired by the growing practice in parts of the civil service where deputations of workers, accompanied by union officials, were allowed to see their heads of department once a year. Such a practice existed in the naval dockyards, and it was something along those lines that the lower-deck societies pressed for.[15]

Yet the societies had no clear idea of what direct representation would involve, and year by year the format of the proposal changed. Sometimes they asked for the right of deputation such as the dockyard workers had. Sometimes they asked to be allowed to petition the Admiralty via commanding officers and commanders-in-chief. At the other times they asked vaguely for representation at the Admiralty. In April 1914 correspondents to the *Naval and Military Record* could envisage direct representation taking three possible forms. One was simply for lower-deck spokesmen to be appointed by commodores of barracks, an arrangement which implied little challenge to authority. Another was through the medium of officially recognised benefit societies. And a third, more detailed, proposal involved the idea of a permanent lower-deck staff at the Admiralty with whom the Board could consult. The joint committees would annually submit the names of three men and the Admiralty would select one of them to head the lower-deck secretariat. In addition there would be a travelling secretary whose job would be to attend lower-deck meetings. The secretariat would be completed by three men selected annually by the commodores of the depots.[16] That schemes so different in their implications for naval discipline could be countenanced under the same heading was indicative of the lack of clarity that still surrounded the notion of direct representation after five years of discussion.

The Fleet criticised the whole concept from the outset. To change over to a system of annual deputations along the lines of the dockyard workers' would be to sacrifice the substance for the shadow of influence, it argued. The annual dockyard delegation was merely a safety valve that produced little.[17] But it was not a convincing argument. Dockyard workers may not have gained all they asked for, but the anonymous petitioning of the lower deck had not achieved any momentous successes, either. Such improvements as there had been were due chiefly to Yexley's persistence as a campaigner and his relationship with Fisher and Churchill.

The Fleet's opposition to direct representation stemmed from Yexley's misgivings about the lower-deck societies. He agreed that they were a vital safety valve, but he opposed the occasional proposals for amalgamating them and creating full-time positions in what would effectively be a lower-deck union. More than most people he appreciated that something as delicate as democracy would be hard put to survive in the Navy.[18] In any event, democracy was desirable only as long as it did not conflict with the legitimate system of command, and trade unionism in the Navy, he believed, was incompatible with the service's potential role as a security force during industrial disputes.[19] As an alternative he wanted to see the lower-deck movement operating efficiently as a clearing house for general grievances.[20] To complement its work there was need for an articulate, influential intermediary who could not be touched by naval discipline and who was capable of crystallising the demands of different sections of the lower deck for the benefit of society at large.[21] It was a prescription for the role he saw himself in, a role that he played to perfection, as the pre-war campaigns over food, clothing, discipline, pay and promotions had shown.

Yexley had a record of achievement that he could be proud of. But it did not entirely satisfy all sections of the lower-deck on the question of the best method of conducting reform campaigns. Indeed, his relationship with Fisher and Churchill aroused considerable jealousy in certain benefit societies and intensified the feeling in favour of direct representation. As the president of the Executive Petty Officers' Society wrote in the *Naval and Military Record* with reference to Yexley, the First Lord ' [. . .] would learn more from a lower-deck deputation in an hour than from an outsider in a week'.[22]

Personality differences aside, there was need for a more permanent, officially recognised channel of representation. However incoherent its expression, there was a growing feeling on the lower deck that a better method of putting forward grievances and requests was necessary. The idea of direct representation was a product of the growing dissatisfaction with numerous aspects of lower-deck life. It was not abstract notions of democracy that motivated the ratings, and the conflict between the idea of democratic representation and the imperatives of a disciplined, hierarchial service was hardly considered. Industrial unrest in the years after 1910 was beginning to find a reflection in the service. As Yexley admitted, ' [. . .] the lower deck, having started to think, has compared its lot with the outside workman and is copying his methods of advancing its position'.[23] The men were less and less prepared to suffer in silence the hundred and one pinpricks and annoyances that service life entailed.

Such was the situation at the outbreak of war. During the next three years the question of direct representation lay dormant. But the pay concessions of December 1917 did not quell interest in further reforms, and from this point on the pay question became closely linked with ideas of direct representation, so much so that some Admiralty officials felt that one could be traded off against the other. It was argued, for example, that if pay were handled in a more generous fashion it might not be necessary to devise a new system for bringing lower-deck grievances to the Admiralty's attention on a regular basis. But the issue of direct representation was not so easily averted.

From mid-1917 onwards various schemes for lower-deck representation were floated as interest in the subject increased. Admiral Beresford supported the idea of a single lower-deck representative being attached to the Second Sea Lord's office.[24] In the press and Parliament it was suggested that a special advisory department made up of ratings be established at the Admiralty.[25] Against this Yexley argued that lower-deck affairs would be best dealt with by an Admiralty welfare department, not by any institution claiming in some way to be representative of the men. He conceived of the welfare department as a vehicle for drawing the ratings and the Admiralty closer together, concerning itself solely with ratings' problems and cutting through the bureaucratic inertia of existing Admiralty departments.[26] His proposal was supported by the *Naval Warrant Officers' Journal*.[27] Meanwhile those responsible for the loyal appeal were simply planning to request that Article 11 of King's Regulations be amended so as to admit the legality of the lower-deck societies.[28]

However, the Admiralty was to reject all such ideas. There was not even to be any relaxation of the formal ban on grievance petitioning. Officers were told:

To allow causes of complaint, whether real or imaginary to be put forward in such a manner is, in the opinion of Their Lordships, not only entirely foreign to the best traditions and discipline of the Navy, but must inevitably tend to alienate the men from their officers. [. . .][29]

The Admiralty's strategy was to try to demonstrate, by practical action, its ability to look after the men's interests. Instructions were therefore sent out advising officers to take a greater interest in lower-deck welfare and to be more vigilant in identifying justifiable complaints. Captains were also advised to consult warrant officers and petty officers about grievances while at the same time being careful not to give the impression that they were recognising or encouraging a committee or combination of men. The paranoia about combinations was as strong as ever.

THE DEVELOPMENT OF ORGANISATION – THE GROWTH OF MILITANCY

In July 1918 the Admiralty got wind of renewed stirring among the lower-deck societies. Literature from the Officers' Stewards' and Cooks' Benefit Association was discovered in the battleship *Centurion*, and one document referred to a mass meeting of all stewards and cooks at the Albert Hall, Portsmouth, in May. However, the tendency among Admiralty officials was to play the matter down and dismiss the activities of the cooks and stewards. There had been no overt signs of dissent for six months and the general feeling was that since the courts martial on HMS *Resolution* unrest had virtually died out.

In fact the lower-deck scene was rapidly becoming inflamed, largely over the inadequacy of pay. Since the increase of 1917 most government employees had received a 12 per cent cost-of-living bonus, and by the spring of 1918 the men at Portsmouth were considering asking for a 25 per cent increase, while at Devonport a much bigger one of 1s 6d a day was contemplated.[30] Discontent was growing, but now sections of the lower deck were organising themselves on far more radical lines than in the past.

During 1918 the lower-deck societies began to revive, and Yexley was working closely with members of several of them, helping them to publicise the complaints of their branch. For some months after the publication of the loyal appeal in July 1917 and the courts martial on the *Resolution* the Portsmouth joint committee had lain low and ceased to meet. Now it was back in business, and in May Yexley was invited to become a member.[31] The secretary of the committee, Frank Tewkesbury, a pensioned chief writer, explained to him: 'At present we meet in secret, with a furtive eye on the door as it were. We are not seditionists [. . .] we want the sword removed which at present dangles over our heads.'[32] That sword was, of course, Article 11 of King's Regulations. Men known to be active in pressing for improvements through their benefit societies were victimised by some commanding officers, and following one such case in 1918 a scheduled joint committee meeting at Portsmouth was cancelled because of 'threats in the air'.[33]

In May 1918 the Workers' Union had proposed to the joint committee that they should forge formal links, and this was now being seriously considered.[34] Yexley spoke against the idea strongly at his first joint committee meeting in June,[35] but decided that developments in the ports would have to be watched closely if such a militant course was to be avoided. He therefore spent six weeks of the summer in Portsmouth, all the time gauging the mood of the lower deck.

Economic grievances were at the forefront, and there was widespread talk of taking strike action. Men on leave from the Grand Fleet were coming home and finding that their wives could not afford enough food to go round.[36] Some 38 per cent of ratings were now married, and they were finding the cost of living exceedingly hard to cope with.[37] Every strike by civilian workers had the effect of fuelling the unrest. John Cummins, an official of the Stewards' Society at Portsmouth, wrote to Yexley about his members' grievances, pointing out, ' [. . .] we are unanimous in the opinion that other methods must be resorted to',[38] while George Simmonds, another official of the society, wrote that the Admiralty's attitude would ' [. . .] cause grave dissatisfaction among our people and will cause many of them to throw in their lot with the Political agitation party, a thing we were very anxious to avoid'.[39] There were vague rumours of a monster political demonstration to be held on Southsea Common. Secret preparations were said to be afoot; on a given day the word would go out and men would quietly make their way to the common. At the same time there were constant rumours of mutiny in the German fleet and wild suggestions were being floated about the possibility of common action between German and British ratings.[40]

The Admiralty chose to adopt a low-key approach. It was an inopportune moment to begin an investigation of the lower-deck societies. In July 1918 the First Sea Lord, Admiral Wemyss, was of the firm opinion that any precipitate attempt to suppress the benefit societies would lead to a 'conflagration'. Undoubtedly there had been a growth of the trade union mentality and methods among ratings, and the question that Wemyss pondered was whether this influence on the societies could now be checked in any way. On balance it seemed preferable to defer action until after the war when Hostilities Only ratings had left the service and were no longer a problem. But Wemyss could not be sure in his own mind that the societies were not already stronger than was generally imagined.

Yexley took the matter more seriously. He feared that a mental attitude harmful to naval discipline was being created. At Devonport, for example, the consensus was that the next loyal appeal should be submitted on behalf of the men by the Labour Party.[41] A vigorous campaign for reforms and even for the democratisation of the service was acceptable and necessary so long as the lower deck maintained its independence of trade unions and the Labour Party. It is the fear that this independence might be compromised that best explains his activities during the next few months.[42]

As the unrest became more pronounced he pressed more and more vigorously for his own version of the welfare department, supporting the joint committee's policy on direct representation through officially recognised benefit societies simply on the grounds that it was preferable to seeing the lower deck join forces with the trade union movement.[43] In August the Admiralty began to bend in his direction with a plan for a standing departmental committee to take over responsibility for general issues of lower-deck welfare. The new Naval Personnel Committee, as it was called, corresponded closely to Yexley's concept of a welfare department. Its brief was to monitor lower-deck affairs, but it was alerted to the serious implications of permitting representation through a combination of ratings. The committee's existence was thus to be kept secret, it was not to have any direct contact with the fleet, and no impression was to be given that it was a grievance committee.[44]

Events were now moving fast. On 29 August the Metropolitan Police and the City of London Police struck in support of demands for a wage rise and union recognition. After one day the strike was called off, with the Prime Minister personally agreeing to a substantial pay increase and recognition of an authorised organisation to represent the men.[45] Within a matter of weeks London firemen who had joined the National Union of Corporation Workers (the present National Union of Public Employees) held a strike ballot to back up a claim for recognition of the union by the London County Council. The government put pressure on the LCC to make concessions, and the firemen's demand was granted in part.[46] These were significant gains for uniformed personnel, who had hitherto been denied the right to organise collectively. And as the Director of Naval Intelligence noted, collective representation of policemen ' [...] is an idea that will germinate in the men's minds and find expression sooner or later'.[47]

YEXLEY'S INTERVENTION: THE CONFIDENTIAL MEMORANDUM

The police strike frightened Yexley and convinced him that only a dramatic initiative would prevent the lower deck from following suit.

If ratings were to try and emulate the police and the fire brigade, he believed, the Admiralty's inevitable response would be to close down the benefit societies and tighten up discipline, and that would be a major setback for the lower deck.[48] He set about drafting a memorandum listing a number of outstanding grievances and stressing the urgency of the situation. Copies of the document were sent to the King, the Cabinet and members of the Board of Admiralty on 4 September. ' [. . .] the lower deck is one great combustible mass,' he wrote. 'Should an explosive point be touched [. . .] the whole Navy would burst into flame. [. . .] men are discussing their "right to strike" and when it shall take place. The public have justified the "Police Strike" and they will justify the Lower Deck when they know the facts.'[49] Altogether he listed sixteen complaints, most of them irritants rather than matters on which the continued loyalty of the men hinged. Yexley was obviously hoping for some rapid concessions, however small, which would at least give the impression that the authorities were concerned with lower-deck welfare and so defuse the situation. Equally, he urgently wanted to establish the fact that *he* was the authorative spokesman on lower-deck affairs, and as such he was pre-empting the more militant wing of the movement. The document was prepared without the knowledge of the lower-deck societies and was not made public until ten years later.[50]

Official reactions to the memorandum were guarded. The First Lord, Sir Eric Geddes, seemed to be deliberately underplaying the issue when he told the Cabinet that, while there was a certain amount of 'dissatisfaction' among the men, there was 'no reason to believe that such dissatisfaction was of an alarming nature'.[51] Even before receiving Yexley's memorandum he had been informed that a naval strike was in the offing and consequently had asked the Chancellor, Bonar Law, to authorise spending on reforms that had already been approved.[52] On double-checking his information Geddes was told privately by Horatio Bottomley, editor of *John Bull*, that '[. . .] there are evidences of abnormal unrest on the part of the lower deck [. . .]'.[53] Admiral Heath, the Second Sea Lord, recognised that there was some unrest but saw it largely as the work of agitators and dismissed Yexley's document as part of a 'cleverly organised movement'.[54] Admiral Fisher, now retired, was much more alert to the potential danger and wrote to George Lambert, the long-serving former Civil Lord of the Admiralty:

After the Police, the next strike will be the Navy! I know the British sailor to his very core! He has been my study all my life, and I have a deep affection for him. The sailors are not being properly engineered, and the authorities will have a mutiny as sure as fate! Everything given them is always done with reluctance and after such pressure as quite takes away the value of the concession, *and it rankles*! Macnamara is an Ass of the First Water and does not realise the volcano any more than the gold stripe people.[55]

Despite the Admiralty's tendency to play down the unrest Yexley's memorandum was given a good deal of attention. The Board of Admiralty meeting on 20 September was largely given over to discussion of it and it appeared on the agenda for further consideration at three subsequent meetings.[56] It seems likely that Fisher's intervention was partly responsible for ensuring that the matter was not put aside. On 7 September Yexley discussed the position with him, and Fisher went immediately to see the Prime Minister to tell him that Yexley was reliable and that the government must act at once to relieve the situation.[57]

On 9 September Geddes invited Yexley to the Admiralty to discuss the grievances. A second meeting followed three days later, and the First Lord began to take action. He called for progress reports from his departmental officials on what was being done about the grievances and began to urge more haste. 'Give me all the reasons why we are not like the Army,' he insisted in connection with one item, and on another he minuted, 'I want to know how this stands tomorrow. I understand it has been under consideration for twelve months.' The 'clear-up', as Macnamara called it, was rapid. Within a month many of Yexley's proposals had been acted upon and, unlike previous occasions when concessions had been made, announcement of the changes was promulgated to the fleet as early as possible. By the end of September the one item still to be dealt with was pay.[58]

THE 1918 GENERAL ELECTION

While Yexley was dealing direct with the Admiralty in an effort to prevent an explosion he was also working hard to contain the radical political activities of the benefit societies. In June 1918 he learned that serious agitation was brewing at Devonport and Chatham. The joint committee at Chatham was proposing to put forward its own candidate, a chief writer, Joseph Cronin, at the next general election, while in Portsmouth a petty officer sick-berth steward, Richard Willis, who was a member of the Labour Party, was canvassing the idea of standing as a lower-deck candidate.[59] As far as the Portsmouth joint committee was concerned parliamentary representation was a second string to its bow, a fall-back strategy if direct representation at the Admiralty was denied. As the committee secretary wrote to Yexley:

I quite agree with you that it is not in the best interests of the Service for the Lower Deck to mix up with the political life of the country, and the upholding of the best traditions of the Navy can be preserved if the Admiralty treat us with confidence.

However, he pointed out, ' [. . .] we shall not hesitate to join in the political strategy if our aspirations are despised'.[60]

Yexley was alarmed at the prospect of the lower deck being linked to the Labour Party in the election. The July edition of *The Fleet* spoke of the 'foolish idea' of having a lower-deck MP and expressed confidence that the Portsmouth committee would not be taken in by it.[61] But in criticising these developments he was being less than candid. During the war years he had continued to cherish the idea of becoming an MP. At the end of 1917 there was a movement in Plymouth to have him adopted as Liberal candidate. Yexley was in close touch with Winston Churchill over the matter, and the idea was supported by the Liberal *Western Daily Mercury*.[62] Thus with Yexley it was not a question of blanket opposition to a lower-deck candidate as such but of opposition to the lower deck joining forces with Labour.

The Representation of the People Act, 1918, had enormously increased the naval vote, allowing men to cast their ballot in the constituency where they were normally resident and for the first time permitting them to vote by post. Yexley saw the possibilities that had been opened up, and at his suggestion the Portsmouth joint committee agreed to write to the Admiralty with a view to securing for the naval constituencies the votes of men with no fixed abode.[63] In August the lower deck at Portsmouth were becoming increasingly interested in having a parliamentary spokesman, and the local Labour Party made a formal approach to the joint committee to consider united action. The committee decided not to take up the invitation for the time being,[64] but as far as Yexley was concerned the danger of some political involvement with Labour was increasing. By September the party had in fact adopted Sick-berth Steward Richard Willis as its candidate in Portsmouth North and he was sponsored by the Operative Society of Bricklayers.[65] Yexley was under pressure to make a move. What finally caused him to make up his mind was a letter from a friend, Chief Petty Officer George Hollamby, informing him that the Chatham branch of the Executive Petty Officers' Society had now written to Portsmouth suggesting a naval strike.[66] This was the deciding factor, and within a matter of days Yexley had resolved to stand.[67]

His first step was to write to both Churchill and Fisher, asking whether they could exert any influence to have him adopted as Liberal candidate for Portsmouth North,[68] but the overture seems to have been without result. Meanwhile the joint committee complained to the local Labour Party that it had adopted its candidate without consulting the lower deck, and even Willis's own society, the Sick Berth Stewards', had disowned him.[69] On 9 October a combined meeting of the local Labour Party executive and the entire joint committee was held at which the party agreed to reconsider its position, and it was eventually decided that Willis should step down. On this basis Yexley allowed his name to go forward as the candidate of the lower deck.[70]

His candidature was supported by the Portsmouth branch of the National Federation of Discharged and Demobilised Soldiers and Sailors, and a parliamentary committee of the lower-deck societies was hastily established. It consisted of representatives from eleven societies.[71] Early in November the Warrant Officers' Society passed a resolution supporting Yexley and announcing that it would write to its members in the fleet and call on them to vote for him.[72] In fact he was supported across the board by the lower-deck societies, with the solitary exception of the Engine Room Artificers, who in characteristic fashion were content to rely on the engineers' and boilermakers' unions to do their lobbying for them.[73] The three political parties were now notified that Yexley was the lower-deck candidate and were asked not to stand against him. Both Labour and Liberals agreed, leaving Yexley in a straight fight with the Tory candidate.[74] But in standing aside the Labour and Liberal parties were not offering him the benefit of their electoral machines. The lower deck were left with just two months to raise funds and develop some sort of organisation. As *The Fleet* commented, for parliamentary purposes they were just a disorganised mob.[75]

On 11 October, the day after his adoption, Yexley wrote to the Admiralty informing them that an independent lower-deck candidate had been selected at Portsmouth and an election committee of ratings set up. He requested information as to whether it would be against King's Regulations for the committee to sign their names to electoral literature. The request took the Admiralty aback. It had already been approached by a number of officers on the active list for permission to stand in different constituencies, and approval had been given as a matter of course.[76]

The prospect of a committee of ratings putting forward a candidate was something it had not bargained for. Clearly there was a potential conflict with Article 11 of King's Regulations, and the question was referred to the newly established Naval Personnel Committee. The committee's recommendation was that Article 11 should be amended so that combinations would be forbidden only on board ship and in the shore establishments.[77] In other words, a ratings' committee would be free to operate when its members were off duty. But this seemingly liberal approach was rejected by Admiral Heath, the Second Sea Lord, who argued that the election campaign would inevitably turn into criticism of the existing regulations and customs, and promises to remedy grievances. He could see no way in which an electoral committee of ratings could avoid breaking Article 11.[78]

Eventually, after a full month's deliberation, the Admiralty issued a Fleet Order announcing that men, whether in or out of uniform, were not allowed to serve on election committees, canvass or take any active part in support of a candidate.[79] It was aimed specifically at Yexley and Cronin and was certain to cripple their election campaigns. On 16 November the order was posted at Portsmouth. At once Yexley telegrammed Macnamara: 'Commander in Chief issued order against naval men assisting. There will be trouble. Yexley.' The threat produced an instant reaction. The same day the Prime Minister and the War Cabinet were alerted, and permission was immediately granted to revise the order so as to allow electioneering by men in civilian clothes.[80] An advance copy of the order was rushed to Yexley on 19 November.[81] It had taken the Admiralty five weeks to reply to his letter, and now the election was less than a month away.

Unlike Cronin at Chatham, who concentrated exclusively on naval issues, Yexley campaigned on a programme with wider appeal, calling among other things for equal pay and employment opportunities for women, Home Rule for Ireland and an end to armed intervention in Russia.[82] However, the election campaign proved to be a very dirty business. Smear attacks were made on him, with suggestions that he was standing under an assumed name and hints that this had something to do with the war. He was vigorously opposed by the temperance movement, whose work in the Navy he had long opposed; and the ERAs' Society bought advertising space in the press to dissociate itself publicly from his campaign and to cast doubt on the representative nature of his lower-deck parliamentary committee.[83] In addition Yexley had no election agent, no funds to speak of, only one committee room, and on election day only one car at his disposal, hired by the Mechanicians' Society. If either he or Cronin ever had a chance of winning the election it finally disappeared when thousands of naval voters were effectively disenfranchised.

There was a colossal muddle over ballot papers for servicemen. In Portsmouth North there were supposed to be 10,200 absent naval voters: it turned out that most of them were not absent at all but based at harbour establishments in Portsmouth.[84] By polling day the bulk of them had not received their voting papers and were turned away from the polls. Only 1,700 of the absent electors actually voted.[85] At the same time an army of Portsmouth dockyard workers who were on ship repair work in the north were not recorded as absent and so they too were disenfranchised. In the Grand Fleet the wrong voting papers were delivered to many ships, and by the time the error had been corrected many men were away on leave. Those who received their election papers appeared to have been the exception rather than the rule. It was hardly surprising if some wondered whether the Admiralty and the Post Office had entered into a conspiracy to prevent men voting.

At Chatham Cronin came bottom of the poll and lost his deposit,[86] However, at Portsmouth North, in spite of the difficulties facing him, Yexley managed to poll a very respectable 7,063 votes against his opponent's 11,427.[87] But perhaps his most important achievement, viewed from a long-term perspective, was that he had managed to thwart the possibility of an organic link-up between lower-deck organisations and the Labour Party.

YEXLEY AND THE CONTAINMENT OF LOWER-DECK MILITANCY

In view of his vigorous intervention in favour of a moderate approach to the questions of direct representation and political involvement, it is necessary to inquire about Yexley's motives. Some have represented him as an Admiralty agent,[88] and indeed there were times when he appeared to be informing on the lower-deck movement. For example, with the growth of naval unrest after 1910 he was asked by the Admiralty to submit a memorandum on the activities of the benefit societies, and he duly obliged.[89] To whom, then, did he owe his first allegiance? Without doubt many within the naval establishment regarded him with abhorrance. Admiral Colville, C-in-C Portsmouth, was appalled that the First Lord had consulted Yexley over his memorandum in September 1918.[90] But in justifying his action Geddes indicated that at the highest level within the Admiralty Yexley was held in a special position of trust:

It appears that two, if not more, of my recent predecessors in this office have had by no means remote relationship and connexion with Mr Yexley, and have found it of benefit to themselves [. . .] to consult him on matters in connexion with the conditions of service of the Lower Deck, and in both cases have found him to be a useful and reliable consultant.
. . . it is quite clear that for years past his relationship with the Admiralty has been one of trust [. . .] .
I thought it well to let you know that although Mr Yexley is desirous of doing all that is possible to advance the legitimate claims of those whom he professes to represent, he has not been considered as an agitator who should be ignored or of dangerous character.

However, the fact that Yexley was now identified with the joint committee request for official recognition of the lower-deck societies sowed seeds of distrust in the minds of Admiralty officials. Aware of his ability as an agitator, they were anxious to know if, in this instance, he was leading the campaign or being led. On this point Wemyss observed that if Yexley was driving he was a more dangerous man than the First Sea Lord had imagined, but even if he was being led he was not being loyal to the best interests of the service.[91]

At one point during that hectic autumn Yexley was under suspicion by DORA personnel of having incited ratings to mutiny. The cause of the suspicion was an article in the *Naval Chronicle* on the police strike entitled 'Strikes and "Strikes" ' in which he commented on its implications for the Navy.[92] The article clearly expressed opposition to industrial action by uniformed personnel, but the Intelligence Service understood the title to imply that a naval mutiny would really be just another strike and as such a matter of no special concern.[93] Consequently DORA officers questioned Yexley at his office. At the Admiralty there was now a certain mistrust of him, a feeling that he was 'running with the hare and hunting with the hounds',[94] and

Geddes remarked in connection with this episode, ' [. . .] a man who plays with fire [. . .] should not expect to be accepted as a fire extinguisher'.[95]

During the next few months Yexley seems to have been in contact with Intelligence Service personnel on at least two occasions at which the activities of the radical wing of the lower-deck movement were brought up. However, the circumstances are not clear and it is impossible to say for certain whether the meetings resulted from continued security surveillance of him or because he was helping Intelligence.[96]

Official concern over his parliamentary candidacy indicates that the Admiralty could not count on him toeing a moderate line, and even his apparent success in steering the lower deck away from the more extreme version of direct representation was not generously received. As Yexley well knew, the alternative to a system of direct representation was for someone like himself to act as unofficial intermediary, yet when in January 1919 he passed on to the Secretary to the Admiralty a request from the Stewards' Society he received a very frosty reply from his old associate, Oswyn Murray:

I think I am right in saying that this procedure by which a definite 'Resolution' of persons in the Service is passed from you to me in a personal and unofficial sort of way is a new procedure, and I am wondering whither it may lead us. It is, of course, quite different in principle from the procedure under which you have from time to time brought to my notice or that of Members of the Board your own impressions of the feelings or wishes of the Lower Deck, [. . .] it could be better if actual resolutions of this kind were forwarded in some more official way.[97]

Yexley's response was equally chill, but it indicated that he was undeterred and still saw himself in the role of an intermediary:

As far as I know, there is no Service channel through which such a Resolution could be passed, as the mere passing of it is a violation of Article 11 [. . .] . However, if you can give me a hint as to just exactly what course you think should be pursued on an occasion like this, it would greatly help.[98]

The evidence, then, does suggest that Yexley's position was at times ambivalent and that his private representations to the Admiralty enabled it at crucial moments to deflect a thrust by the lower deck. Yet it would be wrong to accuse him of conscious duplicity towards the ratings, and indeed the Admiralty was never quite sure how far he would go in pressing their case. His foremost concern was for the

interests of the men as he understood them, but he also wanted the
Navy to be a vigorous fighting service, and he saw no necessary
conflict between the two. If at times he acted for the Admiralty it was
because he viewed the lower deck and the Admiralty as interrelated
parts of the service which was his one interest in life, and in whose
continued health the best interests of the lower deck lay.

SIX

The militant years, 1919–23

During four years of war feeling had been growing and intensifying, but so long as war lasted the Lower Deck contented itself with cursing; as soon as the Armistice was signed [. . .] things assumed an entirely new aspect. The Lower Deck felt it could go 'all out' to get what it had so long asked for and been denied. – *The Fleet*, May 1919

Every dog has his day, and when the seaman's comes round, the civilian [. . .] is likely to feel more than a little sick. – 'Fore and Aft', *Naval Chronicle*, 11 September 1918

Combination will do for the men in the forces what it has done and is doing for civilian workers. – Recruiting leaflet, Sailors', Soldiers' and Airmen's Union, 1919

The flurry of activity at the Admiralty prompted by Yexley's memorandum to the Cabinet and the lower-deck campaign in the 1918 general election still left two major issues unresolved – the level of the ratings' pay and the question of machinery for handling general lower-deck grievances. These were the major interests of the lower-deck societies at the end of 1918, and in the course of the next two years, against a background of increasing militancy, the Admiralty was forced to grapple with them. As it evolved, the strategy of the authorities appeared to be to stall and play for time in the belief that lower-deck passions would cool. Meanwhile limited concessions were made which gave the impression of going some way towards meeting the demands for collective representation but which in the event proved to be of little consequence. When the time was right in 1920 and the militancy among servicemen had run its course, the Admiralty reversed the drift of the previous years and began to take a firm line with the societies. Thereafter, with but a short-lived revival in 1923, the lower-deck movement began a downward spiral that was to continue throughout the decade. That decline was to be a major contributing factor in the mutiny at Invergordon eight years later.

THE JERRAM COMMITTEE AND LOWER-DECK PAY

In October 1918 the Admiralty had established the Naval Personnel Committee with Rear-Admiral Sir Thomas Jerram as chairman. This came close to Yexley's concept of a welfare department. Apart from its general brief to monitor lower-deck society activities, it was to be available all year round for consultation with the Admiralty on matters relating to pay and conditions. One of the first tasks assigned to it by Admiral Tothill, Fourth Sea Lord, was to look into the question of simplifying the existing structure of naval pay and allowances.[1] But the real lower-deck concern, the generally low *level* of pay, was not tackled, and neither the War Cabinet nor the Admiralty showed any sense of urgency in this area. Separation allowances were increased in November, but no move was made to grasp the real nettle, and at the end of December 1918 the Naval Personnel Committee was still preoccupied with individual anomalies in the pay structure of different branches rather than with the general level.[2]

Lower-deck impatience was growing daily. The unfavourable comparison between service pay and civilian wages was becoming increasingly obvious. The problem became more acute when men were given twenty-eight days' leave after the Armistice. It was the first long, general leave since before the war, but many had to return to their ships in the Grand Fleet before it expired because their furlough pay was insufficient to maintain them at home.[3] They were now close to breaking point.

Just before Christmas Fisher, still active on behalf of the ratings, prevailed on J. L. Garvin, editor of *The Observer*, to write a strong editorial on the need for a 'strict and searching inquiry' into naval pay. An accompanying article by Yexley argued that all branches of the service were worse off than they had been in August 1914.[4] There was no doubting the seriousness of the situation, and this publicity strengthened the Admiralty's hand in Cabinet. The very next day Macnamara reviewed the situation for his Board colleagues:

I view the condition of the Lower Deck [. . .] as needing prompt and sympathetic consideration – or there will be trouble. [. . .]

The Treasury must be told definitely that it is probably asking for trouble with the Fleet [. . .] .[5]

Without delay the Board approved a memorandum to the Cabinet on the need for a pay increase. It pointed out that recruiting was likely to suffer and that even now there was a falling off in the numbers joining; with pay at its existing level, few men would re-engage for a second period. Noting that strongly worded articles had recently appeared in the press, the Admiralty urged that the matter be dealt with liberally and at once, and asked for permission to announce that the pay issue was well in hand.[6] The Cabinet consented and the news was released on 27 December.[7] Geddes informed the Prime Minister of the gravity of the situation and obtained his agreement that the body to look into lower-deck pay would be strictly naval, with no involvement of War Office personnel, and that whatever recommendations were handed down would be accepted more or less in their entirety.[8]

On 28 December the Board of Admiralty decided to reconstitute the Naval Personnel Committee as a committee of inquiry on lower-deck pay under Admiral Jerram.[9] The committee was to have twelve ratings attached to it in an advisory capacity and was to hear evidence from lower-deck witnesses at the three home ports.[10] Its composition came in for some criticism, especially the fact that it was to be chaired by a naval officer. In the *Naval Chronicle* there was a call for a prominent public figure to preside over the inquiry, with representatives of the Labour movement among its members. At the Admiralty the latter point was supported by Macnamara, but the Board turned it down.[11] However, among the lower deck generally the setting up of the committee was seen as a victory. The important thing was to co-ordinate the demands presented to it and to ensure that the advisory members made a real impact.

In November 1918 representatives of the three lower-deck joint committees had met to agree on the requests for the loyal appeal. On the question of pay the more militant Devonport line prevailed, and the claim put forward was for a general increase of 1s 6d a day for all ratings. It meant an increase of over 80 per cent for able seamen but was still conservative in view of the abysmally low rates of pay. As Admiral Jerram himself noted, it was hardly sufficient for the lower ratings.[12] Evidently lower-deck thinking at the home ports was out of touch with the more militant mood in the Grand Fleet, especially on the question of pay. When the Admiralty's intention to review pay was announced the Commander-in-Chief, Beatty, established two committees under Admirals Tweedie and Goodenough to inquire into the feelings of ratings in the fleet. The men held meetings at Rosyth and Scapa to decide their demands and early in the new year made it plain that, in their view, the appropriate rate for an able seaman was 7s 8d a day, double what the joint committees had in mind.[13]

The Jerram committee's hearings were due to begin at Portsmouth on 21 January. Elections were held among the lower deck at the home ports to chose the witnesses, and the lower-deck societies made sure that most of those elected were members.[14] Next it was necessary to agree on a common programme of requests for the whole lower deck, and on 18 January over 100 delegates met at the Connaught Rooms in London for this purpose. Of course, the meeting was held in breach of King's Regulations, but in such a period of unrest the Admiralty was most unlikely to take disciplinary action. At the end of the day it was decided to compromise on the pay claim and ask for a 4s a day all-round increase, back-dated to 1 October 1918. Among the other requests to be put forward, the most important were for an increase in the rate of pension from 1d to 2d per day, the introduction of widows' pensions at two-thirds the rate of a man's and the retention of separation allowances, which, like many of the wartime concessions, had been introduced only for the period of hostilities.[15]

In addition the meeting decided that the advisory members must act as a united body. The original Admiralty plan was for the four advisory members from each port to attend only the hearings at their own depot, but at the Connaught Rooms it was decided that all twelve representatives must attend all sessions. The first lower-deck witness on the opening day of the hearing was to seek Jerram's assurances that advisory members would attend all sessions, otherwise they would withdraw as a body. The lower deck were flexing their muscles. Within an hour of the demand being put to Jerram at the first session of hearings the Admiralty had wired approval.[16] All that remained was for the witnesses to present a solid front in arguing their case. On the eve of the first day of the inquiry many of the witnesses had met at the Trafalgar Institute in Portsmouth and had been schooled in what to say.[17] Fifty-six of the seventy witnesses from Portsmouth were nominees of the societies, and, with the exception of the Engine Room Artificers, who chose to go their own way, a united front was presented to the committee on all major issues.[18]

The Jerram Committee visited the three home ports between 21

January and 5 February, 1919, altogether taking evidence from 240 elected witnesses.[19] The environment in which the hearings was held was highly charged. The country was in turmoil as a result of industrial disputes. In the closing days of 1918 there had been a major cotton strike. In January troops had been used against demonstrating engineers in Glasgow. The coal miners were out in some areas, and there was a threat of an industry-wide strike on 19 March if nationalisation was not agreed to and pay increased by 30 per cent.[20] Much of the Cabinet's time in January and February was taken up in discussion of industrial disputes. Ratings would have to be used for strike-breaking purposes in some cases; by the middle of February the Board of Admiralty was drawing up contingency plans for a general strike, and in these circumstances it would be folly to allow disaffection to spread throughout the lower deck.[21]

Already there had been trouble on some ships. For several weeks there had been serious unrest among men on minesweepers in the Grand Fleet. The trouble reached a peak on 3 January when some crews at Rosyth refused to go to sea in protest against low pay. Most of the discontent was in the auxiliary service, whose crews were anxious to be demobilised, but active-service ratings were also affected. The Admiralty was forced to concede a £2 per week bonus to auxiliary men, but on the lower deck there were still those who asked whether a rating's life was really worth a mere forty bob. In fact discipline had deteriorated to such an extent that circumspection was needed if officers were to keep control of their crews.[22] On HMS *Kilbride* at Milford Haven ratings refused work and hoisted the red flag:[23] eight men were court-martialled on charges of non-violent mutiny, seven of them receiving sentences of from three months to two years with hard labour and dismissal from the service.[24]

In the army, men quartered at Folkestone had mutinied; demonstrations by soldiers took place in half a dozen other centres, and on 8 January 1,500 soldiers protested in Whitehall.[25] Servicemen were much affected by what they saw in the civilian world, but the spread of militancy was by no means a one-way process. Indeed, the new First Lord of the Admiralty, Walter Long, argued in Cabinet that Bolshevism originated not so much on the civil side as within the military and then spread to civilian workers.[26]

The lower-deck witnesses asked Jerram to announce his findings by the end of March, but the government could hardly afford to wait that long and after only two days of hearings a decision was made in principle to raise the level of pay substantially. On 29 January an interim bonus of 1s 6d was announced.[27] From this point on, the questioning of witnesses was perfunctory and they were heard in groups. Once the hearings were over the committee, minus the advisory members, returned to the Admiralty to work on their report. Not until this task was complete were the advisory representatives called back, and then only to verify that the committee's summary of the evidence was accurate.[28] Such failure to involve the lower-deck advisory members in the final stages came as a great disappointment to many ratings, who had assumed that they would have a hand in drafting the report.[29]

WELFARE REPRESENTATION OR LOWER-DECK UNIONISM

Meanwhile the Admiralty still had to come up with some long-term scheme for dealing with men's requests and grievances. At the start of the year Yexley again warned that if it wanted to prevent a movement towards amalgamation among lower-deck societies it should make some concession in this direction, preferably in the form of a permanent welfare department.[30] In the press and in Parliament the newly elected Liberal MP Colonel Malone, a Royal Marine officer, restated the idea of attaching lower-deck ratings to such a department, something that Macnamara had already shown his support for at the Admiralty.[31] During the debate on the Navy Estimates there were numerous references to greater organisation among the lower deck. In fact ratings were simply following the example of Civvy Street, where they saw other servants of the Crown rapidly becoming unionised as a result of the government's adoption of the Whitley proposals.

The pressure on the Admiralty was considerable and time was running out if trade union recruiting in the service was to be prevented. Even before the Jerram committee had finished its hearings the Second Sea Lord, Admiral Heath, circulated an urgent memorandum among the Board of Admiralty.

I desire to bring to the notice of the Board that, in my opinion, there is no doubt that an organised attempt is being made by socialist and syndicalist circles to introduce into the Navy a Lower Deck Union on Trade Union lines [. . .] .

The position with which we are now faced is this: If we do nothing, there is the possibility that the Lower Deck Union will become an accomplished fact. If, on the other hand, we are prepared to allow the men a recognised means of presenting their grievances — real or imaginery — and aspirations collectively, I believe that the danger of an unauthorised Union will be averted. [. . .]

It is, I think, essential to provide an authorised and controlled means for the Lower Deck to ventilate its feelings.[32]

The warning was taken seriously, and within ten days it was announced that, in view of the success of the Jerram committee, a permanent system of welfare committees would be established on similar lines. As Yexley saw it, almost at the point of being forced to take unconstitutional action the men were now being offered an alternative that enabled them to stay within the law.[33]

At the time of the Armistice a dozen lower-deck societies were functioning,[34] and shortly afterwards there were reckoned to be 10,000 members. Lower-deck militancy at the end of the war had helped recruitment, and the establishment of the welfare system appeared to offer the societies an expanded role. Among the most important developments was the amalgamation of the societies catering for petty officers and junior ratings in the seaman branch, these jointly forming the RN Seamen's Signalmen's and Telegraphists' Society in 1919.[35]

In August 1919 a brand-new society for Marines, the Royal Marine NCOs' Benefit Society, was established with the specific aim of ensuring that the Marines' voice was heard on the welfare committee.[36] Throughout the service, ratings, especially the younger ones, began to flock to the societies. The growth in the movement was a mirror image of the growing interest in trade unionism ashore, where membership was double the pre-war level.[37] Membership of the CPOs' Society more than doubled in 1919.[38] In April the Seamen's Society claimed almost 7,000 members, and in the twelve-month period following March 1919 the Stokers' Society's membership practically doubled, standing at 5,000 in July 1920.[39] Meanwhile at Chatham both the seamen's and stokers' societies were sufficiently large to require full-time secretaries.[40]

Some sections of the lower deck were acutely conscious of the way the movement was weakened by class divisions.[41] Concern about the problem led them to consider ways of rationalising and strengthening their organisation, and it was this which led them to renew contact with the Workers' Union. In December 1918 the secretaries of the Chatham branches of the seamen's and stokers' societies met Charles Duncan, the union's general secretary, to discuss the possibility of material assistance.[42] The idea was to centralise their operations in a London office with a full-time general secretary. The Workers' Union had offered space at its head office, and the offer was being seriously discussed at the three naval ports. As S. H. Browett, secretary of the Seamen's Society, explained to Yexley, 'If this scheme is taken up by all the Lower Deck Societies it would of course give us much greater power.'[43] ' [. . .] this lower deck diversity is the most disquieting symptom and the one that exposes the weakness of the Lower Deck [. . .].'[44] There was agreement in principle among the three joint committees that the idea was sound, and as a preparatory step a meeting of officials was held in February 1919 to harmonise rules and agree on a uniform scale of affiliation fees.[45]

Meanwhile an even more significant link between the lower deck and radical trade unionism was being forged. The Sailors' Soldiers' and Airmen's Union (SSAU), an outgrowth of the wartime Soldiers' and Workers' Council, had appeared on the scene. The union received a major boost from the Folkestone army mutiny.[46] The soldiers who demonstrated in Whitehall had borrowed a leaf from the lower-deck book and were demanding the right to elect a standing committee to advise the War Office on service matters affecting the welfare of the men.[47] Now the union began to hold meetings up and down the country to generate support for the introduction of this machinery in the army and Navy. By the end of January John Maclean, the Scottish revolutionary leader, was claiming widespread success in winning the support of soldiers and sailors.[48]

With most of its potential members leaving the service, the SSAU became primarily an organisation of recently demobilised men, but servicemen were invited to become honorary members with a view to taking out full membership on leaving the forces.[49] Naval branches of the union were established at the three home ports and Harwich, while the headquarters were housed in the *Daily Herald* offices, with George Lansbury and a few trade union officials acting as an advisory committee to the leadership.[50]

However, the SSAU never really got off the ground. An inaugural rally was planned at the Albert Hall on 16 February with prominent trade unionists on the platform. The Admiralty was already extremely worried about the effect of seditious speeches on ratings on leave, and in Cabinet the First Lord pressed for agitators to be prosecuted with vigour. The Home Secretary indicated that steps would be taken to deal with the problem, and within a matter of days the SSAU rally was cancelled.[51] DORA personnel had been responsible for preventing an earlier gathering at the Albert Hall organised by the *Daily Herald*, and it seems quite probable that the SSAU's was similarly sabotaged.[52] At the same time the union was constantly plagued by lack of funds, despite the belief of the Intelligence Service that it was financed by the wealthy wife of Lieutenant-Commander Kenworthy, the Liberal MP for Hull and one of its most prominent members.[53]

In May there was a contingent from the Portsmouth branch of the SSAU among the 10,000 people in a Labour march from the Trades Hall, Fratton, to a meeting on Southsea Common.[54] But by this time the union was in serious difficulties. A half-baked plan for soldiers to demobilise themselves and for sailors to seize the ports on 11 May, six months to the day since the Armistice, proved a total failure.[55] The organisation managed to limp along for several months more, but its influence among active-service ratings was negligible. It continued to hold meetings to condemn the war against Russia, and during the summer and autumn, assisted by the London Trades Council, unsuccessful attempts were made to merge with the National Union of Ex-servicemen. Thereafter, with the Portsmouth branch of the union riven by in-fighting, little more was heard of the organisation.

The courtship between the lower-deck societies and the Workers' Union also came to a temporary halt after February 1919. This was due partly to the problem of financing the cost of a central headquarters, but also to the fear many men had of being too closely identified with the Labour movement. Indeed, it was still very risky to be prominently associated with lower-deck society work. In 1919 at least two well known delegates to the Portsmouth joint committee – John Norton, Tewkesbury's successor as secretary, and CPO Durrant – were drafted out of turn, and this led to charges in the House of Commons that the Admiralty was victimising benefit society members.[56]

However, the flirtation with the Workers' Union had served to bring the three joint committees closer together. Inter-port meetings were now held on a quarterly basis at the head office of the General Federation of Trade Unions with the general secretary, W. A. Appleton, present.[57] The idea of forming one big organisation for the lower deck was widely supported. The seamen's and stokers' societies were seriously considering a merger, and at Chatham the two organisations jointly opened a permanent office in October.[58] Altogether the societies had consolidated their position and were ready to play a more active role in looking after the interests of their members.

THE 1919 PAY SETTLEMENT

Meanwhile in the spring of 1919 lower-deck attention continued to focus on the Jerram committee, and by April, with still no public announcement of its recommendations, impatience began to grow. The Grand Fleet was now being dispersed, and rumours had it that the object was to prevent any large combination of ratings from forcing the pace on pay and other questions.[59]

The committee reported to the Admiralty at the end of March. Recognising that naval pay immediately before the war had been inadequate, it recommended, among other things, that the rate for able seamen be raised to 4s a day, back-dated to October; that the pension be increased from $\frac{1}{2}d$ to $1\frac{1}{2}d$ a day, and that widows' pensions should be established at two-thirds the rate for men.[60] Within the Admiralty there were some who regarded the proposals as insufficient. For example, Macnamara felt that the pay recommendations were inadequate for junior ratings and proposed instead 5s a day for able seamen. He was also inclined to concede in full the lower deck's request for a 2d a day pension rate.[61] But from the other services and the Treasury there was stiff resistance even to the Jerram proposals as they stood.

At the end of April, with the Cabinet still deferring any decision, the First Lord, Walter Long, spelled out the dangers of delay. He believed that any attempt to offer less would lead to serious trouble and told his Cabinet colleagues that unless a definite promise was given to Parliament immediately it was quite possible that agitators would get at the men even in the course of the following week.[62] The miners' militancy was paying off and the lower deck were aware of it. A week later Long was so alarmed at reports of unrest coming in that he telephoned Lloyd George in Paris at the Peace Conference and obtained the Prime Minister's support for bringing the matter to a swift conclusion. The Cabinet was told:

The immediate settlement of this question was now of the greatest importance, and he thought that if this settlement was delayed over the weekend it would be at the gravest possible risk.

With the SSAU urging self-demobilisation within the next few days and seizure of the ports the situation in the Navy was 'as grave as it could be'.[63]

Cabinet approval was therefore given to the Jerram recommendations on pay and pensions, though with back-dating only to 1 February. However, pensioners who had not been recalled for war service were not to benefit from the pension increase, and widows' pensions were yet again refused.

Lower-deck representatives met at a reconvened meeting in the Connaught Rooms on 19 May to consider the award, and the mood was less than euphoric. As they saw it, some 200,000 men who had been in the service when the requests were served but had now been demobilised were to be cheated of their just desserts.[64] The meeting resolved to continue to press for a full 4s pay increase, pension improvements for all men, the introduction of widows' pensions and the back-dating of concessions to October 1918. The chairman, CPO Lock, warned the government that, while the lower deck wanted to remain apart from outside troubles and Labour influences, they would have no option but to join hands with the trade union movement if that proved to be the only approach likely to pay dividends.[65]

1919: A YEAR OF UNREST

In times as turbulent as these it was always on the cards that disaffection would break out, and the Admiralty was aware of it. In the summer of 1919 ratings had been on strike duty in the course of police, dock and railway disputes, and hundreds had been drafted to Yorkshire to man pit pumps. In August the Admiralty expressed a desire to see them withdrawn from this work:

They find themselves in contact with men of an unsettled state of mind, even of revolutionary ideas; and is it not more than probable that, being in a state of anxiety themselves as to their own position, they may absorb some of these ideas themselves.[66]

During the same period a number of serious cases of indiscipline occurred among men serving in the Black Sea, the Baltic and north Russia. These ratings were being employed in an undeclared war against the Bolshevik government which had been in progress since the Armistice and involved five light cruisers, nine destroyers, seven minesweepers and a battalion of Royal Marines.[67] Signs of trouble first appeared in the Sixth Battalion of Marines, who had expected to be sent home after service in Germany. Between February and September 1919 there was a progressive deterioration in the discipline of this unit, involving several instances of refusal of duty and culminating in an episode in September in which the Chatham and Portsmouth companies refused an order to advance and the Lewis gun sections threw down their weapons.[68] As a result eighty-seven men were court-martialled on charges of insubordination and refusal of duty. Thirteen were sentenced to death, twenty to five years' penal servitude, and fifty-one were given two years' hard labour.[69]

On board ship discontent built up gradually during the summer months. By and large it was not due to sympathy with the Bolsheviks. Earlier in the year one lower-deck correspondent to the *Naval Chronicle* had probably voiced a majority view when he wrote: 'Bolshevists and pacifists need not rub their hands at the growing discontent and disaffection in the Navy, since the sailors are not partial to either one.'[70] Their attitude simply reflected a general distaste for a war whose justification they did not know or did not accept. As Rear-Admiral Cowan, the Senior Naval Officer in the Baltic, told the Admiralty:

[. . .] as weather conditions get worse [. . .] signs of irritation crop up, and cases of incipient insubordination occur, and always the same tendency shows up at the investigation, i.e. the desire to know why we are out here [. . .] why has it been inferred in Parliament that all out here are volunteers [. . .]?[71]

In June the crew of the gunboat *Cicala* refused to sail up the river Dvina and obeyed later only when Cowan indicated that he was prepared to fire on them.[72] In September men of the cruiser *Vindictive* at Copenhagen demonstrated on the quarter deck after being refused leave following a lengthy period at sea, and a number of stokers attempted to interfere with the vessel's fans so as to incapacitate the stokeholds. For this two ratings were court-martialled on charges of mutiny and sentenced to five years' penal servitude.[73] In November Hostilities Only ratings in the minesweepers refused duty after the expiration of the period they had signed up for. The following month disaffection spread to the flagship *Delhi*. In addition to the grievance about having to fight an undeclared war the crew complained of inadequate food. After dinner one day the hands refused to turn to, locked themselves in the recreation deck and went back to work only when the captain threatened to blow the ship up.[74]

However, the most concerted acts of indiscipline occurred in October 1919 among destroyer crews, many of whom had been in the Baltic constantly from April to August and had been in contact with disaffected British soldiers at Reval. During the summer months they had been greatly disturbed by a wireless message broadcast to British ships by the Bolsheviks in Petrograd, calling on them to emulate the refusal of duty of French sailors at Odessa and American soldiers and sailors at Archangel.[75]

At the beginning of October men of the First Destroyer Flotilla were enjoying sixteen days' home leave at Sheerness. Rumours started to circulate that they would be going back to the Baltic, and twenty to thirty men discussed the idea of refusing to sail.[76] On 10 October, with the flotilla at Rosyth, there were similar rumours and two men from *Wryneck* deserted at once. The next day the destroyers *Velox*, *Versatile* and *Wryneck* were signalled to prepare to sail for the Baltic. Word went round; 'My name's Walker,' was the response – in other words, 'I'm not going' – and some ninety ratings broke out of their ships. They made for Edinburgh, and at Aberladi station forty-four of them decided to travel to London to protest at the Admiralty. Most were long-service men. They agreed that they would behave in an orderly manner, there would be no ringleaders, and if the Admiralty wanted a spokesman it would have to pick one out. A petition was drawn up by LS Henry Baker:

After due consideration we have decided to come straight to Whitehall to have our grievances investigated and settled. It must be clearly understood that we have not in any way refused to work or cause unnecessary disturbance, but we have taken the only possible course open to us under such short notice to have our grievances settled.

On arrival at King's Cross they were stopped by the police; forming up into fours, they agreed to go quietly and were escorted to the detention quarters at Chatham barracks.[77]

Meanwhile an identical movement was afoot in Devonport. On 9 October a detachment of troops returning from Russia landed at Plymouth: 150 of them broke loose and started a riot.[78] This seems to have infected the atmosphere in the town, and on 12 October some thirty to forty ratings under orders to sail for the Baltic travelled to London with a view to petitioning the Admiralty about their grievances, only to be arrested at Paddington station.[79]

The mass refusals to sail compelled the Admiralty to study the men's grievances, and two committees of inquiry were established under Rear-Admiral Clinton-Baker and Captain W. Henderson. Apart from general grievances over the amount of time spent at sea, the lack of leave, inadequate canteen facilities and the unpopularity of the war against the Bosheviks, there were two very specific complaints. One was that, since the war had not been officially declared, men killed in action were not regarded as war casualties and their dependants were not entitled to a pension.[80] The second was that they were not getting the extra 2s 6d a day which soldiers in south Russia were allowed. At the Admiralty the Accountant General, Charles Walker, minuted that the extra money was not being paid 'as presumably the men have not been affected either by any special hardships or by the cost of living'.[81] He was ignoring the fact that the ships had been in action against Russian destroyers and cruisers, had been shelled from forts on shore, attacked by aircraft and torpedoed by submarines and had suffered a total of 127 officers and men killed or lost.[82]

Macnamara suggested that an attempt be made to obtain Treasury permission for a small increase, and Clinton-Baker's report recommended the full 2s 6d.[83] But the new First Sea Lord, Beatty, turned the proposal down: 'I am not in agreement that extra pay should be given for service in the Baltic.' The men should be informed that the army's 2s 6d was simply a 'Colonial Allowance'.[84] It was hardly a sympathetic response from one whose own financial gain from the Great War had been a gift of £100,000 from the State. By way of consolation the Admiralty announced that seven days' extra leave would be granted as soon as possible and that a special clasp would be issued for Baltic service.[85] That it was not medals so much as cash and consideration that the lower deck wanted became evident when the first welfare committee met in October.

THE WELFARE COMMITTEE SYSTEM, 1919–20

In the course of the summer of 1919 details of the welfare committee system were announced. One rating from each branch of the service at each port, a total of fifty-four men, would meet at an inter-port conference to be held annually at each port in rotation. Representatives from the same branch would decide on the detailed class requests, while the conference as a whole would agree on the general requests. The meeting would elect from among the

representatives eighteen men to an act in an advisory capacity to the
Admiralty while the requests were being considered. The
representatives would be free to discuss issues such as pay, promotion,
messing, canteens, uniform and pensions but not matters to do with
naval policy, discipline and individual or ship complaints.[86]

From the outset there had been a certain amount of scepticism on
the lower-deck about the welfare committee scheme. After the
experience of the Jerram committee Yexley expressed reservations
about the requests being judged by a committee of officers.[87] There
was also some concern about how the election of delegates would be
conducted. Before the Jerram Committee the delegates at Portsmouth
and Chatham had been chosen by ballots supervised by officers, and
men felt that the presence of officers inhibited them. For the welfare
committees the Admiralty's policy was that men should be free to
conduct their own meetings and elections without interference, but it
was made clear that officers would intervene if it proved necessary for
disciplinary reasons.[88]

Then there was the question of the role of the lower-deck societies.
A really democratic system of welfare representation required the
existence of organisation among the ratings to serve as a forum for
discussion and reporting back. The lower-deck societies appeared to
be the obvious vehicles for this. *The Fleet* could not imagine how the
system would be able to function if men were not allowed to meet
within their societies and discuss the things that concerned them.[89]
The Bluejacket argued that the societies and the joint committees
should actually be responsible for drafting the welfare demands.[90] But
was it the Admiralty's intention to allow the societies this role? In
announcing the new welfare system it had said that Article 11 would
be amended so as to permit ratings to meet at the inter-port
conference, but all other combinations were still illegal.[91] As Admiral
Heath, Second Sea Lord, had said when the welfare arrangements
were still under consideration:

Any relaxation of the regulations will be but the thin end of the wedge which
will split the discipline of the Navy. From an organisation for representing
the aspirations of the Lower Deck it would be but a short step to one very
much akin to the equivalent of the 'Soldiers' and Workmen's Committee'.[92]

In fact the Admiralty had no intention of recognising any role for
the societies in the welfare system, though the heady days of 1919
were not an opportune time to make the point explicit. The

Admiralty's strategy was to ride out the period of militancy and then later to re-establish a firm grip on the lower deck. Indeed, the welfare system was specifically designed to remove any justification for men to approach members of Parliament or to have any contact with naval trade unionism.[93] Rather than recognise a role for the societies, the welfare committee system aimed to undermine them, and thus were sown the seeds of a major conflict that was to reach a climax twelve months later.

The first inter-port conference met at Portsmouth in October 1919. As in the case of the Jerram hearings, the lower-deck societies ensured that their members were well represented among the delegates. The chairman, Chief Writer J. E. Lane, a rising force in lower-deck politics, was also chairman of the Portsmouth joint committee, and the requests that emerged closely mirrored the concerns of the lower-deck movement. At Portsmouth the system was that the delegates selected by the different branches were invited to attend a special meeting of the joint committee where they were presented with a draft programme of requests.[94] To a large extent the general proposals emanating from this quarter were a restatement of the issues left unresolved by the Jerram committee, such as that the new rates of pay be back-dated to October 1918, pensions to be paid to widows, and wartime concessions such as separation allowances and free travel warrants to be retained.[95] And recognising that, to be effective, the welfare system needed to be rooted in permanent lower-deck organisation, the suggested programme of proposals asked for the joint committees of the benefit societies to be designated as port welfare committees and as such be the medium through which requests would be processed in future.[96]

Because there had been no systematic prior discussion of the requests by the lower deck and no sifting of suggestions, the final list of proposals was heavily overloaded. No fewer than 307 general and class requests were forwarded to the Admiralty, ranging from issues of universal importance to petty requests of interest to only a small number of men.[97] Inevitably it meant a delay before any official reply would be forthcoming, and indeed it was July 1920 before the Admiralty responded.[98] During this period many ratings, frustrated by the slowness of the welfare system, the apparent ineffectiveness of the benefit societies, and the lack of progress in unifying the lower-deck movement, grew restive and began to talk again about the need for a more militant approach.

In August 1919 a rating had written in *The Fleet* that young men now joining the service were steeped in the ideals of trade unionism and if the societies did not amalgamate these men would break away and start their own movement.[99] In spring 1920 a letter to the editor from a chief yeoman of signals expressed the view that thousands of ratings who at present took no part in the lower-deck movement would join a *real* society with a concerted policy, but would have no truck with a fragmented movement.[100] In July the *Naval Chronicle* carried a letter signed 'Advance', generally thought to have been written by Chief Writer Lane, the chairman of the lower-deck advisory group on the welfare committee, which outlined three options for the lower deck. They could content themselves with the welfare committee system as already constituted; they could ask for pay and pensions to be assessed by a National Wages Board; or – and this was obviously the preferred option – they could form a lower-deck union affiliated to the Labour movement.[101]

CONFRONTATION WITH THE ADMIRALTY

All the time the Admiralty was quietly watching developments and preparing for the day when it would take decisive action against the lower-deck movement. Early in 1920 Admiral Madden, C-in-C of the Atlantic Fleet, who in 1917 had advocated caution in lower-deck matters, drew to its attention his fears about the societies. They were losing their character as benefit societies and tending towards trade unionism. Electrical artificers were joining the Electrical Trade Union, and so were some torpedo men and petty officer telegraphists. He pointed out that most of the court-martial sentences on the men found guilty of indiscipline in the Baltic had been commuted, and suggested that this showed the power of the lower-deck societies. It seemed to him that the movement was becoming more centralised, more powerful, and he thought it would be advisable for the Admiralty to state that ratings who belonged to illegal societies would render themselves liable to punishment. He was supported by the Director of Naval Intelligence, who argued that, now the welfare system was established, every possible step should be taken to discourage the societies' further development. Their membership had grown rapidly during 1920. The Admiralty's own inquiries indicated that no fewer than 42 per cent of the lower deck were members and that in ten out of fourteen branches more than two-thirds of the petty officers and men belonged to them.[102] In contrast to those who wanted to take drastic action others, among them Captain Chatfield, the Fourth Sea Lord, counselled patience. They argued that it was rash to move so swiftly at a time of unsettled opinion among the lower deck. It was true the discipline and morale of the fleet had suffered as a result of prolonged concentration in home waters and more especially through the large influx of Hostilities Only ratings, with their pronounced civilian views. But the proponents of this line felt that it was a passing phase. Once the fleet was scattered around the oceans of the world and removed from bad political influences that came through associating with the civilian population at home, lower-deck ratings would revert to being more like sailors and less like politicians. At the same time men would become more reliant on their officers – a relationship that had suffered to the detriment of discipline in recent years. Chatfield indicated that a carefully drafted statement on discipline should be issued at the right moment, but that would not be until after the reply to the welfare requests. His view was that it should talk of the importance of maintaining discipline, recognise the societies as a beneficial force provided they kept to their original functions, and conclude by re-affirming Article 11 of King's Regulations. The strategy was endorsed by Macnamara and Beatty, and with Intelligence reports coming in that attempts to undermine the loyalty of serving men could be expected in the summer the Admiralty sat back to await its chances.[103]

When the delegates to the 1920 inter-port welfare committee convened in Devonport on 19 July answers to the 1919 committee requests had still not been promulgated. They were therefore unable to make an intelligent start on formulating new ones. Moreover the Admiralty had recently announced that requests previously proposed and turned down were not to be re-submitted. This high-handed attitude annoyed the delegates, and there was renewed talk of joining up with a union.[104] For four days they waited, unable to proceed with their business until an announcement on the previous year's requests had been made. When it came on 23 July it was apparent that only about a quarter of the requests had been approved, mainly the less important ones.[105] Immediately the delegates issued a statement to the press threatening to abandon the proceedings in view of the futility of the 1919 committee.[106] No attempt was made to begin the work of formulating new requests. Delegates were in contact with Nancy Astor in an effort to win some parliamentary support for their position, and on 29 July a deputation of twenty-one representatives led by the committee chairman, Chief Writer King and Chief Writer Jimmy Lane travelled to the Admiralty for an interview with Beatty to find out what their lordships' intentions were.[107] There was a heated discussion lasting three hours. Lane told Beatty that they were not looking for sympathy but for changes in the welfare system.[108] The delegates were not satisfied and on 4 August, having received no assurances that the system would be made more effective, passed a resolution saying that they were unwilling to be part of an arrangement that left the lower deck twelve months behind the times, and would prefer to revert to the pre-1919 system of handling grievances. The next day the C-in-C at Devonport ordered the welfare committee to disband. In a letter to the *Naval Chronicle* one rating (probably Lane) wrote:

If all the Chaplains of the Fleet went down on their bended knees to proclaim the beneficient intention of the Admiralty insofar as the welfare business is concerned, there are a good many that would not harken to clerical protestations.[109]

It was clear that there was a yawning gulf between lower-deck and Admiralty ideas about how grievances and requests should be dealt with, and many men seemed ready to turn to trade unionism. A week after the dissolution of the welfare committee the *Naval and Military Record* carried another letter from 'Advance'.

The Navy is governed by a class drawn from less than 3 per cent of the population, and they have made the efforts of the Welfare Committee, drawn from the other 97 per cent, abortive. The Navy must not despise the lawful and constitutional methods adopted in the industrial world for securing their needs. They must unite in one solid, lower deck union, with civil officials and officers and offices in London, and a programme of activity on similar lines to other unions, and of course, affiliation as desired.[110]

Later in the month a plan to unite the lower-deck societies along these lines was actually discussed by the Chatham joint committee. The idea was that there would be an amalgamation of all societies. The general secretary would be not an ex-naval man but someone with a close knowledge of the Labour movement. There was to be a general council of six members, two from each port, to act as an advisory body to the general secretary. Matters requiring reference to the societies generally would be decided by a vote, each constituent body having the same voting strength. The estimated £1,000 cost that would be incurred in the first year was to be raised by affiliation fees based on membership.[111]

The Admiralty's first reaction to these developments was relatively mild. Beatty was in favour of issuing the planned disciplinary order immediately, but the Board Secretary suggested holding off until the autumn. Instead a statement was issued observing that there was a growing tendency for men to make speeches on general service matters at meetings and to give interviews to the press and write letters and articles. Such actions, it was pointed out, might infringe King's Regulations and were certainly against their spirit.[112] In the circumstances it was no more than a gentle rebuke.

Discontent over the collapse of the welfare committee was quite widespread. The Cabinet learned from Intelligence agents in Coventry that ratings on leave were indignant over the treatment of the deputation that had seen Beatty at the Admiralty. The men had expressed the view that the loyalty of the Navy could not be relied on if the present attitude of the Admiralty was maintained. The Intelligence Service reported that ratings were taking more interest in politics and were following industrial developments very closely.[113] Political and industrial militancy in the country was at an unprecedented pitch. Everywhere councils of action were being formed within the Labour movement to prevent the government from engaging in hostilities against Russia. Lenin went so far as to liken the situation in August 1920 with that of Russia in the spring of 1917.[114] And in the first week in September the TUC, in a more militant mood than ever before, met in conference – at Portsmouth.

The previous week there had been a rally of 3,000 ex-servicemen in Trafalgar Square which, Intelligence agents reported, was frankly revolutionary.[115] The Home Office also noted evidence of considerable efforts to undermine the loyalty of the forces, with the National Union of Ex-servicemen (NUX), now incorporating many former SSAU members, particularly active at Portsmouth. On 3 September many ratings were present at a meeting of the local branch of the NUX when it was addressed by TUC delegates from the miners' union. The ratings declared that they would refuse to work in any mines in the event of a strike. Throughout the week TUC conference delegates were circulating among ratings telling them of the need for organisation. Some delegates from the building trade union actually went aboard some ships to talk to them. On 5 September the Southsea branch of the Labour Party held a demonstration attended by several thousand people, including many sailors, and the crowd heard David Kirkwood, the Scottish Labour leader, urge ratings to disobey if ordered to proceed to Russia. On this occasion the Home Office informant noted, 'There is already talk amongst the men of getting into an "outside" organisation since they have lost faith in the Welfare Committees [. . .].'[116]

Talk about lower-deck trade unionism continued into the autumn. On 24 October *The People*'s 'Man Behind the Gun' wrote:

[. . .] the proposed union of all lower-deck societies in a much closer co-operation than has hitherto been possible is being steadily and successfully brought into being. It is harrassed and retarded by cross-currents purposely set up, and by the faltering, and in some cases insincere, actions of a few who pose as leaders. Of the ultimate triumph of this deal we have no doubt whatever.[117]

But already the security services were closing in. On 16 October the *Workers' Dreadnought*, organ of the Workers' Socialist Federation, had published an article, 'Discontent on the Lower Deck', which called on naval ratings to support the working class, and on 20 October the offices of the paper were raided by the Special Branch. A few days later a Bolshevik courier, Veltheim, was arrested leaving the house of Colonel Malone, MP, and carrying a number of documents bound for Russia, one of which showed that Malone had received £300 from Russia for agitation among the lower deck. Sylvia Pankhurst, editor of the *Workers' Dreadnought*, and Malone were arrested and charged under the Defence of the Realm Act with attempting to cause disaffection in the armed forces.[118] Both were tried and sentenced to six months' imprisonment.[119]

Now at last the Admiralty decided to go ahead and draft the planned order on discipline.[120] The arrests frightened the lower deck. The seamen's and stokers' leaders at Chatham had had much correspondence with Malone and were afraid of being implicated. At Yexley's suggestion both now sent letters to the Admiralty declaring their continuing loyalty to the King and to the service.[121] Meanwhile scapegoats on the lower deck were found and two ratings, Crook and Springhall, were discharged from the service for having links with Sylvia Pankhurst.[122]

In December the time seemed right for the authorities to press home their advantage, and on 22 December Admiralty Fleet Order No. 3657 was issued, which was to put paid to the wider organisational aspirations of the lower-deck movement. Following carefully the approach advocated by Captain Chatfield almost a year earlier, the order set out to define the legitimate functions of the lower-deck societies once and for all. Their benefit work was mentioned approvingly, but their activities were to be restricted to their proper sphere. The Admiralty claimed to have documentary evidence that outside influences hostile to discipline and good order were operating within the societies, and announced categorically that any move to amalgamate would be seen as contravening the letter and the spirit of King's Regulations.[123] The societies had won the official recognition for which they had been pressing for nearly two decades, but the price they paid was the loss of any hope of being able to engage in the wider political aspects of welfare in the future. At one stroke they had been recognised and gagged.

THE WELFARE CONFERENCE SYSTEM, 1922

The lower-deck societies now went into decline.[124] The knowledge that they were being watched for subversive activities made men steer well clear of them. In Portsmouth some society meetings were now attended by officers, on the instructions of the commander-in-chief at the port.[125] In January 1921 *The Fleet*, which since the war had been acting as the official organ of some of the societies, began a series of articles on what was wrong with them. Inadequate benefits and domination by senior ratings were cited among the reasons, especially by the younger men. There were important disagreements between some of the societies – the seamen and stokers, the largest societies, for example, being particularly resentful of the absence of proportional representation in joint lower-deck organisations and of the plan to give equal voting rights to all constituent bodies in the proposed amalgamation of lower-deck societies.[126] But the biggest factor in their decline was that, shorn of political influence, they were no longer attractive to the ratings, while to become too prominent in their affairs was regarded as the surest way of being drafted to some far-flung outpost of empire. In the spring of 1921 400 members of the Seamen's Society at Chatham dropped out, and by the end of the year the societies generally had lost up to 50 per cent of their members.[127] Organisations such as the artisans' Portsmouth branch were functioning only intermittently; at Chatham the seamen and stokers were having difficulty in maintaining their permanent office, and in early 1922 *The Fleet* commented that the end seemed to be near for them.[128]

Meanwhile the internal feuding within the joint committees and the personality clashes involving leaders of the movement were contributing to the weakness of lower-deck organisation. At Chatham the disagreement between the seamen's and stokers' societies and the joint committee over the terms of the proposed amalgamation led to those two bodies withdrawing from the joint committee, and very soon it was moribund.[129] At Portsmouth the joint committee chairman, Lane, was a controversial character, hero-worshipped by some, detested by others, and as the committee split into pro- and anti-Lane factions attendance began to drop off.

It was against this background of decline and disintegration that the Admiralty began to think of reviving the welfare system. In 1921 the commanders-in-chief at the home ports were asked for their opinion. There was no great enthusiasm – indeed, the commanders-in-chief at Chatham and Devonport were very much opposed.[130] As Admiral Browning observed, ' [. . .] the "Welfare" system as it existed in 1919 and 1920 cuts at the foundations of discipline [. . .] . I cannot but regret the initiation of the system.'[131]

However, a modified system of welfare *conferences*, not committees, as before, was introduced. Henceforth the conferences were to be held every two years. Meetings of the delegates in the ports were to be attended by officers appointed by the commanders-in-chief: they were not to participate but could give advice if asked. There were to be no advisory representatives and no opportunity would be afforded for the lower deck to deal directly with the Admiralty. The principle of direct representation had been abandoned. As in 1920, requests raised on a previous occasion and turned down were not to be reintroduced. Moreover the welfare conference would have less authority than before, as matters relating to naval canteens and financial support for ratings in distress or their families were now to be handled by NAAFI and the Royal Naval Benevolent Trust respectively. Finally the Admiralty also pointed out that requests involving large financial expenditure were unlikely to be granted.[132]

There was widespread apathy when the first conference met in May 1922. It was not easy to formulate worthwhile requests that had not already been turned down or were not excluded. Heading the list, though it had previously been rejected, was the basic request that the joint committees be recognised as port welfare committees. This proposal was put forward simultaneously in Parliament by the Portsmouth MP, Sir Thomas Bramsdon.[133]

With Lane acting as the chairman of the conference, the joint lower-deck committees at the ports were again responsible for whatever cohesion and pattern the programme of demands had. But in the absence of any co-ordinated discussion of priorities by ratings at the base the list was again overloaded. Fifty-six general requests and 200 branch claims were presented, but when the results were announced over a year later, with only fourteen of the general requests approved, few were surprised.[134] With all the restrictions surrounding its operation the welfare system had become largely irrelevant.

THE ROUT OF THE LOWER-DECK SOCIETIES

Only with the first hints in September 1922 that a cut in pay was being contemplated did lower-deck organisation revive. In spring 1923 a committee under Sir Alan Anderson was appointed by the government to inquire into the remuneration of State servants. In flat contradiction of the Jerram findings its report argued that in 1914 ratings had not been underpaid and that existing rates were too high and should be reduced.[135] The suggestion snapped the societies back into life. Lane proclaimed that the lower deck should resist any attempt to cut the Jerram scale.[136] Throughout 1923, with increasing intensity as the November general election approached, a major campaign was mounted against any cuts.

The threat to pay became a rallying cry for recruiting members to the societies.[137] In the space of three or four months the seamen's society had recruited 1,000 new members, and in September alone the stokers' society increased its membership by 500.[138] At Chatham a co-ordinating committee of seamen and stokers was formed to lobby over the question of pay.[139] The Admiralty feared that the next step would be the formation of squadron joint committees among seagoing ratings. There had already been renewed talk of forming a central lower-deck body to represent men ashore and afloat.[140] Meanwhile at Devonport in October the joint committee held a dinner for the three Plymouth MPs, Nancy Astor, Shirley-Benn, and Kinlock-Cooke, together with the Parliamentary Private Secretary to the First Lord of the Admiralty, and obtained promises that each of them would oppose any pay cuts.[141]

Some dramatic initiative was now needed to arouse opposition to the cuts. The next welfare conference was not due to meet until May 1924 – after the start of the financial year and perhaps too late to raise objections.[142] A correspondent in the *Naval Chronicle* called for the conference to be brought forward, but there was no chance of that being allowed.[143] By October 1923 a month had passed since Anderson's report had been presented and it would be another month before Parliament could discuss it. In the circumstances an open letter signed by Lane, Powell, the secretary of the Chatham stokers, and Vale, secretary of the Devonport seamen and one of the two men court-martialled after the 1917 Grand Fleet petition, was sent to the naval dockyard members of Parliament. It was a straightforward, low-key statement of lower-deck opposition, respectfully drawing attention to some weaknesses in Anderson's argument.

This was the Admiralty's cue to intervene and stop the campaign. For some time the joint committees had been under observation, and in August 1923 the commanders-in-chief at the home ports had actually been asked for their views on the idea of suppressing them.[144] The general feeling was that no urgent action was necessary,[145] but the Admiralty was cautious and advised the commanders-in-chief to keep a close watch on the committees.[146] They were different from the lower-deck societies in that they did not administer benefits and were not recognised officially. In fact their real function was strictly political, and the Admiralty was especially concerned over the role on them of naval pensioners, who were not subject to naval discipline.[147]

When the joint letter from Lane, Powell and Vale was issued the Admiralty moved quickly. On 30 October Admiral Fremantle, commander-in-chief at Portsmouth, sent his chief of staff to interview Lane about the letter. Lane was defiant: he admitted breaking King's Regulations and agreed that he was in effect running a port welfare committee against Admiralty orders, justifying it on the grounds of the inefficiency of the official welfare machinery. He told the chief of staff that it would be impossible to suppress the joint committee, and that even if men were punished others would go on meeting in secret.[148]

But the Admiralty was now prepared to meet the Portsmouth joint committee head on, and Lane was asked to convene a meeting on 6 November. With a full delegation in attendance, the chief of staff presented himself at the meeting and read out Article 11 and Fleet Order 3657. He warned the delegates to keep within the bounds of King's Regulations, announced that the commander-in-chief's next move would depend on their actions and, refusing to admit any discussion, left the meeting.[149]

This dramatic intervention had its desired effect, and the societies were stopped in their tracks. If anything more were needed to deter agitation it was provided by instructions now issued for naval officers to attend society meetings as observers. The practice established at Portsmouth was extended to Chatham and Devonport. The effect was naturally to reduce attendance. In some cases societies accepted the officers' presence, explaining to them politely that as long as the surveillance went on, attendance would be rather poor.[150] But other organisations resisted the intrusion. At the February 1924 meeting of the Devonport Seamen's Society the officer was refused admission on the grounds that he was a non-member and was kept waiting outside while the meeting debated the merits of the case.[151] The commodore at Devonport barracks thought it more than possible that on the next occasion the officer would either not be informed of the venue or would not be allowed in.[152]

Meanwhile Robert Young, MP, the former general secretary of the Engineers' Union, wrote to the Labour government's First Lord, Chelmsford, on behalf of the Engine-Room Artificers' Society:

[. . .] no business can be done in the presence of strangers. Trade Unionists are apprehensive of this line of action [. . .] in some men's minds this interference is being resented as being in part, at least, resorted to because of the advent of Labour to administrative function at the Admiralty.[153]

The First Lord's reply was to the effect that, now the societies had been given a sharp reminder of where the borderline between lawful and unlawful action lay, there was no intention of making the practice of sending officer observers a permanent one except where the societies requested it.[154] This represented a concession of sorts, but the order was not withdrawn, and society meetings were subject to observation at any time. In general the action had served its purpose, the intervention of the chief of staff was a turning point in the history of the lower-deck societies, and never again would their membership approach the level of 1923.

The years 1919–23 saw the lower-deck movement at its peak strength. In the immediate post-war years members of the societies were insistent that the wartime promise of a better life should be redeemed, and they envisaged for their organisations a continuing role in determining their conditions of service. In many ways this reflected contemporary developments in the wider Labour movement, where militancy and utopian idealism went hand in hand. But it was a development that the Admiralty was not prepared to acquiesce in. Finding itself forced to ride the storm of militancy in 1919–20, it never lost sight of the need to circumscribe the activities of the benefit societies. When the time was right in December 1920 it moved decisively to restrict their wider aspirations. It was the beginning of the end for the lower-deck reform movement as a permanent force. Rather than provide the societies with an expanded role the Admiralty-devised welfare system sought to undermine them. The revival of 1922 proved short-lived, for by that time the central issue had been effectively settled. The societies had fought for direct representation and lost. Yet direct representation was the only way they could hope to have a continuing collective influence on service conditions.

SEVEN

The movement in abeyance

At present the men repress their feelings because, with the labour market in a very bad state, few are tempted to risk their fate as civilians, therefore they growl and bear with conditions as best they may. – 'Lancaster', *Naval Chronicle*, 3 April 1925

Has a naval man any rights? We should say so – quite a lot; all the same our advice to individuals is 'for goodness sake don't go chasing them or you will hit up against a snag every time. Rights are things that can only be chased in the abstract; they are dangerous devils when handled in the concrete.' – Lionel Yexley, *The Fleet*, August 1928

The Admiralty had weathered the storm of 1919–20 when militancy among ratings threatened to get out of hand. Thereafter the authorities were at pains to keep lower-deck protest under control. The welfare system and the tight rein on benefit societies were part and parcel of this, but the Admiralty also adopted other tactics. Signs of dissidence, real or imagined, were stamped on quickly, and exemplary punishments were handed out to miscreants. The Admiralty's ultra-sensitivity to the threat of Communist subversion helped create an atmosphere in which men with legitimate complaints were reluctant to speak out for fear of being branded as 'sea lawyers'. Access to Members of Parliament and the political process in general was deliberately restricted. Ratings came to have less scope for participation in parliamentary elections and were discouraged from becoming involved in the normal democratic process of political debate. In general the Admiralty sought to insulate the lower deck from civilian influences while at the same time trying to strengthen its own paternalistic system of man management. At one level the policy succeeded, but the absence of any regular means, within the service or without, by which ratings could communicate general grievances on important issues with a reasonable expectation of being listened to was a major flaw, and the Admiralty would pay the price in 1931.

DISSENT AND COUNTER-MEASURES

The naval authorities were ever alert to signs of dissidence, and occasionally an example would be made of someone, even when only on suspicion, to keep the rest in line. An incident on the battlecruiser *Hood* in the spring of 1921 illustrates the point. Two ratings, John McKirdy and Thomas Guthrie, were court-martialled, charged with a mutinous practice. It was claimed that they had displayed red bunting in their mess, which the captain interpreted as a sign of revolution. He believed it was intended as an inducement for others to mutiny. Both men were acquitted, but two others were then court-martialled in connection with the same offence, the master-at-arms, Walter Batten, on a charge of concealing a mutinous practice, and Stoker John Hall, accused of endeavouring to incite men to commit an act of mutiny. Again the prosecution failed to prove its case against Batten, but Hall was found guilty and carried the can for the episode, being sentenced to three years' penal servitude.[1]

Occasionally a man regarded as having 'advanced views' would be quietly got rid of. Such was the case of Able Seaman Len Fagg, who was discharged, 'Services No Longer Required', in 1923. Fagg was a twenty-six-year-old rating who had served throughout the war in the Grand Fleet. While in the service he became an avid reader of radical literature, joined the Communist Party in 1921 and, though duty prevented him from being active, made no secret of his membership. While on the light cruiser *Dragon* in 1922 he became an active member of the Seamen's society and was responsible for recruiting many of his messmates. He was also a member of the ship's canteen committee and fell foul of authority that year when he protested against the commander's proposal to allot £25 of the canteen funds towards the cost of a lower-deck wedding present for Princess Mary, who was about to be married to Viscount Lascelles.[2]

In October the following year, arriving back in Chatham from a Mediterranean tour just as protest over the proposed pay cuts was reaching a crescendo, he was immediately drafted into barracks and given twenty-four hours' notice of his discharge. At the time he had passed the professional examination for leading seaman and the educational test for petty officer; he had two good-conduct badges, and his service record showed that in the past year his performance had been rated 'exceptional' and in the five previous years 'superior'. No explanation for his discharge was ever proffered; there was no question of his being an incompetent seaman – indeed, all the evidence points to the fact that the Navy simply wanted to be rid of a potential troublemaker at this critical juncture.[3]

A similar case in 1927 involved Able Seaman Michael Doyle, except that on this occasion the Admiralty's action attracted more publicity. Doyle had been observed visiting a Communist Party bookshop in October 1927 while on leave. When he returned to his ship, HMS *Effingham*, three days later he was searched, but the only literature found on him was copies of *Punch* and *War Cry*. Nevertheless he was sent into barracks, two weeks later being examined by the commander and a Special Branch officer and questioned as to whether he was a Communist Party member. He denied the suggestion, but within a matter of weeks was discharged from the service. His case was brought up in Parliament, and the Parliamentary Secretary to the Admiralty was asked whether it was illegal to visit a Communist establishment. The answer was, of course, no, but it was pointed out that the comanding officer had the right to take steps to prevent undesirable literature from being brought on board. Though no trial had been held it was decided that Doyle was exerting an unsatisfactory influence on his shipmates and was 'unsuitable for retention in the Service'.[4]

News of discharges such as these soon became known on the lower deck, and cases occurred often enough to provide men with a constant reminder to do nothing that might draw attention to themselves.

In general they kept their heads down, and certainly in the early 1920s complaints were reduced to a minimum by the threat of immediate sea posting for those who complained.[5] In 1922 there was an unsavoury case involving a chief mechanician who was drafted out of turn after being elected to represent the stoker branch at the forthcoming welfare conference. Subsequently a letter came to light which explained what had happened behind the scenes. It had been sent from one commissioned engineer to another, and *The Fleet* printed an edited version:

There is a Mechanician being sent to you [...] who is to relieve a Mechanician going on draft. He is to be put on board —— and, when —— is near completion he is to be transferred to the next latest ship to leave so that you are to keep him at —— all the time.[6]

The message was clear. The man was being got rid of, and the welfare conference would have to do without his services.[7]

Throughout the 1920s the Communist Party attempted to capitalise on naval grievances. Its propaganda met with little response, but the reaction of the authorities indicates how fearful they were of any radical ideas gaining support in the service. In 1921 Rear-Admiral Cowan, commanding the battlecruiser squadron in the Atlantic Fleet, observed that discipline 'hangs by a very slender thread, chiefly by reason of the mass of mischievous and revolutionary literature, which floods the country [. . .] '.[8] During the campaign of agitation against the pay cuts in 1923 the party launched a drive to recruit members on the lower deck. The journal of the Young Communist League invited ratings who were discontented to contact Walter Newbold, the Communist member of Parliament, and there were plans to flood the garrison towns with propaganda. Towards the end of 1924 the Communists began to try to get literature into the ships, using newspaper boys, who were allowed on board in harbour. As in many such cases, Home Office and service Intelligence learned about the strategem almost as soon as it was formulated, and as a result commanders-in-chief at the home ports were warned to increase searches.[9]

In spring 1925 the Communist Party's *Sailors' and Marines' Programme* was published, listing demands for the reform of service conditions, and the question of radical literature circulating in the Navy once again began to worry the Admiralty.[10] An investigation was carried out at Plymouth, following Conservative Party complaints that left-wing papers such as *Lansbury's Labour Weekly, The Workers' Weekly, The Communist, Forward, The Workers' Dreadnought* and *The Bulletin* were on sale in Devonport dockyard. The sale of newspapers in naval dockyards had actually been prohibited in January 1911 during an earlier phase of labour militancy, but by this stage most daily papers were available on board at the ship's canteen, with the exception of leftward leaning ones such as the *Daily Herald* and *Reynolds's News*. At Devonport left-wing literature was on sale at a kiosk outside the dockyard gates. There was nothing the authorities could do about this, and prohibited journals did circulate from hand to hand among an underground readership on the lower deck. However, the Metropolitan Police, who were responsible for dockyard security, were put on the alert about seditious literature getting past the dockyard gates, security was tightened up, and it appears that lists of dockyard employees, graded according to their left-wing proclivities, were maintained by the police.[11]

In late 1925 and spring 1926 the Communist Party stepped up its attempt to reach the lower deck by means of leaflets mailed to ratings in ships.[12] Hundreds were sent out, dealing with low pay in the service and linking sailors' grievances to industrial disputes ashore. One, entitled *The Admiralty's New Swindle*, issued in December 1925, warned of trouble arising from the protracted miners' dispute with the coal owners, and of the role that ratings would soon be called on to play in it:

I tell you there are going to be some lively doings shortly [...] . [The employers] set about the miners three months ago [...] [the government] know that the trouble will only start again in May [...] . In the event of the workers standing up against them, the Bosses and the Government intend using the Army and the Navy against us [...] .[13]

Service mail was being monitored, and in the *Naval Chronicle* ERA Lewis Hanbidge had already drawn attention to a certain unrest among ratings and a feeling of insecurity caused by Special Branch examination of lower-deck correspondence.[14]

The Admiralty was so concerned about the effect of *The Admiralty's New Swindle* on the men that a statement refuting its arguments was drafted and despatched to commanders-in-chief to be read out to ships' companies and placed on notice boards.[15] This of course only served to give the leaflet more publicity. The statement was carefully phrased so as not to arouse lower-deck feelings, and prudence dictated that part of the original draft be left out of the final version: 'Although the Navy will never be called upon to interfere in strikes and industrial disputes, it is the fundamental duty of all Governments to preserve order and maintain supplies in times of emergency.' But a general strike seemed inevitable; the Navy would, if necessary, be used against the strikers, and there was no sense in the Admiralty's giving a hostage to fortune by claiming there would be no strike duty. Not only was strike-breaking anticipated but arrangements had already been drawn up for private firms which benefited from naval assistance to compensate the Admiralty and for some ratings to be paid double for their work.[16]

One month before the General Strike more leaflets entitled *Soldiers, Sailors and Airmen, Don't Shoot Workers, Don't Scab on your Brothers* were found in ships and shore establishments. Already a dozen leading Communists had been tried and given prison sentences under the Incitement to Mutiny Act.[17] Yet in spite of the serious nature of this latest leaflet the Home Office decided that, in view of the industrial situation, there should be no prosecutions. And this time the Admiralty was careful not to give the leaflet extra publicity or give the impression of panicking by making mention of it in general orders.[18]

In subsequent years updated versions of the *Sailors' and Marines' Programme* were issued periodically, usually to coincide with welfare conferences, pressing demands such as the right to form a lower-deck union, to stand for Parliament and engage in political campaigns, and the abolition of regulations against writing to the press.[19] Navy chaplains were viewed by the authorities as a bulwark against the spread of such radical ideas, and their usefulness in this respect was one of the reasons why the Admiralty turned a deaf ear to the growing chorus of voices asking for the abolition of compulsory church service on Sundays. As the Chaplain of the Fleet noted:

The Parade Service is an integral part of the silent teaching of Discipline and Loyalty in the Navy. If abolished the well-being of the Service on disciplinary side would undoubtedly suffer. The one chance Chaplain has of talking to the men as a whole and explaining many things in everyday life they do not understand, e.g. newspaper articles; all this is most important owing to the growth of a bad form of socialism.[20]

There is no evidence that the *Sailors' and Marines' Programme* had a direct influence on the formulation of welfare demands or that it brought in naval recruits to the Communist Party. But what was important about such literature was that each time a wave of new propaganda hit the lower deck it was met with determined efforts by the authorities to rout out any dissidents, and this left the ratings ever more conscious of the need to keep their own counsel where complaints were concerned.

NAVAL RATINGS AND THE POLITICAL PROCESS

In addition to their fear of the effects of written propaganda, the authorities were also concerned about the possibility of men attending and participating at political meetings. In 1926–27 reports of ratings addressing groups in Hyde Park were becoming fairly common. This presented a difficult problem. The authorities were determined to stop the practice, yet there was fear of adverse publicity if strong-arm measures were used. All the Admiralty could legally do was station naval patrols in Hyde Park and, if necessary, arrest men for offences against the naval disciplinary code. Yet the sight of armed patrols so far from the naval ports was bound to draw attention to the limitation of sailors' civil rights. The Admiralty was caught on the horns of a dilemma.

In August 1927 instructions were sent to commanders-in-chief announcing that a small naval patrol would be posted at Hyde Park from Saturday to Monday each week and that men caught addressing meetings would be sent under escort to their port division. However, at the Admiralty there was still concern about the prospect of patrols arresting men in public and perhaps provoking a bigger incident. Consequently, after only three weeks the instructions were amended to the effect that men known to have participated at meetings would only be arrested when they returned to port.[21] From now on it would be a case of keeping ratings under surveillance on leave and taking disciplinary action away from the glare of publicity.

Not only were they being denied freedom to read what they pleased and to do and say what they wanted off duty, but their political rights in parliamentary elections, won as recently as 1918, were now under threat. In the first place their right to a ballot at all times was not being upheld. The debacle in 1918 when many absent servicemen failed to receive postal ballots has been described. At the next general election in 1922 the pattern was repeated, with large numbers of naval voters disenfranchised. In Portsmouth Central there were 3,134 absent naval voters, but less than half received their ballot papers. Only 897 postal votes were cast by ratings, and the outcome of the election was a narrow defeat for the popular Liberal, Sir Thomas Bramsdon, who had long been associated with campaigns for lower-deck reforms.[22] Altogether the system of proxy or postal balloting on a large scale was regarded by the authorities as too troublesome, and in 1929 it was finally decided to disenfranchise ratings in foreign service and allow postal ballots only to men serving in ships in home waters.[23]

In addition there was a whittling away of the right to engage in electioneering, a right which had been fought for so vigorously by Yexley and Cronin in the teeth of Admiralty opposition in 1918. The position in the 1918 and 1922 elections was that men could not attend political meetings or canvass in uniform but were free to do so out of uniform. In the spring of 1924, in the aftermath of the Admiralty's 1923 skirmish with the Portsmouth joint committee, a new order was inserted in King's Regulations reinforcing the rule that there should be no kind of political activity in ships and establishments and no active propaganda.[24] Then, in October, with another contest imminent, the scope for electoral activity was narrowed still more. An Admiralty directive to commanders-in-chief at the home ports announced that under no circumstances were men to identify themselves publicly as supporters of a particular candidate or party, either by joining an election committee, speaking or appearing on a platform or canvassing.[25] General orders along these lines were issued at Portsmouth and Devonport, but not, apparently, at Chatham – an indication, perhaps, of how arbitrary the measure was. There was some protest on the lower deck, and for several years afterwards criticisms were voiced in the House of Commons, but to no avail.[26] As Hore-Belisha, Liberal MP for Devonport, commented some years later:

By restricting the right of free expressions of opinion on political questions, or the seeking of information at public meetings, the Government are taking away from the Navy [. . .] their right as citizens to know and make known what it is they are voting about.[27]

In 1927, when the authorities once again turned their attention to the question of servicemen's electoral rights, the 1924 regulations were reaffirmed and the Servants of the Crown (Parliamentary Candidature) Order announced that, in future, ratings could no longer stand for Parliament while on the active-service list.[28] In previous elections those who wanted to put up as candidates could do so as active servicemen and then, if elected, opt to be removed from the active-service list. But now a man would have to gamble his service career *before* he knew the election result. It made the prospect of a lower-deck member of Parliament that much more remote, and it was yet another area where the rating's rights as a citizen were being eroded. *The Fleet* assumed that the measures were specifically intended to minimise any service support for the newly formed Labour League of Ex-servicemen, whose objective was to work for the return of a Labour government on an anti-militarist platform.[29] The League may have been the Admiralty's main target; however, all indications are that it was opposed to servicemen getting involved in any kind of politics at all. And it was perhaps because of this that there were constant complaints from the lower deck that before general elections they were never given adequate information as to what their rights were.[30]

Scope for direct political activity was thus greatly reduced, but so also over the years were the chances of having their grievances handled for them by Members of Parliament. Since before the Great War MPs representing naval constituencies had formed themselves into a committee for the purposes of lobbying. The lower deck looked to this body for support in their reform campaigns. The Dockyard Committee, as it was called, was not an official Commons body, and its existence was a constant source of annoyance to the Admiralty, who felt that it encouraged the ratings to work up grievances. For a rating to approach an MP on a service matter was forbidden. The original welfare committee system had been devised in part to stop men from contacting MPs and have questions raised in the House.[31] Yet it failed in this respect, and in the early 1920s the dockyard Members bombarded the Admiralty with questions on lower-deck affairs. During the 1923 election campaign, conducted against the background of threatened pay cuts, the lower-deck societies had lobbied vigorously and with great effect among Members of Parliament and parliamentary candidates. Commenting on the access that the lower deck had to Members, *The Fleet* pointed out in 1925:

Parliament is becoming a great big Welfare Committee for the Navy and never before in the history of Parliament have the affairs of the Navy been so predominantly advocated. Hardly a day passes without some question being asked about the comfort of the sailor.[32]

However, since the 1923 lobbying campaign the Admiralty had been concerned to limit the number of questions asked in Parliament on behalf of ratings. It was not thought to be practical politics to try to prevent all communication between men and their elected representatives, but from then on Admiralty answers to questions in the House tended to be evasive, and whenever possible the reply was that if ratings would care to use the correct service procedures their complaints would be looked into.[33] The 'correct procedure' excluded any possibility of a collective grievance being stated. Rather it involved individual ratings taking their complaint to their superior officer and then, if not satisfied with the answer, appealing over his head up the naval hierarchy. Only a foolhardy man would contemplate the mere idea. To appeal against a decision of an immediate superior was to jeopardise one's future career. Anyone whose case was adjudged to be unfounded ran the risk of punishment for making a frivolous complaint. The effect of the Admiralty's new policy with regard to contacting MPs was, therefore, simply to seal off another important safety valve.

As the decade passed the Admiralty gradually tightened up still more its policy on parliamentary questions. MPs who tabled a question on lower-deck matters were written to by the Parliamentary Secretary asking them to be good enough not to proceed with it.[34] Moreover after 1929 the Admiralty decided that, as women now had the vote, steps should also be taken to block any opportunity for them to complain to Members of Parliament on their husbands' behalf. Practice here was to inform MPs that sailors' wives should be advised that naval grievances were to be processed through the regular service channels.[35]

The reduced scope for approaching MPs at the end of the 1920s is indicated by one case involving a rating in the battlecruiser *Repulse*. In 1929 he wrote to his constituency MP for the Isle of Thanet to complain about leave arrangements. The author of the letter was traced by the captain and punished with twenty-eight days' detention. This prompted Will Hall, Labour MP for Portsmouth Central, to ask in the House of Commons about the propriety of the sentence. The Admiralty was unwilling to commit itself on such a sensitive issue and, as ever, reluctant to court adverse publicity in public discussion of the case. After some weeks of indecision the Parliamentary Secretary decided that 'Hall should be spoken to privately and not answered by mail'.[36] Hall appears to have been satisfied with his private, verbal reply. The question was conveniently swept under the carpet, and the lower deck were left to draw the obvious conclusion: complaining to MPs could be very risky and was likely to be unproductive.[37]

WELFARE CONFERENCES AND LOWER-DECK SOCIETIES IN DECLINE

Hemmed in as they were by Admiralty restrictions, the welfare conferences were never seen as a satisfactory outlet for grievances, and few paid much attention to them. The fact that the conference had only advisory status meant that the men would have to trust the Admiralty to look after their interests, but, as Yexley pointed out, the weakness of the system from the outset was that the men had no faith in the Admiralty's sincerity.[38]

In 1924, when elections for welfare delegates were held at Portsmouth, only 461 of 11,000 men bothered to vote. No more than nineteen out of a possible 4,800 seamen and thirteen of the 1,800 stokers participated in the election.[39] In the debate on the Navy Estimates in 1925 it was argued from the Labour benches that, in the interests of a contented fleet, the welfare conference should have greater freedom of expression and that every facility should be given for the rectification of grievances.[40] Yet before the next conference in 1926 the Admiralty reimposed its ban on any requests that had previously been turned down, leaving the welfare delegates with little of substance to discuss. They were reduced to such proposals as that a better quality of boot and a lighter form of cap be issued, and that two types of navy tobacco be supplied, one for cigarette and one for pipe smokers. Even then out of fifty-eight general requests put forward only one was fully approved, while forty-four were rejected and others were still under consideration three years later.

So farcical was the situation with regard to the number of requests turned down that, for the next conference, the Admiralty had to lift its ruling and declare that after a period of five years a rejected request could be resubmitted.[41] Yet before the 1930 conference, the last before the Invergordon mutiny, the Admiralty announced yet another restriction on the freedom to raise grievances. Now the officers present at the various delegate meetings were to be empowered to veto at the outset any requests they deemed improper.[42]

Although the Admiralty was well aware of lower-deck feelings about the welfare system it refused to make any structural changes to render the arrangement more effective. Among Admiralty officials there were those who favoured abolishing the welfare conferences on the grounds that they wasted too much time and money and led to few significant changes.[43] Others recognised their importance as a safety valve even if they achieved little, and proposals to alter or scrap the system were not seriously considered. Even under a Labour administration, which might have been expected to be more sympathetic to the need for an effective grievance system, this remained the case. When, in 1929, Lewis Hanbidge, acting editor of *The Fleet*, tackled A. V. Alexander personally about the inadequacy of the welfare scheme the first Lord showed little interest.[44]

In their benefit work the lower-deck societies were largely eclipsed after 1922 by the Royal Naval Benevolent Trust, which had been set up on a service-wide basis with Admiralty support specifically to administer grants to naval ratings and families in financial difficulties.[45] Likewise in these years the societies were formally excluded from the welfare process and they were less and less able to use MPs to raise issues on their behalf. In the years after 1923 they rarely strayed beyond the bounds of permissible action laid down in Fleet Order 3657 of December 1920. Some of them printed the AFO's strictures on welfare work on their membership cards and at the head of their monthly minutes to remind members of the legal position. Yet they still remained under close surveillance by the Naval Personnel Committee, and there was always a feeling of mistrust towards them at the Admiralty.

For example, in 1925 the authorities suddenly became concerned about the activities of the ERAs' society. The January issue of the society's journal, *The Naval Engineering Review*, had been bold enough to discuss the protocol of the League of Nations and the question of whether soldiers and sailors had the right to decide whether or not to fight. It had also carried a commentary on a recent speech by the commander-in-chief at Portsmouth, and this was seen as a breach of King's Regulations. The Second Sea Lord's view was that the organisation's aims went beyond the legitimate scope of society activity and that the *Review* displayed a socialist tendency. All in all he was inclined to suppress the publication but for the fact that such a course might prove counter-productive in the long run. However, those responsible for such dangerous literature were not to be allowed to go unchecked, and the society's executive committee were summoned before the commander-in-chief at Portsmouth to have this breach of their charter pointed out to them and to be warned against future misdemeanours.[46]

In such a climate the lower-deck societies were never likely to prosper, and indeed, during the latter half of the 1920s, with few exceptions, they declined steadily. For a time the Wireless Telegraphists' Society enjoyed a period of prosperity. Membership doubled during 1926 to reach a total of 530 and nearly 700 three years later.[47] Yet this was still significantly less than a quarter of the entire branch, and the telegraphists were now reckoned to be the most vigorous lower-deck organisation.[48] In September 1926 Yexley doubted that there were more than 5,000 active paid-up society members in the entire lower-deck. Several societies were on the point of collapse, and though there was occasional talk of amalgamating those that remained the administrative difficulties always proved too great.[49] *The Fleet* itself had long ceased publishing the minutes of their meetings, partly because there was so little to report but also because Yexley was no longer in such close touch with the lower deck. There was now a considerable age gap between him and the younger ratings, on top of which he was also in poor health. In 1928 he was forced to relinquish the editorship of the paper temporarily, and from that point it was clear that *The Fleet* was no longer a significant force for reform.

THE STIFLING OF GRIEVANCES

In various ways, then, in the course of the 1920s the Admiralty closed down outlets for the ventilation of lower-deck grievances. Meanwhile, lacking any enthusiasm for the welfare system, it set out to foster the idea that the all-important relationship was the one between the individual rating and his commanding officer, rather than between the lower deck as a collective body and the Admiralty. It sought to do so by placing greater emphasis on the divisional system.

On board ship men had long been split into divisions for certain functions, and each division had its divisional officer who was supposed to take an interest in the welfare of his men and advise them on personal matters. The system was extended to the naval depots in 1925, largely to counter radical influences. The case for its introduction was put by Admiral Fremantle, commander-in-chief at Portsmouth:

It is common knowledge that organisations exist for the dissemination of propaganda adverse to loyalty, patriotism, and discipline, and favourable to sedition and insubordination [. . .] .

[. . .] the position remains thoroughly unsatisfactory and, in my opinion, the system of internal economy as regards relations between officers and men would be a source of serious apprehension at any time when subversive propaganda were active and successful.[50]

However, if the personal links between officers and men were to be strengthened ratings would have to have more incentive to use the service channels for proffering complaints. This was unlikely to happen as long as junior ratings regarded their divisional officer as someone who found fault with them and as long as the complainant risked punishment for bringing unfounded charges against his superior or making a vexatious complaint.

For years this aspect of King's Regulations had been a bone of contention, but in 1928 it was also seen to apply to officers. In a famous case Captain Dewar and Commander Daniel of the battleship

Royal Oak were court-martialled and punished for complaining quite justifiably about their admiral's behaviour.[51] The patent injustice of the system caused the Admiralty to revise the procedure in 1929. The new rule exempted from punishment those who genuinely believed their charges to be true even when they were unable to substantiate them. Yet it was still a risky business, and there was always the possibility that a man who gave misleading evidence in good faith would be unable to prove that he was not telling a deliberate lie.[52] There were positive drawbacks as well. Men could complain only of an injustice they had suffered personally: no one else was entitled to raise the matter on their behalf. Likewise, written complaints were barred: all grievances had to be stated verbally – a further deterrent for anyone unsure of his ability to articulate a case.[53] Altogether the change did not amount to much; men would be no more inclined to use the procedure than before, and it was hardly enough to compensate for the absence of an outlet for general grievances.

In a crisis ratings were still likely to resort to the old traditional means of drawing attention to disabilities – mass leave-breaking, performing badly in regattas, downing tools or simply failing to report for duty. As early as 1925 one lower-deck writer in the *Naval Chronicle* noted that 'there appears to be a suppressed resentment which leads to work being performed listlessly, badly, and with as little output as possible. In short, a system of ca-canny.'[54] These were the tried and trusted practices, and two classic instances occurred in the twelve months preceding the Invergordon mutiny.

In the Mediterranean Fleet the battleship *Revenge*, previously a happy ship, became a very unhappy one overnight when a new captain, J. A. G. Troup, took command in 1930. From the outset he presented himself as a strict disciplinarian and told the crew in effect that he would make them or break them. He worked the hands exceptionally hard, and defaulters were punished severely, especially leave-breakers. When the ship was at Golfe Juan men who had broken leave during the previous six months were not granted the twenty-four hours' general leave that was customary when visiting Riviera ports. The upshot, in the time-honoured tradition of the service, was a deliberate mass breaking of leave. Some men deserted, and Troup was jeered when he went ashore.[55] As the men had hoped, the incident led to an Admiralty inquiry, something which complaints through the regular channels were unlikely ever to achieve.[56]

A more celebrated case occurred a few months later on the

submarine depot ship *Lucia*. The *Lucia* had long been an unhappy ship. Though she was away twice a year on cruises, leave was only given as though she were a harbour vessel; in general, less was granted than in other Devonport ships. She had little in the way of recreational facilities. The crew were subjected to many petty annoyances: just before the incident an order curtailing the hours for smoking on the upper deck had particularly annoyed them, and meal hours were often foreshortened. The men were worked hard, and the day they refused duty was the fourth successive one of extra work. It was a Sunday, normally a rest day. Weekend leave had already been cancelled but they expected leave on Sunday afternoon. When, instead, they were piped to turn to and clean the ship in readiness for painting they stayed below and closed the hatches. Twenty-seven were arrested, Leading Seaman William Carter was dismissed from the service and four others were court-martialled, with sentences of up to six months' hard labour.

There was a storm of public protest; the officers involved had their appointments terminated, the prison sentences were commuted, but Carter's dismissal stood.[57] A court of inquiry was told that the men did not seem to know how to make complaints in the proper manner. Significantly it also heard about an earlier episode, well known to the crew, in which a shipwright had raised a perfectly legitimate grievance with the first lieutenant but was punished for making a frivolous complaint. As the court commented:

The shipwright's request was not unreasonable but it was unsympathetically received and treated in a manner likely to discourage others from being brought forward, thereby tending to choke a vent which modern conditions demand should be kept completely free.[58]

Events such as those on the *Revenge* and *Lucia* often represented the only form of protest available in the late 1920s and early '30s. Effective constitutional means of raising collective grievances were completely lacking; the men were isolated from Parliament; the lower-deck press was no longer the force it had been, and unless pushed beyond endurance they chose to keep a low profile. The situation was critical in the sense that if ever a major complaint arose there was no mechanism for dealing with it expeditiously. Indeed, it was not even certain that the authorities would become aware of it in time. In Parliament in January 1931 Colonel Malone called for a judicial inquiry into the administration of naval law and in particular the machinery for dealing with grievances, only to be told by the First Lord that there were no grounds for it.[59] Invergordon was only seven months away.

EIGHT

The road to Invergordon

[. . .] during the three years of Welfare history very little of a satisfactory nature has come to the rating of the Lower Deck. 'Welfare' is a misnomer; 'A Spoofing Committee' would more correctly describe the machinery. – W. Stoddard, president of the ERAs' society, quoted in L. Hanbidge, *W. Stoddard: a Biographical Sketch*

This threat to their income must cause uneasiness to many, and it is regrettable that no means exist whereby those affected may defend themselves, or suggest alternative methods of securing the desired saving on naval expenditure. – 'First Artificer', *Naval Chronicle*, 21 August 1931

For six long years they dallied and juggled the wedge so thin,
For six long years we wondered how far they would drive it in,
But you spoke and we believed you, 'Your money is permanent,'
And now you're clipping the plain AB by twenty-five per cent.
                              AB John Bush, 'Invergordon, 1931'

In important respects the Navy was a better place for ratings in the inter-war years than it had been previously. This much was reflected in the falling rates of desertion – 258 cases in 1926–27, compared with 1,896 in 1906–07. It was also reflected in the decline in the number of men buying themselves out – a reduction from 1,070 to 197 between 1906–07 and 1926–27 – though no doubt the bleak employment prospects outside the service influenced these trends.[1]

There were no dramatic improvements in conditions, but over a period of time incremental changes altered things for the better. As the Navy became a more technical service there was greater emphasis on brain than brawn. An important change in victualling arrangements came with the growth of 'general messing', under which meals were prepared and cooked centrally by a properly trained staff.[2] The formation of the Navy, Army and Air Force Institutes (NAAFI) in 1921 as a co-operative canteen organisation covering the whole service, and replacing the multiplicity of private operators of former years, brought uniformity and meant that canteen administration would be a much less contentious issue. Shipboard living conditions improved in some respects, and a greater emphasis on personal hygiene reduced the incidence of venereal disease by more than half between 1912 and 1932.[3] On a day-to-day basis discipline in this increasingly technical Navy tended to be more relaxed than before the war. There were far fewer summary punishments and fewer courts-martial: in 1922 only one-sixth as many as in 1901.[4] In the same year the maximum period of penal servitude was reduced to three years, while changes were introduced in court-martial procedure that benefited the defendant by allowing the 'prisoner's friend' to play a more active role.[5] The temporary separation allowances of wartime became permanent marriage allowances in 1920, and in 1926 naval widows finally became entitled to a State pension as of right.[6]

Yet reform was still overdue in many areas, and even where some progress had been made the lower deck still had cause for real complaint. For example, technical developments also had their negative side, and the growing quantity of weaponry and machinery meant that the space left to accommodate ships' companies was more and more restricted.[7] Overcrowding was sometimes a problem, and the men associated it with the high incidence of tuberculosis, which became a matter of grave concern in the 1920s. Every year of the decade 1,200 – 2,000 ratings were invalided out, and of the various causes the most worrying was TB. The death rate was twice as high as among civilians, and yet for many years the service paid no disability pension to most of the men invalided with the disease.[8] Even in the late 1930s the incidence was as high as it had been thirty years earlier.[9]

Discipline may have grown more relaxed in some ways, but some things still cried out for reform. There was no adequate system of appeal against court-martial sentences; the birching of boys had been reintroduced for some offences, and the amount of caning was on the increase in the training establishments in the 1920s.[10] After the war the old-style autocratic officers were never so much in evidence again, but even so the gap between fore and aft persisted. There were still ladders reserved for officers only, special boats for officers and their wives, and officers' balls held on the quarter deck with the crew having to holystone out the cigarette burns the next morning.[11] Snobbery ensured the persistence of a barrier between blue serge and gold braid. As the Jerram committee had pointed out in rejecting the ERAs' claim for officer status, it was necessary to uphold 'the principle that an officer should not work with his hands'.[12]

The 1920s saw the mate scheme at its nadir: scope for commissions from the lower deck was so limited that only five mates a year were being promoted in the seaman branch. The main stumbling block was the traditional opposition of the naval establishment to ranker officers. In 1918 the Second Sea Lord had warned of the danger of creating too many mates in terms that had become familiar: 'To be a good officer, it is also necessary to be a gentleman.'[13] That prejudice remained throughout the period. In the mid-1930s only 3 per cent of officers came from the lower deck, and selection boards for cadet applicants were still primarily concerned with parentage and accent.[14]

The question of marriage allowances was also the subject of strong resentment. When the system became permanent in 1920 the Admiralty imposed an arbitrary age limit of twenty-five on qualification for the 7s 6d a week. It meant that married men under that age who had been receiving a separation allowance for their wives now had to manage without. The welfare conference delegates requested in 1922 that marriage allowance should be paid at twenty-one but were turned down, and repeated calls by MPs for the age to be lowered were rejected.[15]

The head of the Naval Personnel Committee observed in 1924 that the word 'hardship' was often heard in connection with the lower deck because there had been so much home and harbour service in recent years, with the result that a larger percentage of the men were married. The Admiralty's hope now was that, with the largest concentration of men in the Mediterranean, they would be in a position to save more and spend less, an enforced absence from Britain helping them to balance their budgets.[16] The hope that foreign service would automatically ease the economic burden of married men was a forlorn one, especially in view of the cost of living on some foreign stations. Moreover the tendency to longer periods of foreign service only gave rise to other grumbles − over the length of tours of duty abroad, which put a severe strain on marriages, the shortness of foreign-service leave, and the inability of men to take their wives and families overseas with them.

THE CONTINUING THREAT OF PAY CUTS

Of themselves these disabilities were unlikely to lead to widespread unrest, though they might fuel discontent arising from other causes. The question of pay was an altogether more serious matter, and it became a persistent source of lower-deck worry during the 1920s. The Jerram award had more than doubled rates at the lower level, but ratings were still not satisfied that they were being adequately paid. Increasingly they compared themselves to other groups of workers, and in 1920 envious eyes were turned towards the police, with their basic weekly rate of £3 10s fixed by the Desborough committee following the 1918 strike.[17]

Prior to the 1920 Welfare Committee there was a strong feeling on the lower deck that pay for all ratings ought to be increased by 2s a day, half of it permanent and half subject to fluctuations in the cost of living.[18] But the welfare delegates never got as far as formulating a proposal on pay. Indeed, it was largely on this issue that the committee foundered. The Admiralty answer to the 1919 welfare requests, issued just after the 1920 delegate meeting got under way, rejected most of those involving further expenditure, pointing to 'the great permanent improvement in pay' in 1919 which left no justification for further concessions.[19] As Colonel Malone told the House of Commons, the dissatisfaction was considerable, especially in view of the police award.[20] The latter had had their strike, won the right to collective organisation, and now appeared to be reaping the material benefits. All this contributed greatly to the growing support in autumn 1920 for the formation of a lower-deck union.

By 1921 the cost of living had risen by more than 40 per cent since the last pay rise, but the economy was already beginning to move into recession, and when the next welfare conference met in May 1922 the economic climate had altered completely.[21] The cost of living was falling, and no proposals were submitted for higher pay. Thereafter the problem was to safeguard existing rates, not to increase them, for in autumn 1923 the Anderson committee had called for a reduction. Its report started from the assumption that, because there was no difficulty in obtaining recruits in 1914, the rates of pay in force then must have been adequate. As *The Fleet* commented:

That was the argument and the principle on which every sweated industry in the kingdom worked: pay the workers not what they earn but what you can get them for [. . .] .[22]

At the Admiralty there seem to have been different views on whether or not the 1914 rates had in fact been adequate. The Naval

Branch argued that total emoluments in 1914 had compared well with shore wages.[23] Nevertheless the Board of Admiralty issued a memorandum on the Anderson report, denying that pre-war rates were sufficient and objecting to the comparison between unskilled labourers and army privates on the one hand and able seamen on the other. 'The AB,' declared their lordships, 'most emphatically is not an unskilled man.' They insisted that the 1919 Jerram scale was intended to be permanent and that it would be a gross breach of contract to tamper with it:

Although nothing was said when the new rates of pay for men were issued in 1919 as to their being rates for all time, it may be said that they were considered, at the time, to be the permanent rate of the future.[24]

Already Anderson had been told:

The view of the Admiralty is that the men at present in the Navy would undoubtedly consider it a breach of faith if any reduction were made in their rates of pay and that this view could not be contested in the case of men serving under a current engagement [. . .] .[25]

The Secretary to the Board recorded his general disapproval of the committee's handling of the question, referring to it acidly as ' [. . .] a committee of three businessmen, having no prior acquaintance with the subject'.[26]

Yet for all its indignation the Admiralty was only too ready to accept that future rates of pay might have to be cut, and indicated its willingness to co-operate.[27] Indeed, before the Conservative government fell at the end of 1923 the Sea Lords had agreed in principle to accept the Anderson report.[28]

Meanwhile the suggestion that pay in 1914 had been adequate deeply angered the older ratings, who remembered the hardships of those years and even more vividly the difficulties with the rising cost of living during the war. It was this strong feeling that lay behind the resurgence of the lower-deck societies in 1923. In *The Fleet* Yexley argued that if the cuts were ever made it would mean the break-up of many ratings' homes.[29] Even the present rates of pay were not always enough to keep a wife and children, as was indicated by the regular calls on the RNBT for supplementary grants.[30]

At Plymouth in October 1923 the joint committee had obtained promises of support from the three local MPs, and Lady Astor had announced, 'When the question of reduction of pay of the Navy comes up I will show no quarter, and anything I can do short of making a scene I will do.'[31] With the future Prime Minister, Ramsay MacDonald, also having given a commitment to maintain naval pay during the 1923 election campaign the lower-deck lobby against the proposed cuts appeared to have been successful.[32]

However, the matter was not yet disposed of. In the early weeks of the new Labour government the Board of Admiralty discussed the fact that no formal decision had been taken on the Anderson proposals. The Sea Lords were in agreement that they should be accepted, but the two Labour appointees, Frank Hodges, the Civil Lord, and Charles Ammon, the Financial Secretary, dissented.[33] Hodges argued that it was impossible to justify a differentiation in pay for men doing the same work, and he and Ammon concurred that no case had been made out for a reduction. But on this they were outnumbered, and the Board went on formally to endorse the principle of the Anderson report.[34]

The Navy Estimates for 1924–25 removed the threat of an immediate cut, and under questioning the Financial Secretary told Parliament that, as far as serving ratings were concerned, their rates would not be reduced.[35] But the statement conveniently sidestepped the question of whether *any* cuts in pay were still proposed. Indeed, cuts were still very much on the agenda. Under Treasury pressure the Admiralty was in the process of drafting revised pay scales, and, at a conference of the three armed services just nine days after the Financial Secretary's statement, Admiral Sir John Kelly, the Fourth Sea Lord designate, accepted on behalf of the Navy the principle of a 9d decrease in the daily rates at the lowest level for able seamen. However, the War Office favoured even larger reductions for all three services, and no general agreement could be reached on the details of the cuts. Successive interdepartmental committees attempted to produce a generally acceptable formula, during which time the Admiralty gradually gave in to the War Office view.[36]

Meanwhile the politicians continued to be evasive. In the November 1924 election Stanley Baldwin made a commitment to keep existing rates as permanent, and in July 1925 Sir Bertram Falle, Conservative MP for Portsmouth North, repeated the promise on behalf of the Conservative leader even as cuts were still being discussed:

The pensions of ratings [. . .] are permanent rates. I understand that the ratings are being told that the Government propose reducing and cutting down their pay. Such statements are devoid of truth.[37]

On the return of a Conservative government aggregate cuts of 15–16 per cent in naval pay were decided for men joining in the future. The Admiralty chose to apply not a uniform percentage but a flat-rate reduction of 1s a day for petty officers and men; at the lowest level able seamen would therefore be 25 per cent worse off.[38] No one at the Admiralty seems to have been concerned with the inequity of this. All appear to have been more impressed with the argument that able seamen were overpaid. As the head of the Naval Personnel Committee commented:

Undoubtedly the lower deck are very well off. Some of the higher ratings keep motor bicycles and can afford to take the more expensive seats at local entertainments and their meals at places which officers patronise. In some cases they are able to buy their houses [. . .] .[39]

There is no evidence of any high-level resistance, by the First Lord or from Admiral Beatty, the First Sea Lord. All the Sea Lords concurred in the eventual revision in rates of pay which was to apply to men recruited as from October 1925.[40] The Sea Lords' acquiescence stands in marked contrast to their vigorous opposition to, and talk of resignation over, the Treasury's call in the same year for less spending on new cruisers. Beatty – regarded by Sir Maurice Hankey, Secretary to the Cabinet, as the only First Sea Lord apart from Fisher capable of standing up to the Cabinet – saw his fight against cut-backs in money for ships as the most important battle of his life. Yet he apparently accepted without demur the reduction in pay.[41]

The policy of introducing two rates of pay for men doing the same work was a long-term prescription for trouble. Men already in the service were to be reprieved, but the Admiralty no longer regarded the 1919 rates as sacrosanct, despite the fact that in 1920 they had referred to the Jerram increase as 'permanent'.[42] Now the official announcement of the new scale noted that it was to be ' [. . .] clearly understood that men are not entitled to a right of any rate of pay or any emolument under existing scales'.[43] The two-rate system meant the gradual introduction into the service of men who would not be able to afford the standard of living of their messmates, who would be unable to meet their mess bills and for whom marriage would be financially impossible. It would engender jealousy, and sooner or later there would be pressure to bring down the pay of those on the 1919 rates.

At the Admiralty there was a suggestion that the welfare conference for 1926 should be abandoned, in view of the dissatisfaction likely to be caused by the cuts and the protests that would certainly follow.[44] Yexley was in agreement, but for different reasons. He felt that it would be a crime to convene a welfare conference as long as men were on different pay scales and saw things differently. The exercise was bound to be divisive.[45] But it was precisely this argument that seems to have reassured the Admiralty. As the head of the Naval Branch conceded,

[. . .] there will be for many years to come two sets of ratings in the service with different interests and different outlooks on the welfare question, and this state of things will tend to prevent any serious trouble occurring.[46]

To ease the effect of the cuts the delegates proposed that increments in pay be granted to ratings every three years, but this was turned down. The Admiralty objected to having large numbers of able seamen in the service and was deliberately refraining from making their pay scale too attractive.[47] As the decade wore on and as the proportion of post-1925 men increased, the issue was to become a serious problem. But now there was no vocal lower-deck movement, no vigorous campaigning to alert the country, and no ready access to sympathetic MPs. All that remained of a once vigorous reform movement was a handful of ailing death benefit societies forbidden to speak out and a welfare conference to which no one paid any attention.

THE ECONOMICS OF SUBSISTENCE

To a keen observer the effect of the cuts on material standards of living could already be seen in the late 1920s as the first generation of post-1925 recruits began to work their way through the service.[48] NAAFI revenue was down: in 1925 men had spent on average $2\frac{1}{2}d$ a day on beer, but by the early 1930s it had fallen by 40 per cent.[49] The Royal Naval Benevolent Trust was having difficulty raising funds from the lower deck, while at the same time increasing demands were being made on its resources by needy ratings and their families.[50] Since men under twenty-five were ineligible for the marriage allowance, the worst-off were able seamen on the 1925 pay scale who had married while still under twenty-five. Out of a total basic weekly pay of £1 3s 2d,[51] plus 1s 8d in lieu of rum if he happened to be an abstainer, an AB would have to support a wife and a home as well as himself. A typical family budget might involve 12s 6d for rent, 3s for light and cooking, 2s 6d for coal, 2s for insurance, 5s hire-purchase instalments on furniture and 1s for the boot club. Even without expenditure on food, clothes or amusement the weekly bill would hardly be less than 26s.[52]

In addition he also incurred bills in the service. The cost of subsistence varied according to location and ship. Vessels with general messing involved ratings in little expenditure on extra rations, and for this reason alone many preferred them. The traditional system of broadside messing under which ratings catered for themselves was preferred by those who set great store by their food but it also tended to mean more outlay, and ratings would commonly have to foot mess bills in excess of their messing allowance from their own basic pay. An average mess bill could run to 10s a month, but on the West Indies or China stations, where canteen food was dearer, 18s–25s on 'standard ration' ships was commonplace. Clearly no younger men on the new rates could afford this and maintain a family back home.[53] It was not unknown for them to ask to be excused a draft to certain ships where mess bills were known to be high.[54]

Another important factor was that rented accommodation in the home ports was expensive. In the late 1920s the difficulty of finding somewhere to live at a reasonable price was remarked upon in the lower-deck press. At Devonport in particular there was considerable overcrowding, and thousands of people lived in damp, insanitary houses.[55] The average rent for a room was 11s a week but it could sometimes go as high as 15s.[56] Some men lived in unfurnished rooms and bought furniture on hire-purchase to avoid the high cost of furnished property, but then the hire-purchase commitment could be crippling. As a result, many of those serving in home waters chose to live away from the naval ports, perhaps in their wife's home town. But then there was the problem of train fares on leave.

In the early post-war years the cost of rail travel was a major burden on ratings. In wartime, with the railways under government control, they had been allowed to make return journeys at the single fare. In addition two free travel warrants a year cushioned the cost of going on leave from remote Scottish bases. Servicemen had become used to this concession, but in May 1920 it was withdrawn.[57] Neither the government nor the railway companies would agree to subsidise travel to and from leave at the wartime level, and cheap fares came to an end in April 1922.[58] The effect, in some cases, was to prevent men from taking their leave at home. Only after the matter had been raised by MPs in the House and by the welfare conference did the Admiralty negotiate with the companies to secure some concession in train fares, and from November 1923 men were allowed to make return journeys at the single fare plus a third.[59]

Despite welfare requests the Admiralty persistently refused to reintroduce free travel warrants. Men were therefore worse off than they had been during the war, and the cost of going home on leave was to become a serious problem later in the decade as some found it more and more difficult to make ends meet.[60] A return ticket from Rosyth to towns in southern England could cost as much as £4. In many cases it was a question of saving up by strict economy and self-denial over a period of months to make one return journey home. Even those who lived in London claimed that they could only afford to travel home from Devonport once in two months.[61]

The dismal family circumstances of men on the 1925 rates was decribed in a report by the commodore of Portsmouth barracks some years later:

As regards food, tinned milk, 3d for bones for making soup, cheap bits of frozen meat, bread and butter, tea, cook-shop food, appears to be the general mode of living, while vegetables are only a weekend affair. When a pair of boots has to be mended some other thing has to be done without.

So hard-pressed were some families in rented rooms that they would share Sunday dinner with the householder to spread the cost a little.[62]

In the circumstances it is not surprising that the post-1925 entries looked to the future with some trepidation. In February 1930 *The Fleet* published a letter to the editor from one young rating:

Pay never worried me: it does not do so much now. But I am looking ahead. I can see a growing bubble of discontent bursting in a few years' time – when we think how impossible it will be for an AB or LS with the new scale of pay to support a wife and family and keep them respectable and pay for rent or rooms. [. . .] I cannot see it possible to support a wife, etc., on that; to do so a man would have to give her every penny of his pay. Even a PO or Chief on new rates would have to scrape. Something will have to be done about it sooner or later.[63]

It was a common complaint that in its recruiting drives among the unemployed the Admiralty made little effort to explain that rates of pay were now lower. The result was that men were joining the service without fully realising how much of a disadvantage they were going to

be under.[64] Later in the year a correspondent to *The Fleet* declared
that the time had come for post-1925 entries to make themselves heard
throughout the Navy.[65] In October 1930 the allowance of 3*d* a day in
lieu of rum was withdrawn from men under the age of twenty.[66] In
spring 1931 the Admiralty turned down yet another request in
Parliament that the qualifying age for marriage allowance should be
reduced to twenty-two, and during the debate on the Navy Estimates
Mr J. Kinley was led to remark, 'No one need pretend that the Navy is
a happy family of very happy men who would not leave if they had an
opportunity. No one need pretend that the Navy is satisfied.'[67]

Generalisations about the level of contentment among older ratings
in the late 1920s are hard to make. Service conditions were rather
better than in pre-war years. But this was perhaps not the comparison
that the men themselves made. They judged their conditions in terms
of what it seemed reasonable to expect, and their expectations were
higher now. In the wake of the 1919 pay rise ratings enjoyed a modest
improvement in their standard of living. Lower-deck families could
move from single-room accommodation to two rooms, from two rooms
to a small rented house.[68] Yet during the 1920s nagging doubts about
the permanence of the post-war improvement and the security of their
position persisted. As Admiral Lord Cunningham later reflected,

[. . .] the constant juggling with pay and allowances in the interests of
economy, all had their effect. The sailors had come to believe, not without
justification, that the pundits in Whitehall knew nothing of the manner in
which they lived [. . .] .[69]

There was general dissatisfaction with the welfare conferences and
the lack of any effective channel for general claims for improvements
in conditions. The amount of foreign-service duty rankled with some
married men.[70] Others found the routine of the peacetime Navy
irksome. But at bottom it was the bearing of peacetime conditions on
living standards that was of most importance.

The Navy in the 1920s was no place to seek quick advancement,
and by the end of the decade there was a marked stagnation in
promotion.[71] In the early post-war years an able seaman could expect
to be promoted to leading seaman with a higher rate of pay at the age
of twenty-four, but by the 1930s the average age at promotion was
twenty-seven. Similarly petty officers had formerly reached the rank
at twenty-eight, but in the early '30s the normal age on promotion was
thirty. It was not uncommon for a quarter of a ship's able seamen to

have more than twelve years' service, and large numbers of older ABs implied a discipline problem. They were 'old hands', they knew the ropes and were not going anywhere from a career point of view. Some would be older than the petty officers over them and consequently not easily kept in line.[72] These were the men whose pay was soon to be cut. For some time there had been a niggling feeling among them that one day, in spite of the promises, a reduction would be enforced. And some of them had already had their pension prospects undermined.

The Jerram committee had fixed the pension at $1\frac{1}{2}d$ a day $- 10\frac{1}{2}d$ a week after twenty-two years. In March 1930, in a further quest for economy, the Admiralty announced out of the blue that the pension would henceforth be reduced to $8d$ a week. This meant that men on 1919 rates of pay who began their second period of service after 31 March 1930 would get 25 per cent less pension than men on identical rates of pay who had already begun their final ten years.[73] Another differential was being introduced. It was a serious blow for men who intended to make the Navy a career. For those already in their second period it was a narrow let-off. They could take comfort in the knowledge that they had already entered into an agreement to serve for twenty-two years with a 1919-level pension at the end, and that agreement was binding. Or so they thought.

THE MAY COMMITTEE AND THE 1931 PAY CUTS

In the course of 1931, as the slump deepened and unemployment pushed past 2·5 million, the Labour government came under increasing pressure to retrench. Orthodox economists stressed the need for less public spending, and in March the government appointed a Committee on National Expenditure under the chairmanship of Sir George May. During the spring there was a growing chorus of demands from employers for cuts in wages such as had already been made on the railways. The National Confederation of Employers' Organisations called for reductions in all State and municipal wage rates.[74] In June an interim report of the Royal Commission on Unemployment Insurance advocated lower unemployment benefit. The following month the report of the Macmillan committee on trade and industry accepted the need to reduce real wages.[75]

Most important of all, the May committee's report, presented to the government on 31 July, urged extensive pruning of State expenditure, including wage cuts for civil servants, teachers, the police and the armed forces.[76] These were sweeping economies, and J. M. Keynes warned the Prime Minister that if they were implemented they would lead to 'a most gross perversion of social justice'.[77] As far as the forces were concerned, the report offered two alternatives: an allround reduction in pay or the application of 1925 rates to men on the 1919 scale. 'No officer or man serving His Majesty,' the committee argued, 'has any legal claim to a particular rate of pay [. . .] .'[78]

On 21 July 1931 the men of the Atlantic Fleet had begun their summer leave. When, on 1 August, the May report was made public they had plenty of time to study its implications. Newspapers in the home ports and the left-wing press made much of the proposal to enforce 1925 rates all round.[79] Throughout August the threat of service pay cuts were kept alive.[80] Not only was there the prospect of 1925 rates being extended to everybody, but the lower 1930 pension would be introduced generally, along with cuts in clothing allowances and payments in lieu. The Communist Party made a special effort to get its propaganda across. In Chatham during Navy Week, the senior service's annual public relations recruiting exercise, the Young Communist League staged a public meeting which was attended by ratings in uniform. Harry Pollitt, the party secretary, went down to address the rally, and a reinforced naval patrol was called out to clear away the uniformed men in the audience.[81]

Admiral Sir John Kelly's official report on the mutiny that was to follow indicates his belief that there was a leakage of the government's intention to implement the May proposals, and that this spawned secret lower-deck discussions.[82] The point ties in neatly with conspiracy theory. The Admiralty's subsequent hunt for ringleaders and outside agitators reflected a view commonly held in sections of the service that lower-deck ratings in general were incapable of staging such a protest unaided, and that the action had elements of a deliberate attempt to subvert the Navy. However, there was no leak. The reality was less dramatic, less sinister, but no less dangerous from the Admiralty point of view. The May report seems to have been studied more carefully by the men than by the senior officers.[83] And as Lieutenant-Commander C. R. Benstead of the battleship *Rodney* noted, the report only spelled out what most intelligent ratings had long suspected.[84]

Seventy-five per cent of lower-deck ratings had joined up before 1925. Many of them were veterans of the Grand Fleet and were fully aware of the agitation that had led to the 1919 pay awards. Some had experience of collective organisation in the lower-deck societies before their demise and had been active in the campaign against the Anderson proposals in 1923–24. These men had watched with more than a little interest over the years as the rate of naval pay had been discussed and reviewed by politicians and committees of inquiry. They knew at first hand what sort of living standards 1925 rates would mean, and they viewed the 1919 pay scale as something that had to be defended. A temporary sacrifice of income shared equally by all sections of the community to overcome the immediate economic crisis was perhaps acceptable, but any permanent departure from the 1919 rates had to be resisted.

On 1 September *The Fleet* carried an anonymous letter to the editor from a rating in the Mediterranean whose tone captures well the prevailing mood of apprehension and bitterness and the hint of a reaction should the full 1925 cuts be enforced.

What I want you [Yexley] to realise is that you are not going to be permitted to rest on your laurels, for it seems that a bigger problem is confronting the Lower Deck in the near future than ever occurred in 1919. [. . .]

There has recently been published the recommendations of the Royal Commission on National Expenditure, and under the 'Services' heading there appeared the recommendation that the pay of all Naval personnel should be reduced to the 1925 rate. We all realise that such a recommendation may not be adopted, but we all rather fear that it might. We all sincerely hope that the many solemn promises that Parliament made to us in 1925 will not be broken, but so very many promises, not necessarily appertaining to the Navy, *have* been broken that we all feel somewhat dubious of getting better luck.

It is a bit too premature to get pessimistic about it, I will admit, but I believe that just at present this matter is exercising the minds and discussions of the Lower Deck to the almost total exclusion of anything else. We are all wondering what will happen if the powers that be do adopt such a course. Will it be a case of Hobson's Choice – like it or lump it? Will we get the opportunity to resist such an obviously unfair measure, and if so will the existing Welfare machinery be strong enough to deal with such a job? I for one doubt it. [. . .]

Did any of the commissioners visit a sailor's home to see how his pay is spent during the course of their enquiry? Did they ever visit and live with sailors aboard a small ship to see how that pay is *earnt*? Obviously they didn't, [. . .] .

If they want to know where expenditure in the Navy can be reduced they have only to ask the average AB – if they can get him to talk; but in the meantime we are all asking, What is going to happen – If?[85]

The letter indicates that even in the Med. there was no shortage of information and discussion among the lower deck, and that fleet was now dispersed in small groups on its annual summer cruise of the eastern Mediterranean.

The ratings of the Atlantic Fleet were less isolated during their summer leave at home. They were in a position to discuss the implications of the cuts and could hardly have failed to see that other sections of the community were organising for resistance. Unemployed workers in Bristol had staged a protest demonstration at the TUC against reductions in unemployment benefit. A similar demonstration had occurred in London, while teachers and policemen indicated that they were not prepared to accept pay cuts without protest.[86] By the end of the summer leave period a consensus had almost certainly formed among important sections of the lower deck that if the full 1925 cuts were introduced the men would refuse to accept them. They were drawing on their collective consciousness of the 1919 campaign. As in 1919, it would be 'up to the fleet' to take the initiative. But for the time being the men were keeping their cards close to their chest.[87]

In any case no viable channels of protest were open within the law. The welfare conferences were known to be valueless where major grievances such as pay were concerned. The letter to *The Fleet* revealed a lack of confidence in the system, and restrained articles in the *Naval Chronicle* during the summer of 1931 regretted the absence of any effective constitutional procedure through which men could state their case.[88] Had the lower-deck societies been as strong as they were before 1923 it is likely that they would have initiated a press campaign, drawing public attention to the seriousness of the situation. But this route had been closed.

Equally, there was no approach to the Members of Parliament in the home bases. At Devonport this could perhaps be explained by the fact that in 1923 the three local MPs had publicly proclaimed their willingness to speak and vote against any cuts in pay, and now the lower deck counted on their automatic support. As it happened the promises of 1923 were forgotten and these MPs made no protest. Lady Astor, who had once vowed to give no quarter on their behalf, even expressed concern at the ratings' unco-operative attitude.[89] In any event this avenue was effectively blocked as a result of deliberate Admiralty policy, and no approaches were made to MPs to warn them of lower-deck feelings. At Portsmouth neither Will Hall nor Bertram Falle had any idea of what was in the offing.[90]

Only one public figure appears to have sensed something in the wind and tried to alert the Admiralty. W. A. Appleton, General Secretary of the General Federation of Trade Unions, had long-standing contacts with activists in the lower-deck movement. He had worked closely with a number of the societies at the end of the war and in 1917 had vigorously supported their campaign for a pay increase. On 9 September, less than a week before the outbreak of mutiny, he had questioned Admiral of the Fleet Lord Wemyss as to the contentment of the lower deck and advised him to 'watch the fleet'. This cryptic warning was duly passed on to the First Sea Lord, but to no avail.[91] What the basis of his information was – a direct approach from someone in lower-deck circles, a sailor's wife, or simply intuitive understanding – is not clear.[92] But his unease was in marked contrast to the apparent lack of awareness at the Admiralty of what lay in store.

By 1 September 1931 the National Government had decided to implement the May proposals. The 1925 rates were to apply to all men, but no announcement was to be made until after the Chancellor's emergency budget speech on 10 September. When the Atlantic Fleet anchored at Invergordon on the 11th for the start of its autumn exercises the men were without any official information on what lay ahead. There was still a strong feeling that the cuts would not materialise. There was a reluctance to believe, despite the May report, that previous government and Admiralty promises about the permanence of the 1919 rates would be broken. Since publication the government had signified neither acceptance nor rejection. Most men had interpreted silence in this quarter as a reassuring sign. What they failed to appreciate was that Parliament had been in recess since before the publication of the report and consequently had had no opportunity to question Ministers. The intentions of the National Government would be revealed only when Parliament reassembled.

The lower-deck mood was thus predominantly one of guarded optimism that the whole thing would blow over, or that at least only a temporary pay cut of 10 per cent all round would be made. On 5 September the *Daily Express* confidently predicted that the Chancellor would announce a 10 per cent cut in pay for all State servants in the forthcoming emergency debate.[93] But intermingled with these hopes were underlying fears that the upshot might be much worse. At Lieutenant-Commander Benstead noted, 'we were not at ease'.[94]

On 10 September, the day of the budget speech, a White Paper was issued stating that the 1925 rates would apply all round as from 1 October.[95] The first word of this was broadcast by the BBC on the six o'clock news, but as with all radio messages very few ratings heard it, and anyway there were no details.[96] The next day the *Daily Express* repeated the White Paper's statement that 1925 rates would apply to all, with pensions reduced to the 1930 level.[97] An identical story appeared in the *Scottish Daily Record*.[98] Rather misleadingly the *Daily Mirror* announced that pay would be cut by 10–20 per cent.[99] Further reports in the press the following day, Saturday, indicated that teachers' pay was going to be reduced by 15 per cent and that 3,000 of them had already staged a march in protest. The pay of police constables was to be reduced by only 7 per cent, although the May committee had recommended a total cut of $12\frac{1}{2}$ per cent.[100] On service pay details were still lacking, and there was an unwillingness to accept that the cuts would be as much as 25 per cent. It was still not clear either whether the post-1925 ratings would be affected by any economies.

By late Sunday morning, 12 September, the entire fleet had at last received full confirmation of the new pay scales – but from the *News of the World* rather than from the official Fleet Orders. Before the official notification had been posted on most ships the Sunday papers were brought on board by men returning from the Presbyterian church service in Invergordon.

Despite the rumours and garbled reports that had been circulating for days, the final realisation that the cuts were really going to take place came as an enormous blow. The men were furious. For one thing there was the sheer size of the reduction – 25 per cent at the lowest level. But along with this was the inequity of the revision. The largest proportion was being borne by the lowest paid. Officers were only faced with an 11 per cent decrease. This was hardly a case of equal sacrifices for all. The cuts were regarded as a breach of contract, a repudiation of the oft-repeated assurance by politicians and the Admiralty that the 1919 rates would remain. Quite simply, ratings felt that the Admiralty had betrayed them.

Then there was the cut in pensions, a further breach of contractual obligations, it seemed, towards men already on their second period. Savings here would not become effective for a number of years and would make no contribution to solving the present economic crisis. For some the reduced pension was of more significance than the cut in pay. As a letter to *The Fleet* written the day before the mutiny by a rating in the Persian Gulf indicated, most of the men' [. . .] are resigned to the reduction of pay as being necessary in view of the present crisis, the point that has surprised all is the attack on the pensions, which was totally unexpected'.[101]

The timing of the announcement was another cause of bitterness. The new rates were due to be introduced in two weeks and would be in effect by the time the fleet returned home from the exercises. Men had been given no opportunity to make necessary adjustments to their domestic budgeting, no time to talk to their wives. Facing a sizable number was the very real prospect of furniture bought on hire-purchase being repossessed, and destitution for their families. Obviously the cuts had been decided some time before, and it was wrong to give so little notice.

THE 'BREEZE' AT INVERGORDON

The men most affected were the older, married ones, staid hands, perhaps with children. The average age of those most deeply implicated in the subsequent action was twenty-eight, which meant that they had joined as boy seamen in 1919.[102] From this point on they began to assert themselves on the lower deck. Petty officers made themselves scarce, and the younger ratings were kept out of it, some accused of letting the others down by enlisting on lower pay.[103] Wherever men congregated pay was the sole topic of conversation. And in the course of the next thirty-six hours of debate and argument the majority of the lower deck were won over to the view that the cuts had to be fought by one means or another.

Gatherings ashore in the naval canteen at Invergordon on 12 and 13 September also discussed the cuts and helped to harden the general resolve to take protest action. At the Admiralty, where conspiracy theories of mutiny tended to gain credence, and in subsequent histories these canteen 'meetings' were accorded more importance than they really warrant. Claims that representatives were elected from each ship, a secret code of signals established and a committee set up to organise the mutiny can be discounted. They originate from a pamphlet, *The Spirit of Invergordon*, published by International Labour Defence (ILD), a front organisation of the the Communist Party, which was allegedly written by Able Seaman Len Wincott.[104]

Wincott claimed to have led the mutiny, and after being discharged for his part in it he joined ILD. The mutiny became an important element in Communist Party propaganda, and the Admiralty's predisposition to view it as the work of a few ringleaders was complemented by the party's claim to have the support of the ringleader-in-chief.[105]

Quite simply, the focusing of attention on the canteen meetings ignores the sheer difficulty of organising a general mutiny on a dozen or more ships. As Able Seaman George Hill, one of the prominent activists on board the cruiser *Norfolk* and a close associate of Wincott explained:

[. . .] you can only hope that the intentions of ALL other ships involved will be maintained. There is no sure way of knowing. This automatically ruled out any 'lead ship' as such, or more important an overall leader in a lead ship, who as circumstances develop can issue a directive to all other ships. So the question of who led the mutiny does not arise.[106]

Meetings and discussion had been taking place on board the various ships ever since the extent of the cuts first became common knowledge. There was considerable support for some form of protest action; the majority were agreed in being no longer prepared to carry on working for the kind of money they were now going to be paid. The most effective form of collective action was to refuse to put to sea. It would have to be done in a concerted fashion and, since there could be no overall direction, this automatically meant that the 'down tools' would have to be when most of the big ships were due to sail, on the morning of Tuesday, 15 September. *Valiant*, *Hood*, *Rodney* and *Nelson* were due to sail between 8 a.m. and 10 a.m. that day. At individual meetings of ratings held on the various ships it was generally agreed that if *Valiant* refused to sail the rest would 'chuck their hand in'.

At 6 a.m. on 15 September, the normal time for seamen to turn to and scrub decks, only the *Hood*, *Norfolk* and *York* could report a full muster.[107] In *Valiant* the petty officers and a few leading seamen presented themselves for duty, but no seamen turned to. Only seventy-five of *Rodney*'s seamen were present. Sixty of *Nelson*'s were absent from duty. Fifty-seven were missing in *Dorsetshire*, while in *Adventure* the hands fell in reluctantly. Despite the patchiness of the response, it was a remarkable demonstration of solidarity, given the illegal nature of the action.

Before the start of the forenoon watch the captains of various ships attempted to address the crews with a view to restoring discipline, but without effect. Lower-deck attention was focused on *Valiant*, whose cable party had refused to unmoor and work the anchors. She was also experiencing difficulties in hoisting her boats, and the forenoon watch of stokers had refused to go below. At 8.00 a.m. as colours were hoisted in all ships, and with *Valiant*'s preparations for sea still visibly incomplete, there was spontaneous cheering by ratings throughout the fleet. The mutiny proper had begun. Other ships now joined in. The stokers of the forenoon watch in *Norfolk* refused to go below; thirty-five stokers from *Dorsetshire* failed to turn to; and up to fifty seamen and stokers in *Adventure* were missing when the captain cleared lower deck to address the crew shortly after 8 a.m.

Between 8.00 and 9.30 a.m. was the high point of the mutiny. At 9.16 Rear-Admiral Tomkinson, Senior Officer Atlantic Fleet, signalled to the Admiralty that four ships had failed to sail. Those already at sea were recalled to harbour, and at 9.31 a.m. the exercises were cancelled. The immediate objective had been achieved; the fleet had been prevented from sailing. But beyond this objective, aims were vague. The men anticipated a response of some sort, and most of them would have settled for an early announcement that pay cuts were to be limited to 10 per cent. However, the initiative now lay with the Admiralty. In the meantime the crews pursued their action in different ways, again reflecting the fragmented nature of the protest. In some ships the general feeling seems to have been that the measures already taken were sufficient and that it was proper to return to work according to normal harbour routine. In others no work was done all day.

Though technically a mutiny, what had really occurred was a strike. Naval Intelligence was later quick to follow up the possibility that the use of the strike weapon was related to trade union influence. The Devonport-based ships, especially *Rodney*, *Adventure* and *Norfolk*, were judged to have been among the worst affected, and the Director of Naval Intelligence pointed out that 45 per cent of the men from this division came from the Midlands and the North.[108] The point is certainly not without relevance – ratings were well aware of the practices of industrial workers, though to suggest a direct link between the proportion of Devonport men born north of a line from London to Bristol and the behaviour of their ships at Invergordon is clearly too simple. The tendency for an increasing number of sailors to come from northern industrial towns and urban districts remote from the traditional naval catchment area of the southern home ports and their hinterland had been general since the turn of the century and was accompanied by a distinct change in the mentality of the lower deck. But a more immediate influence is likely to have been the mutiny of the *Lucia* nine months earlier. That incident was fresh in mind at Invergordon and, as on that occasion, men simply stayed on their messdecks or massed on the forecastle to demonstrate their solidarity with other ships.[109] As Fred Copeman, one of the mutineers, described the action:

It was a simple affair, worked out in the simple way that comes natural to sailors. Go on the forecastle. If you're on the forecastle no one else can get there. The hatches from the seamen's messdeck lead directly to the forecastle. If the marines are with you no one can do anything about it. Every ship did it the same. The mutiny was a spontaneous, commonsense form of strike action. It wasn't planned.[110]

The quick response expected from the Admiralty was not forthcoming, and as the mutiny extended into its second day so many men's resolve began to waver. The sense of isolation and the lack of communications had an unnerving effect. They were now involved in a very serious action and would have welcomed a way out. The longer the mutiny lasted the more prone were they to splits and divisions. The ships had been prevented from sailing, but the next move was up to the Admiralty. All the men could do was to respond, and there was no way of concerting their response.

In London the Cabinet had refused to agree to a postponement of the cuts on the grounds that this would undermine its whole economic strategy, but it did accept the Admiralty's suggestion that the ships should be brought home.[111] A signal to this effect in the middle of the Wednesday afternoon informed the fleet that hardship cases would be investigated. With many ratings beginning to waver, the men were in no position to improvise a united response. The signal split the lower deck, provided those who wanted it with a means of getting off the hook and effectively took the steam out of the mutiny. There was no clear-cut decision as such to return to duty, and some of the supposed leaders were back at work while their followers continued to hold out.[112] But by 7 p.m. on Wednesday 16 September the crew of *Valiant*, the first to refuse orders, had fallen in for work and psychologically this tipped the balance. The mutiny was effectively over. At 9.30 p.m. the cruiser squadron sailed on schedule, and an hour and a half later the battleships put to sea for home ports.

AFTERMATH: VICTIMISATION AND SURVEILLANCE

On Thursday evening, 17 September, with the fleet steaming home, the House of Commons held an emergency debate and Sir Austen Chamberlain, First Lord of the Admiralty, announced that there would be no victimisation of men involved in the protest action.[113] The subsequent dismissal of over two dozen ratings was due, according to the Admiralty, to their continuing to agitate on return to port. Developments in the naval towns during the following weeks and months constitute an interesting sequel to the affair. There is no hard evidence of further organised agitation among the ratings, but the incidents shed an interesting light on the mentality of the Admiralty, its attitude to the lower deck and its methods of rooting out dissidents.

As soon as the disturbances at Invergordon became known Naval Intelligence and MI5 began investigations into the organisation of the mutiny. Indeed, it seems possible that security intelligence was taking an interest in lower-deck affairs before it, with detectives in sailor's uniform operating in the naval ports.[114] Whether this was routine work or prompted by reports that all was not well with the fleet is unclear. At the first sign of unrest at Invergordon Major Sam Bassett, a Royal Marine officer temporarily attached to MI5, was sent to investigate.[115] And on Friday 18 September, before any of the ships had arrived home, security intelligence agents were put to work in the home ports.[116]

With the ships back home on Saturday 19 September, intelligence agents eavesdropped on sailors in pubs, especially in Devonport, and tried to engage them in conversation. From this source reports began to reach the Admiralty of plans for further meetings and protest action. At Chatham and Portsmouth intelligence sources heard rumours that ratings intended to protest outside the Admiralty on the Monday morning.[117] No real evidence was ever produced to substantiate the rumours, but on the basis of such hearsay security intelligence began to construct a lurid account of continuing agitation and conspiratorial gatherings. From Devonport the C-in-C wired the Admiralty that he had 'definite confirmation' that an illicit signal had been made to *Rodney* from *Nelson* on the passage south from Invergordon which read, 'HMS *Nelson* will now take over pivotal ship, keep your end up and do not forget 0800 next Tuesday'.[118] What substance there was in this remains obscure, but together with other fragments of hearsay it was put forward as proof that a further demonstration was planned for Tuesday 22 September, when all ratings would walk off their ships.[119] The Board of Admiralty remained in continuous session throughout Sunday, and the C-in-C, Devonport, sent his chief of staff up to report to the First Sea Lord. On Monday morning, 21 September, Major Bassett was summoned from Portsmouth to brief the Prime Minister, and later in the morning the First Lord attended a Cabinet meeting to give an account of the latest position.[120] He reported in dramatic terms that it was very serious. Communist agents were active in the ports; the lower deck had a complete organisation to resist the cuts; petty officers were disaffected, and plans were afoot to walk off the ships on Tuesday morning. He told the Cabinet that if thousands of ratings broke out and marched into the towns serious rioting would ensue and the revolt might induce other classes of the community to join in. The Admiralty had considered using force to stop such action. The First Lord had examined the possibility of sealing off the dockyards, but it was decided that the Royal Marines at home ports were not to be trusted and the men might batter down the dockyard gates.

The recommendation of the Sea Lords was that, rather than simply offer some concessions to hard-pressed individuals, the government should immediately announce that as a result of its inquiries the cuts would be restricted to a maximum of 10 per cent for all ratings. The Cabinet agreed, and it was decided that the Prime Minister would make an announcement in the Commons that afternoon.[121] By evening the fleet had been notified of the change of policy on pay.

While the sense of grievance among the lower deck was strong, and a reduction in the level of cuts imperative, the signs are that the government was panicked into making the concession and that it was merely an act of expediency. The suggestion that the new 10 per cent limit was a result of the Admiralty inquiries is scarcely correct. Committees to investigate cases of hardship began work at the three ports only on the Monday morning as the Cabinet was taking its decision, and their deliberations continued for two more days. The pay cuts were revised only because of fear of further protest action. Yet evidence of anything of the sort being planned was of the flimsiest nature. Even the C-in-C at Devonport, who first raised the alarm about secret meetings, seems to have been reasonably satisfied on the Sunday when he wired the Admiralty, 'Situation remains same as yesterday. Moderate elements appear to have the upper hand at present and are advising no action to be taken Tuesday although extremists are still urging action on that day.'[122] The local press was also more sanguine about the weekend's events. The *Portsmouth Evening News* reported that in the course of the two days everything had been normal in the town and there were no exceptional cases of leave-breaking. At Plymouth the *Western Morning News* noted that 'there was never at any time a suggestion of any demonstrative spirit among the men' and that rumours of secret meetings were 'without foundation'.[123]

Altogether, intelligence personnel seem to have decided from the outset that the mutiny must have been the work of conspirators and proceeded to make every effort to turn up supporting evidence. Various scenarios were put forward. Sir Vernon Kell, head of MI5, advised the Deputy Chief of Naval Staff that ratings from the *Norfolk* and *Dorsetshire* had probably been influenced by German communists, possibly veterans of the 1917–18 naval mutinies, when they visited Kiel during their summer cruise in 1931.[124] However, Fred Copeman and Len Wincott, who were on that cruise and subsequently became prominent Communist Party activists, totally dismiss any suggestion that the lower deck were at any time influenced by the party.[125] Similarly, intelligence agents reported that the lodges of the Royal Antediluvian Order of Buffaloes on board ships had been used as a cover for secret meetings. Much of the evidence for this came from statements made to intelligence agents by ex-Chief Writer Jimmy Lane, the lower-deck leader in Portsmouth. He was clearly antipathetic to the 'Buffs' and at the same time keen that no hint of suspicion should fall on the lower-deck societies such as might lead to their suppression. In short the case against the Order seems to have been based on hearsay spiced perhaps with a touch of malice. Yet on the strength of this the innocuous Buffaloes became a scapegoat and their right to hold meetings on board ship was withdrawn.[126] Within MI5 there was a belief that the conspirators had actually been organising secretly for two years. The Director of Naval Intelligence contended that there were people in the Labour Party who had either 'pre-knowledge or contemporary knowledge' of events at Invergordon. He also claimed there was evidence that the so-called plot to walk ashore on 22 September had been elaborated at Invergordon, this in spite of the fact that the men could have had no idea that they would be back in port that day.[127]

Seven weeks after the mutiny two dozen ratings were dismissed from the Navy, 'Services No Longer Required', to be joined by a number of others in the following months. Since the First Lord had said that no one would be punished, the reason given was that they continued agitation on returning to home port.[128] The First Lord's amnesty had been difficult for some at the Admiralty to swallow, and soon after the event Admiral Field, the First Sea Lord, wrote to Beatty expressing regret that the ringleaders could not be punished. Still, he pointed out that he was compiling a list of those who had agitated subsequent to Chamberlain's Commons statement and told Beatty, '[. . .] we shall find a way of getting rid of them'.[129]

However, continued agitation in any organised form would seem to have been largely a figment of the imagination. Those discharged denied any involvement, and when pressed by the First Lord for details Naval Intelligence was forced to admit that the evidence would not hold up in court.[130] The likelihood is that victims were selected arbitrarily from among those thought to have been prominent at Invergordon, with others the Admiralty simply wanted to be rid of. All the signs are that there was no central co-ordination of the mutiny: refusal of duty was the simplest and most natural form of action the ratings could take. However, leading personalities did emerge on individual ships – men such as Stoker Arthur Harwood and AB John Emerson in *Nelson*; ABs George Day and Marshall Brockway together with Marine Coleman in *Valiant*; Stoker Alfred Fowler, Bandsman Alley and ABs Cyril Bond and Willie Ryder in *Rodney*; Stoker Tom Winstanley in *Warspite* and ABs Copeman, Wincott and Hill in *Norfolk*. Their role was to generate support for the refusal of duty and then to maintain the commitment among their messmates. But there was no sense in which they constituted an overall executive body or acted as representatives of the men before the officers. Most of them were unacquainted with one another, and none was widely known or had any influence outside his own ship or even his own department.[131] Officers were hard put to identify ringleaders even on their own ships. *York*'s captain was quite unable to say who were the principal agitators. After two days of mutiny his counterpart in *Norfolk* compiled a list of seventeen suspects, none of whom, judged by the evidence available, stood out as a dominating character. His belief, like that of many other officers, was that the chief ringleaders were from *Rodney*. But then *Rodney*'s captain could not even identify the subversives among his own crew.

Naval Intelligence compiled a list of 120 men throughout the fleet who, it claimed, had played a major part in the incident. Twenty of them were leading hands or Royal Marine NCOs. Fifty-one had seen service in the war, meaning that they were personally acquainted with the pitifully low pre-Jerram rates of pay and knew about the struggle to get them improved in 1919. Nine had actually joined the service before 1914 and had seen the rise of the lower-deck reform movement and the earlier campaign for some constitutional channel of representation before the Admiralty.[132] Try as they might to categorise these 120 into grades of subversive, Intelligence was unable to draw up a list of leaders. Some were given 'five star' rating as agitators. One man, thought to have masterminded the action of the Portsmouth ships from on board *Nelson*, was codenamed 'Red Admiral', while his counterpart in *Rodney* was known to Intelligence as 'Gandhi'. But as the Director of Naval Intelligence admitted, 'were they replaced there is little doubt that their places would be taken by the other men named'. His blanket recommendation was therefore that all on the list should be discharged or 'otherwise eliminated'.[133]

Thus the selection of men for dismissal would seem to have been quite arbitrary. It has all the marks of an act of expediency carried out in breach of promise and timed to avoid political disadvantage. By mid-October the Board of Admiralty were urging the First Lord to authorise the ejection of the suspects, and in advocating strong action the Director of Naval Intelligence even expressed the view that 'this would be good for electoral purposes'.[134] But the Board were also mindful that discharging the men from the service would lead to much adverse publicity, and Chamberlain, the First Lord, was unwilling to sanction it before the forthcoming general election.[135] In the event the decision to dismiss twenty-four ratings *en bloc* subject to the Prime Minister's concurrence was taken at a Board meeting on 29 October, the day after the election.

The reaction of the establishment to the events at Invergordon was characterised by a deep feeling of paranoia. In his report on the mutiny Admiral Kelly stated that some naval schoolmasters were 'of a type which is frankly Socialist in outlook'. He recommended the greatest possible care in future when recruiting for these posts, and King George V marked this passage in red pencil on his personal copy.[136] Many of the ratings who took part were branded as being 'under Communistic influence'. In November 1931 Naval Intelligence calculated that there were no fewer than eighty-one such individuals in the Atlantic Fleet alone, a figure which would have struck the average lower-decker with wonder while representing for the Communist Party a degree of success beyond its wildest dreams.[137] The zealous search for a link between lower-deck agitation and communism appears even to have led security intelligence to the questionable practice of employing *agents provocateurs*. This is evident from the case of two party officials, Alison and Shepherd, who went to prison in 1931 for trying to incite a mutiny. On that occasion one of the activists at Invergordon, Telegraphist Stephen Bousefield (who may have been an Intelligence spy all along) was used to bait a trap for the two Communists.[138]

Naval Intelligence was later to assert that the idea of spying on men had always been rejected, but the claim is dubious in view of a Board decision later that 'agents should not in future go on board ships or undertake espionage work away from the home ports'.[139] In fact intelligence surveillance of the lower deck was stepped up after Invergordon with Major Bassett's permanent attachment to MI5.[140]

Men continued to suffer as a result of the mutiny. In subsequent months discharges on a smaller scale continued. However, in view of the public uproar over the dismissal of the twenty-four ratings Naval Intelligence urged caution in future and advised the Admiralty to justify any further discharges as part of a normal weeding-out process for reasons of economy.[141] Despite the First Lord's amnesty it also became policy that no one who had been implicated should be allowed to re-engage for pension without special permission.[142] Ratings blacklisted as a result of the mutiny were kept under surveillance by security intelligence for well over a year afterwards.[143]

That surveillance did take place and that information gleaned from it was used in unethical ways is indicated by the case of Fred Copeman. After being discharged he got a job as a rigger in London and became active in the National Unemployed Workers' Movement. In May 1932 the right-wing employers' organisation, the Economic League, wrote to the Admiralty pointing out their interest in countering subversive activities in industry and asking for any information they could have about him. The Admiralty duly obliged with the information that he had been discharged, 'Services No Longer Required', and was understood to be acting in London as an agitator on behalf of the Communist Party. In fact at the time Copeman was not a member of the party, but he lost his job on the suspicion.[144] The incident reflects little credit on the Admiralty, and

the helpful response to the Economic League contrasts with the cold
rebuff of those who wrote to the King and to their lordships for some
explanation of their dismissal.

The blind reaction of the Admiralty to what was supposed to have
happened on the lower deck derived from its lack of first-hand contact
with the ratings. Senior officers were out of touch, and there was no
open investigation. Indeed, any idea of an inquiry was strongly
resisted.[145] The instinctive reaction was to sweep the whole affair
under the carpet, to give no opportunity for criticism of the way things
had been handled. The Deputy Chief of Naval Staff put the argument
against an inquiry in the most dramatic terms:

The whole Navy, including the nine Commanders-in-Chief, will be 'On
Trial', i.e. Authority will be 'On Trial'. [. . .] The whole thing would flare up
again instead of dying. *This is exactly what the King in his wisdom wishes to
avoid.*[146]

In particular there was opposition to any suggestion that a Commons
select committee should investigate. As the Permanent Secretary
explained.

The Trade Union members of the Committee might be expected to advance
the view that a strike on a wages question ought not to be regarded as a
breach of Service discipline.[147]

The Admiralty wanted public discussion to end as soon as possible.
The Deputy Chief of Naval Staff pointed out:

[. . .] it is most *desirable* that the debate in the House of Commons on the
Navy Estimates should be completed before the 14 March, in order that any
further discussion of their mutiny six months previously be concluded before
the Atlantic Fleet ships reach their Home Ports on that date.[148]

At all costs the ratings had to be kept out of any debate about the one
event which most concerned them.
    The mutiny and its aftermath were a sorry episode, mishandled
from beginning to end. The Admiralty's failure to respond promptly
had made it last longer than necessary. The subsequent moves against
suspected ringleaders involved victimisation and a good deal of
injustice. And at bottom it can hardly be denied that the Admiralty
brought the mutiny on itself. Lack of awareness of what had really
gone on among the ratings at Invergordon matched the earlier failure
to realise the consequences of reducing pay and pensions. The long-

term causes dated back beyond 1931 and lay in the decision to block vital channels of representation in the early 1920s and to apply a flat-rate pay cut in 1925. Few people at the Admiralty seem to have been aware of this, though it became abundantly clear to Rear-Admiral Tompkinson – too late for action – in the course of the mutiny. As he later reported:

There was another important factor in the subsequent spread of the trouble, viz. the conclusion which rapidly became prevalent, that the ordinary Service channels for complaints were in this case valueless, and that the men had no other course than the one they took. [...]
  The more the officers urged upon the men the futility of their action and encouraged them to resort to the proper Service methods the more did it appear to many who had hitherto been opposed to the outbreak that the proper Service methods would have no effect and the only method to secure a real consideration of the complaint was that which had been adopted.[149]

Who was ultimately to blame – the May committee which recommended the cuts, the National Government which enforced them, or the Board of Admiralty under Admiral Sir Frederick Field which acquiesced in them? The Anderson committee first recommended the reductions, but as part of a national economy measure called for by the Bonar Law administration and decided in Cabinet. The decision was a political one and the Conservative government of the day must bear much of the blame. The Admiralty too should have seen the dangers more clearly than it did and represented them with greater force to the Cabinet. The lower-deck poet John Bush asked accusingly:

Would you ask your sleek Committee by whom was the probe begun
To manage on twenty-eight bob a week or try it on twenty-one?[150]

The point is well made, whether the 'sleek committee' be Anderson's or May's; Bonar Law's, Baldwin's or MacDonald's Cabinet; Beatty's or Field's Board of Admiralty. The fact is that, throughout, the measures were taken by men who were largely unaware of the economic realities of life as experienced by the lower deck. And with no effective channel of representation there was little likelihood that they ever would be made really aware of them.

NINE

The end of collective representation

The Welfare Conference was brought into existence to discuss things, and unless the members are allowed to give full and free expression to their thoughts it might as well be done away with altogether – better a little 'hot air' on the surface than a stifled underground discontent! – *The Fleet*, September 1920

When Naval history of the Twentieth Century is written it will be recorded that constitutional mass representation was born in 1919 and died in 1932 after a weakly infancy and a delicate childhood. – J. E. Lane, *Naval Chronicle*, 9 December 1932

The crude victimisation of ratings after Invergordon and the increased emphasis on strict discipline smothered any further demonstration of lower-deck dissatisfaction. But the Navy now faced a number of problems. Morale was at an all-time low. Recruiting suffered in the wake of the mutiny. There was an obvious need for the Admiralty to pay more attention to conditions of service, and yet at the same time the welfare conference system was clearly seen for the ineffective mechanism it was. Again, some method of dealing with general complaints and requests had to be devised, but in the ensuing climate of fear and suspicion there was no chance of their lordships experimenting with a genuine system of collective representation by the men's own autonomous organisations. For much of the 1930s the Admiralty agonised over how to deal with demands for improved conditions, fearing that almost any approach would give ratings an opportunity to combine and perhaps challenge legitimate authority. The method finally chosen – the Review of Service Conditions – reflected all the paranoia of a naval establishment largely out of touch with, and not particularly sympathetic to, their ratings. Few significant improvements followed, but at the level of cosmetic change just enough was done to keep the men quiet. The reform movement was no more, and the rest of the decade passed without major incident.

THE LINGERING SORE OF INVERGORDON

Bitterness lingered for some considerable time, however, and the cause was undoubtedly low pay. For four years the men felt the strain of life on the reduced rates. Many of them had to cut the allotment to their families. From the Mediterranean the commander-in-chief reported that half-way through the month ratings would be short of money for a drink in the canteen, the odd visit to the cinema, even their supper. This kept them in barracks or on board ship. Many scarcely ever went ashore. The signs of hardship were everywhere to be found. Takings at the Corradino canteen in Malta fell by nearly 30 per cent.[1]

The limitation of pay cuts to a 10 per cent maximum did not mean that the aim of applying the 1925 rates universally had been abandoned. The government's policy was that the 10 per cent limit was to apply only to a first term of engagement. Pre-1925 ratings who signed on for a second period automatically reverted to the lower rates and the lower pension.[2] In fact there were no fewer than four different pay and pension scales according to whether a man had joined up before 1921, 1925 or 1930 and when he had signed on for pension.[3] Signing on for another term meant being temporarily worse off than more junior ratings who had yet to reach the age for re-engagement. Small wonder that morale was low.

One result was that many were deterred from re-engaging for pension. In 1932–33 there was some official concern about this. Three ships in the Mediterranean Fleet reported that, of a total of ninety-four men eligible to re-engage, not one had done so. Overall, 61 per cent were signing on for pension, as against 70 per cent in the early 1920s.[4] As Admiral Kelly reported from the Home Fleet:

Broadly speaking, it may be said that all Men in their first period of engagement are dissatisfied: those up to say 7 years' service on account of the latter grievance [i.e. different rates of pay for the same job] [. . .] and those from 7 years onward because of the conditions attached to re-engagement.[5]

The opinion was shared by the commanders-in-chief at the three home ports.[6] In view of this the Cabinet agreed in 1933 to cushion the fall in pay for men re-engaging. From that point on they were to remain on the 1919 scale less 10 per cent after re-engagement until they were advanced to a higher-paid rank. Only then would they convert to the 1925 rate for the rank.[7]

As ever, married ratings were in the most difficult position. The current marriage allowance — 7s a week for men over twenty-five — was wholly inadequate, and the Secretary to the Board of Admiralty conceded that 10s a week was the least on which a rating could possibly run a home. He advocated raising the allowance by 3s for men on the 1925 scale, and the proposal was accepted — but only in 1936. Not until 1938 was the allowance for pre-1925 entries increased, when the payment for all married men went up to 17s a week.[8] Nor was any attempt made to lower the qualifying age appreciably. The Admiralty remained firm in the belief that young marriages should be discouraged.[9]

Shortly after the mutiny it instituted a fund from which special hardship payments could be made to young married ratings. The paltry sum of £5,000 was made available for the RNBT to cover the whole service. Benefits were restricted to those under the age of twenty-five, of whom there were probably over 1,000.[10] The maximum payment was 2s a week for men with children, while those without were allowed 1s. Originally intended to last only twelve months, the fund was kept going for three years. In the course of this period 716 men were doled out payments to a total of £4,305. A large number who were entitled to the help refused to apply on the grounds that it was charity. In the Mediterranean Fleet, as a result, only 124 out of 206 eligible ratings drew the benefit.[11] For the same reason a further 114 throughout the service withdrew their application.[12]

Altogether it was a pitiful attempt to ease the burden of low pay, but it was to be the pattern of the 1930s. At best, cases of hardship were to be offered discretionary hand-outs. At this very time the Admiralty was going ahead with plans for a new Royal Yacht costing £825,000.[13] With conscription in the air in 1939 it was no longer politically feasible to discriminate over entitlement to marriage allowance, and a joint committee of the three services met to consider reducing the qualifying age. The Admiralty was prepared to concede only a two-year reduction in the minimum, to twenty-three years.[14] And when the Cabinet decided to go the whole hog and pay marriage allowance to all servicemen over twenty it was done against the vocal opposition of the Sea Lords, who complained bitterly of a policy which was 'contrary to the interests of the service' and 'inimical to the well-being and efficiency of the ratings concerned'.[15]

The price of a roof over their family's heads in the home ports continued to be a major burden for married ratings, as the various inquiries that followed Invergordon showed. In 1932 the Portsmouth committee of the RNBT, led by Jimmy Lane, proposed that the Trust should put up £5,000 to launch a naval housing association which would build low-cost accommodation. As the scheme was intended to apply to Portsmouth only, the Chatham and Devonport representatives on the RNBT vetoed it. But the idea continued to appeal to the lower deck in Portsmouth, and later that year the Barracks Canteen Committee stepped in and offered to make the necessary funds available. An interest-free loan of £6,000 was provided to launch the venture, and the Victory Housing Society was formed, with members drawn from ex-officers and ratings. There were no naval funds to support the scheme, but in 1933 the Admiralty agreed to sell the society a plot of land in Tipnor at a nominal sum. With a £34,000 loan from the Public Works Loan Board the society went ahead and built 132 houses to let to needy married ratings. The rent was 12s 6d a week, little if at all less than the going rate for rooms, but the standard of housing was much better.[16]

It was an admirable exercise in self-help but it barely scratched the surface of the lower deck's financial problems. The only real solution was to restore the 1931 pay cuts. In 1933 men were becoming restive over the continued application of the reduced rates now that the economy was picking up and prices had started to rise again.[17] Their restlessness was reinforced by Lord Beaverbrook's 'Grand Army of Prosperity' campaign in the *Daily Express*, which aimed at stemming 'the tide of panic pay reductions' and restoring the previous levels.[18] At the Admiralty it was noted that the campaign strengthened the men's belief all along that the cuts had been unnecessary and unwise.[19] As the secretary to the Fourth Sea Lord observed, ' [. . .] all officers are afraid that under present conditions the Navy cannot be said to be contented'.[20]

Once again there were rumours of impending trouble when the Atlantic and Mediterranean fleets met for combined exercises. Major Bassett of the Naval Intelligence Department was flown out to Gibraltar to investigate. With his flare for the dramatic he told the Commander-in-Chief, Mediterranean, that the situation was serious and that 13–15 March was when the men intended to take action unless something was done.[21] In the event nothing came of the rumours, nor was pay increased, despite the fact that the government was able to announce a 'give-away' budget in 1933. Only in the following year was half the pay cut restored, and not until 1935 was the full amount of the 1919 scale reintroduced for pre-1925 recruits.[22]

The bad odour surrounding the post-Invergordon Navy clearly affected recruitment. The numbers applying to join in the mid-'30s were satisfactory but their quality caused the Admiralty some alarm. Educational standards were not what they might have been. In 1935 well over 50 per cent of boy seamen joining had but a bare elementary school education, and there was a consequent shortage of Advanced Class boys who might be expected to specialise in signals or wireless telegraphy.[23] There was a particular shortage of artisans and artificers, and standards had to be lowered to attract sufficient mechanics.[24] The recruiting staff officer in Glasgow offered an explanation of the poor response in 1936. Labour exchanges were reluctant to display naval propaganda for fear of incurring the wrath of the unemployed in the neighbourhood, most of whom were 'socialists of the extreme type':

The political views and activities of the 'masses' in the Glasgow district is [sic] firmly believed to be the principal deterrent on Naval Recruiting in general. The great majority from whom the recruits of all branches are taken are rabidly anti-service, so much so, that there have been cases where applicants have stated that they dare not mention the fact that they were joining the Navy to anyone in their neighbourhood for fear of being 'roughed'. Warships are considered a non-productive burden to the Country and men who wish to man them are treated as 'Blacklegs'.[25]

As the Director of Naval Recruiting observed, 'We have a political bogey to contend with.'[26] Not until the threat of war began to loom in 1937–38 did the outlook improve, and only then after a concerted campaign by an enlarged body of recruiting officers.[27]

Meanwhile within the service one effect of the 1931 cuts was to dampen enthusiasm for the Navy as a career. Ratings trimmed their effort to match their pay. In the *Naval Review* it was argued that the existence of two scales had done more than anything else to lower efficiency.[28]

There was a decline of interest in promotion. In 1934 the number of leading seamen qualified and suitable for petty officer rank was below requirements, and the following year the Admiralty had to admit that it could not secure enough suitable men for the job. Ratings had to be appealed to to come forward for promotion; qualifying periods were reduced in a number of departments and the service was forced to resort to expedients such as the promotion of able seamen to 'acting leading seamen unpaid'. Those who accepted these positions even had to buy their own badges and were scornfully referred to as 'love killicks' on the lower deck.[29]

THE PROBLEM OF MORALE

Invergordon forced the Admiralty to take a long, hard look at various aspects of service life as it affected the ratings. A major review of discipline and welfare was conducted by a committee under the Second Sea Lord, Admiral Fuller. From the Admiralty's standpoint the main question was how to restore morale. Officers were extremely sensitive to signs that it was flagging, and at the end of 1931 Admiral Kelly observed that, while ship discipline was high, the behaviour of men on shore was below standard.[30] One of the problems he identified was a lack of authority among petty officers. Kelly believed that fully three-quarters of them were deficient as leaders. There was a widespread feeling that greater care in selection and training was necessary, and it was decided to give them a bigger role in the divisional system.[31]

From the standpoint of naval administration it was recognised that for far too long the Admiralty had paid little attention to personnel.[32] Latterly the Naval Personnel Committee had been largely concerned with matters of vocational training, and there was no department dealing exclusively with 'the human side of naval personnel'. In addition some notice was now taken of the long-standing complaint that too much influence was wielded at the Admiralty by civilian officials with no knowledge of sea life or sympathy with ratings.[33] In view of these factors it was decided to establish a Directorate of Personal [sic] Services based on a merger between the Naval Personnel Committee and the Manning Department. The object was to raise the status of the personnel function, and it was decided that the director of the new department should be an admiral, whereas past chairmen of the Personnel Committee had been merely captains.[34]

A strong faction at the Admiralty, including the First and Second Sea Lords, believed that what was lacking was the spirit and discipline associated with the sailing ship era. Proposals were advanced, and formally adopted, for a revival of training under sail. Four barque-rigged vessels were to be built at an estimated cost of £340,000 and would constitute a training squadron for boy seamen. It was a fair reflection of the mentality of some of those in authority that an investment of this order should have been planned in a form of training that was thirty years out of date. By contrast only £5,000 had been spared for hardship among young married ratings, an indisputable cause of low morale. However, a new Board of Admiralty was appointed in 1935, and on assuming office and learning of the scheme a horrified First Sea Lord, Admiral Chatfield, promptly cancelled it.[35]

Some officers believed that a firm disciplinary stance was the best answer. Admiral Tyrwhitt, commander-in-chief at Chatham, argued that:

[. . .] taughtened discipline is undoubtedly necessary.
There has been a tendency of recent years to minimise acts of insubordination: an air of general benevolence has prevailed [. . .] .
I believe that if this tendency is not checked there may be further trouble.[36]

Such an attitude seemed to find support at the Admiralty, instructions being issued to officers that they were 'expected to put down any further disturbance [. . .] with a strong hand'.[37] Admiral Cowan, the King's principal naval aide-de-camp, expressed himself in a similar vein:

For the last 4 or 5 years in my judgement they [the Admiralty] have failed to check a growing looseness of discipline [. . .] . As regards the men there has been far too much talk of increased privileges, comfort, food etc and too little of achievement and efficiency [. . .] .[38]

Many admirals and other senior officers agreed with him.[39] From this quarter there was little sympathy for the lower deck, who were already felt to be receiving lenient treatment. Admiral Colville, for example, criticised the Board for not resigning when the government announced there would be no reprisals against the mutineers.[40] Already too much attention was being paid to complaints. As Tyrwhitt again noted some months later:

The men are suffering from a 'grievance ventilation' mania. [. . .] It must be realised that the men do not regret Invergordon, nor are they ashamed of themselves. [. . .]
The habit of grousing has become the fashion and any grievance is better than none.[41]

Tightened discipline certainly left little scope for an independent lower-deck movement. There were still, however, some instances of collective resistance. Court-martial returns record only one case of mutinous behaviour after Invergordon, yet there were at least three separate occasions when protest action took place – on board the *Durban* in 1931, the *Guardian* in 1936 and the *Warspite* in 1937. Fearful of provoking a repetition, the Admiralty was concerned that they should be given as little publicity as possible. In the *Warspite* incident the press was asked to play the matter down, and the subsequent court of inquiry was deliberately delayed until Parliament had risen to avoid any embarrassing questions.[42] In the case of the *Guardian* the main evidence against one of the men subsequently punished was that he had been on the *Rodney* at Invergordon and under surveillance since then. Referring to the *Warspite* affair, the Commander-in-Chief, Portsmouth, was reported to be

[. . .] very strongly of the opinion that a certain spirit similar to Invergordon is proved undoubtedly to exist among a few ratings still left in the Fleet [. . .]. [. . .] we are skating on very thin ice if we pass over this occurrence without some drastic attempt to face facts.[43]

Clearly the spectre of Invergordon continued to haunt the authorities. In this climate any organised lower-deck movement would have been hard put to survive. An interdepartmental committee of the three services, the Home Office, the Treasury and MI5 kept a standing watch on the general question of subversive activities in the forces.[44] In 1934 the Incitement to Disaffection Act was passed to reinforce the draconian powers already available to the Admiralty under the Incitement to Mutiny Act of 1797. The Act was introduced to counteract the underground activities of political radicals who, according to the government, were flooding the services with their literature. An occasional Communist Party publication, *Red Signal*, circulated on the lower deck, and the Attorney General, Sir Thomas Inskip, claimed that 50,000 copies of papers and pamphlets of this nature had been produced for the consumption of servicemen in 1933 alone.[45] The Act considerably strengthened the powers of the police in combating such activity. The principal targets of the legislation were people who distributed literature as opposed to those who produced it. Search warrants were made easier to obtain and the power of magistrates was increased. To secure conviction it was enough to show that a person had in his possession a document possession of which by servicemen would be an offence. To do anything preparatory to committing an offence was also an offence.[46] In short the legislation created a hostile environment for anyone aiming to foment unrest in the armed forces. Evidently the measure was entirely effective in preventing the Communist Party from making inroads into the Navy, and although a Communist organiser was assigned to Portsmouth in the wake of the mutiny, in fours years he was unable to recruit a single active-service rating to the party.[47]

The Admiralty was ever vigilant for the slightest signs of radical activity and at times over-eager to take positive steps against miscreants. It had considered legal action against the *Daily Worker* on a charge of incitement to mutiny over the paper's treatment of the *Lucia* affair but was advised by the Director of Public Prosecutions that there were no grounds.[48] A circular letter, 'Notes on Dealing with Insubordination', was issued to officers in 1932 and reissued in 1937 following the *Warspite* affair, when renewed mass indiscipline was feared to be in prospect.[49] Meanwhile thorough surveillance of the Invergordon mutineers was maintained until at least 1933. Naval Intelligence required captains to fill in forms regularly, detailing whether certain men were known to hold Communist views or to receive Communist literature.[50] The *Guardian* and *Warspite* incidents indicate that the post-Invergordon purge of ratings with radical leanings was still under way as late as 1937. In one particularly rash instance in 1937 a stoker charged with disseminating Communist literature at Chatham was sentenced to forty days' detention as well as being dismissed 'SNLR'. The point was, of course, that the Communist Party was not an illegal body and distributing its literature was not of itself a crime. Moreover proceedings had not been instigated by the Director of Public Prosecutions, as the Incitement to Disaffection Act required. The authorities were behaving in a very arbitrary fashion, and the implications dawned on them only after the stoker had been sent to detention. What if MPs were to hear of the case and ask awkward questions about the apparent miscarriage of justice? The Admiralty was relieved to see the stoker spirited back to Civvy Street and liberty without a storm of protest in the Commons.[51]

THE REVIEW OF SERVICE CONDITIONS

The most important outcome of the Fuller committee's examination of naval welfare and discipline after Invergordon was proposals for a further revision of King's Regulations relating to the complaints procedure and for the establishment of machinery to replace the welfare conferences. As Roskill observes, relations between officers and men had been shaken, if not shattered, and the Admiralty's aim was to get back to a position where men looked to their officers rather than to outside agents or channels of collective representation to rectify grievances.[52] The proposed changes in King's Regulations were the latest in a long line of attempts to achieve that goal. The divisional system was to be strengthened, and a new article in the regulations would give men an outlet for raising complaints informally with their divisional officer, thus supplementing the existing formal procedure. Meanwhile the policy of refusing to answer parliamentary questions about lower-deck grievances directly was reaffirmed.[53]

Some senior officers felt that the new access to divisional superiors provided sufficient outlet for representations from the lower deck.[54] Others believed it would in the long run but that the men would need time to adapt to the system. Until then there would have to be another means of sounding out opinion. It had been decided to abolish the welfare system, though a final conference took place in 1932 while the details of a replacement scheme were under discussion.

In its place there was to be a Review of Service Conditions. There was never any firm official view as to what the precise aims of the review should be or how it ought to operate. As Admiral Pound later commented, it was an ill-thought-out scheme.[55] The general intention was to bring officers and men closer together by giving divisional officers and divisional petty officers a greater role in the processing of requests, and at the same time to eliminate organised pressure over particular grievances.

The original idea, as put forward by the Fuller committee, was that, on a given date, divisional officers would distribute forms to their ratings, inviting men to write down a request and return them within twenty-four hours. The divisional officers would, if necessary, hold follow-up meetings of those who happened to have made similar requests to discuss the issue further.[56] A preliminary examination and sifting would take place at a meeting of captains on the flagship. The divisional officers and petty officers would attend, along with any ratings the divisional officers might select to give evidence. Eventually the requests passed on by the squadrons and fleets would be considered by the Admiralty.[57]

From the outset there were numerous critics of the proposal.

Writing in the *Naval Chronicle*, Jimmy Lane predicted that a scheme based on personal complaints by men to officers would be doomed from the start, 'simply because the men will not take the risk of becoming, as they think, "marked men" '.[58] The Secretary to the Board of Admiralty was inclined to agree, arguing that it would generate a good deal of suspicion and ridicule:

[...] suspicion, because so many men have an innate fear that there is 'something behind' an invitation to an individual to take personal action of this kind: ridicule, because a scheme under which every man in the Navy is to be asked to think for twenty-four hours and then to make a wish may be thought to have a strong resemblance to a certain type of fairy story which generally has some ludicrous ending.[59]

However, most of the opposition within the Admiralty stemmed ultimately from the fact that there was no foolproof way of preventing the ratings from taking concerted action to press for reforms. Anything of the sort was highly unlikely in the circumstances, but there was no way of being absolutely sure. Some sections of the naval hierarchy opposed the scheme on the grounds that it was meant to be extended to seagoing ships. Admiral Chatfield, soon to become First Sea Lord, had grave doubts about this, and was supported by Admiral Kelly.[60] The Fuller committee's purpose in including those at sea was to avoid the situation with the welfare conferences where pensioners in the benefit societies were able to exert a strong influence on the requests put forward. Away at sea ratings were less open to this sort of civilian influence, and their inclusion would result in fewer 'politically motivated' proposals. Others, however, feared that inviting ships' companies to put in requests would inevitably lead to meetings on board as well. Admiral Kelly's main worry was that as soon as the review was announced the men would begin to discuss grievances together.[61] As always, the spectre of combination haunted official minds:

The chief objection to carrying out the Review in seagoing ships is that meetings will be held. There is not much objection to meetings when they are carried out under the chairmanship of the D[ivisional] O[fficer]. What we want to do is to remove as far as possible any justification for meetings without the presence of DOs.[62]

In contrast were those who wanted the review totally confined to the seagoing service. The head of the Naval Law branch argued that this would eliminate 'the outside and undesirable influences and organisations more or less inseparable from the old Home Port conferences'.[63] Whatever approach was proposed, there would always be someone at the Admiralty to see it as a recipe for subversion.

How long the review system would remain in being was another question on which opinions differed. The Fuller committee had seen it as a temporary measure until the men had got used to raising issues under the new article of King's Regulations. On further reflection it seemed to some officers that the individual complaint procedure would never suffice by itself, and, however reluctantly, the Admiralty would have to adopt a permanent routine for discovering the opinions of the lower deck *as a whole*. The new Second Sea Lord, Vice-Admiral Pound, summed up the alternatives:

It appears necessary to come to a decision whether the Admiralty review is to be looked upon as something which we should get rid of as soon as possible or as being an essential part of our organisation. [. . .]

It is considered most unlikely that requests affecting a class would ever be put forward by an individual of the right type. [. . .]

The good type of man will be unlikely to take the initiative in consulting others.

Hence, if Class Requests are put forward it will most probably be done by ratings of the sea lawyer or agitator type [. . .] .

If the representations of Class Requests will not be made in a satisfactory manner by the normal service channels, and if no outlet such as the periodical Admiralty Review exists, then it is more than probable that the men will resort to Members of Parliament, Trade Unions, etc. There may also be further attempts to establish Naval Trades Unions. [. . .]

For all the above reasons it is considered that we should perfect the organisation of the Admiralty Review on the basis of its having come to stay.[64]

The argument is revealing of official attitudes. The sort of men who voiced general complaints and requests were almost by definition troublemakers. If they were not given a safety valve to let off steam the outcome might be the formation of a lower-deck union.

However, when the review was first announced in 1932 it was proclaimed as a temporary arrangement.[65] The actual scheme departed from the Fuller proposals in that there were no provisions for lower-deck witnesses to appear before review committees. The Admiralty was careful to avoid any suggestion of 'delegate' spokesmen. All representations on behalf of the men were to be made by divisional officers. Requests were to emanate from seagoing fleets as well as shore establishments. On every ship men were to be allowed to put forward requests through divisional representatives carefully selected by the divisional officers. The requests were to be made by individuals, and no combinations or meetings were permitted for the purpose of elaborating a collective viewpoint. As far as possible the system had to be sanitised. Unlike the welfare conferences, there would be no opportunity for ratings in different ports to get together. But, as with the conferences, certain issues were excluded from the review process, including matters of policy such as the employment, distribution or training of the fleet; matters of discipline or the general arrangement of duties; and general scales of pay.[66]

There was still much apprehension at the Admiralty, and the heart-searching continued right up to the date of the review. Behind it all was a persistent fear that, despite the regulations, men might combine to present a united front. The head of the Naval Law branch believed they would still get together beforehand, and there was always the danger of an unofficial central organisation being set up to confer at the home ports and even afloat.[67] That being the case, it was suggested that the review be carried out with the fleet dispersed as widely as possible, to deny anyone the chance of establishing himself as leader.[68]

With these points in mind the Second Sea Lord was anxious for the announcement of the review to be timed carefully. It would have to be made far enough ahead to avoid claims that too little time was allowed but delayed long enough to prevent organisation: '[. . .] it is desirable to restrict opportunities for the formation of unofficial organisations [. . .]'.[69]

As one of the principal architects of the defunct welfare system Sir Oswyn Murray, Secretary to the Board, showed no enthusiasm for the new arrangement and looked back with some nostalgia to the old one:

After much thought, I am forced to the conclusion that there is no possibility of framing a safe, satisfactory scheme on this basis. [. . .]

Its natural tendency must, I think, be to concentrate the attention of the Service on a few big, expensive and possibly impracticable aspirations. If a man is given a wish once in several years, he is not likely to waste it on asking for a change in the pattern of his badge [. . .] .

The truth is that those features of the Welfare Scheme that are now criticised [. . .] have to a very large extent operated as a safeguard to the scheme [. . .] .[70]

If there were misgivings at the Admiralty, the lower deck too had their doubts, not least because the first review was at least three years distant. They took this as a sign of unwillingness to treat their grievances with any sense of urgency. Lane urged the authorities to bring the date forward.[71] In fact the very opposite happened: originally intended for 1935, the review was postponed another year because of the Abyssinian crisis.

Eventually it was held in autumn 1936. No fewer than 5,000 requests were received, covering almost every imaginable subject. The task of reviewing them would take at least three years, by which time seven would have elapsed since the procedure was inaugurated. Answers would therefore have to be given piecemeal over a period of time. This in itself posed a problem, and it was recognised that the announcement of results in batches would require a little stage-managing to prevent any one batch being too disappointing.[72] The first replies were made public in February 1937, but the process was still not complete on the eve of war in July 1939.

With major economic issues excluded, many of the proposals the Admiralty spent its time pondering were trivial. Messes would not, it was decided, be issued with a fruit knife; there would be no coloured tablecloths for broadside messes. On the other hand a teaspoon would be included in the official messtraps and a surplus boot brush omitted from the regulation service kit.[73] Most of the serious suggestions were rejected, including, of course, one that the review be widened to include such matters as pay.[74] Nevertheless their lordships were generally satisfied with the exercise and there was an air of self-congratulation about the Secretary to the Board's minute:

It [the Review] provided the Lower Deck with an excellent means of 'letting off steam'. The reputation of the Admiralty as guardians of Welfare will have improved.[75]

If the Review of Service Conditions was hardly a stirring success, it had helped the Admiralty to the end of the decade without further overt protest from below.

Yet it was hard to disguise the fact that, in economic terms, or as regards significantly improved conditions, the men had gained precious little. Any consolation would have to come from less substantive aspects of the review. As the Secretary put it:

The satisfaction caused by the giving of reasoned replies to all the requests is known to be widespread. As the requests approved are necessarily a small minority, this aspect is important.[76]

Under the welfare conference system little effort had been made to explain decisions. Now that some sort of justification was being put forward the ratings would doubtless be happy to see their requests turned down.

The Admiralty's satisfaction with the results did not leave it any more enamoured of the review. Some officials still looked forward to the day when it could be dispensed with and reliance placed on individual channels of approach under King's Regulations. Others, while recognising that periodic reviews would have to be a continuing feature of service life, argued that there should be a considerable interval between them. The general view seems to have been that they should not be held more often than every five or even six years. And, as under the welfare conference system, it was proposed to limit still further the variety of issues that could be brought up and to bar requests that had previously been turned down.[77]

From the lower-deck standpoint the review inevitably appeared in large measure irrelevant. Denied the right to advance a collective view, the men had dissipated their efforts over a wide range of relatively unimportant matters, a different proposal being put forward on average for every twenty ratings. Serious grievances about pay had been turned aside.[78] An improved allowance for married ratings in 1938 was seen as a generous increase, but it was no substitute for an all-round rise in pay and it left single men feeling resentful. In the late 1930s an able seaman received less than a farm labourer, a junior postman or a government typist under the age of twenty-one. Petty officers earned less than engineering labourers and about as much as government typists aged twenty-three. Even taking account of total emoluments in cash and kind, an able seaman got no more than about £2 14s a week, while a skilled tradesman ashore was likely to draw more than £4 6s.[79] At the Admiralty it was recognised that pay was still the biggest issue with ratings. Admiral Backhouse, the First Sea Lord, minuted in 1938:

[. . .] there cannot be the least doubt but that pay is the largest factor in the life of the vast majority. In the Navy, Leave and Food come second and third.[80]

Backhouse realised that, despite the ban on pay requests, the most significant feature of the review was that from every branch of the service proposals had come for increasing incomes by one means or another, usually dressed up in the form of extra allowances or non-substantive pay. If the review system were to continue he wondered whether some separate mechanism for keeping pay under consideration should not be devised.[81] It was the old problem that had never been tackled. And there things rested. The war intervened, no further review was ever held, and the Admiralty had still not come to terms with the central cause of recurrent unrest on the lower deck: the absence of any mechanism for processing collective complaints over pay and conditions.

The lower-deck movement in perspective

[. . .] there is no reason why men who have a collective grievance or a collective request should not represent it collectively. – Lieutenant James Callaghan, MP, speech to the National Council for Civil Liberties Conference on Democracy and the Armed Services, London, 10 November 1946

The movement towards reform must come from outside the services and this is my intention when I can resume my normal existence. It will however be necessary to enlist the sympathetic aid of progressive serving officers and of the educated thinking civilians. After this war the usually apathetic public will be 'service' minded. – Leading Telegraphist Charles Thomas, private correspondence, HMS *Capetown*, 11 October 1940[1]

Why did the reform movement appear when it did, and what was its dynamic? The movement was a product of the times, a response to changes taking place in the Navy and conditioned by developments in society at large. In the closing decades of the nineteenth century spasmodic lobbying for improvements had already taken place, but concerted agitation began only at the turn of the century, and it is convenient to date the reform movement proper from there. What caused a sudden increase in the pressure for change? A number of factors can be identified. In the first place the momentum of change in the Navy itself was being stepped up. In 1898 the first Navy Law signalled Germany's intention of becoming a naval power. From that point the struggle for supremacy was on, and the first steps were taken down the path leading to the Great War. The effect was to increase the British public's sense of dependence on the Navy and to thrust the state of the service to the forefront of politics. In this climate 'Big Navy' lobbies such as the Navy League flourished, and it was an ideal opportunity for advocates of lower-deck reforms to mount the stage and voice their case too.

Technical and organisational changes in these years, all by-products of the race for naval supremacy, contributed to the emergence of the reform movement. With Jacky Fisher as Second Sea Lord in 1902–03 the service was extensively reorganised in matters of personnel and training. There was a new dedication to technology which had repercussions on the lower deck. Improvements in gunnery and torpedoes, the introduction of wireless telegraphy and the applications of other scientific developments were all having an influence on routines. The rate of change meant that the men had to adapt. Considerable alterations were made in the methods of training and advancing them. While on the surface naval routine continued much as it always had done, in reality new skills and practices were having to be mastered, a higher all-round level of ability was being demanded and the pace of service life was quickening. In the years preceding the war the greater emphasis on battle practice and the manning of many ships with only nucleus crews led the lower deck to talk of a 'speed-up' in work.

Inevitably the effect was unsettling. Stephen Reynolds described it this way:

[. . .] changes can take place in the Navy with such disconcerting suddenness. Scientists, perhaps, working in the obscurity of a laboratory and the technical journals, invent some new thing [. . .] . In the outside world it would have to fight for recognition, and men would have time to get used to it. But should the Navy adopt it, then the Navy must forthwith adapt itself to it, and even should it affect directly only one class or branch of the personnel, nevertheless in a homogeneous service its effect will reverberate throughout the whole.[2]

Traditional methods were thus being called into question. Forward-looking, educated sailors of the younger generation welcomed the changes, wanted to be part of a sophisticated service, recognised the contribution they were making and demanded that it should be adequately rewarded.

In contrast with this technical modernisation many conditions of service remained archaic in the extreme. The Navy tended to lag a generation behind the standards of civilian society. At the turn of the century conditions on the lower deck had, in many respects, not improved since the early days of continuous service. There was deeply felt resentment over issues such as food and uniform regulations, and around these the reform movement was built.

Among the organisational changes of the decade before the Great

War were the abandonment of overseas bases at Esquimault, Trincomalee, Halifax and Jamaica, a reduction in the patrolling of distant waters, the scrapping of large numbers of obsolete small craft used for the purpose and the regrouping of forces in home waters. All this was part of the preparation for war. As far as the lower deck were concerned it meant that they were closer to home, more in touch with political and social developments and more likely to set up home ashore and take on family responsibilities. In short, they were less cut off from the rest of society, more exposed to its influence. And a major feature of Edwardian days was the rise of the Labour movement.

During the decade and a half before the Great War the position of organised labour bulked large in political debate. Unions were growing rapidly in strength and militancy, the rights of ordinary men and women were being asserted by a burgeoning socialist movement, and there were plenty of examples of working men organising collectively to defend and improve their conditions. Their influence was an important factor in the rise of the lower-deck movement. Some ratings in the artisan branches – carpenters, electricians, blacksmiths, shipwrights, plumbers and engine-room artificers – had direct links with the trade unions, while several other branches also recruited adults – who might be union members – direct from industry. Even before the end of the century the warrant officers had explored the idea of forging contacts with what appeared to be their natural allies in Havelock Wilson's National Sailors' and Firemen's Union.

Yet while developments in the trade union world set an example and conditioned the environment in which the lower-deck movement emerged, too much should not be made of its direct links with Labour. The influence among the men was never strong. Traditionally theirs was a conservative service, and though at times there might be support, as at Chatham in 1906 and Portsmouth in 1918, Labour's general anti-militarist stance meant that it often appeared as the party least likely to benefit ratings. Lower-deck radicals were more likely to identify with the Liberal Party. They understood that to the Tories the Navy usually meant ships, whereas to the Liberals it meant sailors.

Union membership on the part of the naval artisans was a legacy of their employment in civilian life. As individuals they would tend to think and act like trade unionists, but by and large the unions themselves did not seek to extend their membership within the Navy or to develop the principles of unionism among ratings. They were content to service their naval members as best they could, and gave no thought to proselytising servicemen. Thus the engineers' union was always well represented among the ranks of the engine-room artificers, but these ratings were an insular body of men and the main thrust of their policy as an organised group was to defend their relatively privileged position *vis à vis* others. If anything, it could be argued that the ERAs' attitude discredited trade unionism in the eyes of the lower deck.

On the other hand some instances of collective organisation among civilian workers carried more weight. Civil servants were beginning to form embryonic unions in the early years of the century, and ratings could see the obvious connection with their own position as State employees. More particularly workers in the naval dockyards, with whom sailors came into direct contact, appeared to enjoy certain benefits as a result of their freedom to organise. Then also, in a more faltering way, the police were beginning to demand the same right. As a uniformed service the police force shared many conditions in common with the lower deck, and the fact that they were beginning to organise ahead of the ratings served to challenge some of the arguments about the impracticality of collective organisation in a disciplined service. A rank-and-file policemen's paper edited by John Kempster had been in existence since 1893, publicising grievances and calling for the right to consult the authorities over aspects of their conditions of work. Before the Great War a separate movement led to the formation of the National Union of Police and Prison Officers, with a more aggressive approach.[3] The differences between Kempster and the police union, essentially the difference between the paths of in-house consultation and out-and-out trade unionism, prefigured a similar debate that was about to begin within the lower-deck movement. The point is that ratings were not unaware of these developments among the police, and it is tempting to see in Kempster's moderate style of campaigning a model for the approach Yexley was to adopt.

The first two decades of the century were, then, years in which notions of a democracy were in the ascendant. They were part of the international currency of ideas and began to penetrate institutions where such sentiments had never been tolerated. It is not without significance that, in the very period when the lower deck were organising in the Royal Navy, a faint echo of this development was to be heard in the German and United States navies. Before the Great War, under a regime infinitely more repressive than anything the

British ratings knew, deck officers (i.e. warrant officers) in the German navy organised a Union of Retired Deck Officers to lobby for improvements in conditions for the rank, adopting the same techniques of petitioning and pamphleteering as were used by the lower-deck movement. Limited concessions were granted before the Great War, but during the period of hostilities the German naval authorities succeeded in alienating the deck officers, their autonomous organisation was suppressed and the consequence was to be seen in the mutinies of the High Seas Fleet in 1917 and 1918.[4] The flexible, conciliatory line which from time to time the British Admiralty had taken in matters of personnel was quite lacking in Germany.

Even in the American fleet, where conditions generally surpassed those of the Royal Navy, and where in pre-war years the Secretary for the Navy had gone to great lengths to raise the status of ratings, organised effort was occasionally necessary to secure specific improvements. The lower deck had their own societies and their own press. In the early 1900s the latter had successfully campaigned to assert their civil liberties. In the course of the Great War it had argued for a system of democratic representation in which ratings would have a voice in decisions that affected them at all levels from ship to Congress. And between 1919 and 1923 a petty officers' society, whose primary function lay in the area of self-help and recreation, successfully lobbied for a pay increase for sailors.[5]

There is no sign of any direct link between these moves in the different countries, though it is worth noting that *The Fleet* kept its readers informed of developments in the US Navy. Democratic sentiments and ideals of collective organisation were free goods, available for adoption by anyone who cared to espouse them. The point is simply that the time seemed to be ripe for such ideas, independently arrived at, to take root in the three services.

What is also interesting is that the vehicle of collective organisation in each case was the sailors' benefit societies or clubs. The central role of the lower-deck societies in the reform movement is understandable in the context of British naval history. In view of the near absence of pensions for men who died or were invalided in the service, death benefit societies played a useful role and, in the case of the Warrant Officers' Society, had a history dating back more than a century. Self-help activities were second nature to naval ratings, and 'By the Navy, for the Navy' was to become the motto of the Royal Naval Benevolent Trust. Over the years the societies came to provide a focus for sailors' activities when off duty. They were recreational and social organisations, and they helped to foster a sense of solidarity among men of particular branches.

A number of benefit societies came into existence in the last two decades of the nineteenth century when various professional grievances were already coming to the fore. The societies were the obvious bodies to advance them. There were precedents for officers and men to petition the Admiralty for improvements, and some societies adopted the practice from time to time. But the ancient custom of petitioning was circumscribed by a more recent ban on combinations, hence organising a petition was, in service terms, an illegal act meriting severe punishment. At this point, in official eyes, the lower-deck societies overstepped the mark and, from being harmless affairs providing small benefits for widows, became a subversive threat to discipline.

It was at the turn of the century, with the benefit societies beginning to establish themselves, that Lionel Yexley became involved in lower-deck affairs. His arrival on the scene reflected a stirring in the ranks that was already taking place, but he was almost certainly the most important factor behind the sudden increase in the pressure for reform from 1899. Yexley's contribution through *The Bluejacket* and *The Fleet* was to argue the case for reforms in general terms that transcended the divisions between different branches of the service. Without ignoring the parochial concerns of individual groups he chose to press larger issues that were of importance throughout the Navy. In particular he set out to defend the interests of the great mass of junior ratings in the seaman and stoker branches who were not members of the benefit societies. If the reform movement was ever to be anything more than a number of small groups, each treading its own path, often in jealous competition, seamen and stokers would have to be involved. Yexley understood this well. Under him the lower-deck press was thus a force for drawing the lower deck together and making them conscious of their common interests. It was an 'All Navy' approach.

Yexley's style was to adopt a particular cause, subject it to close analysis and argue the case for the particular solution that he favoured, canvassing the support of influential people in the press, Parliament and the service itself. He would argue that the lack of any rights of representation made it essential to treat ratings as a special case. Once having achieved a degree of success, he would claim full credit for the resulting changes and then move on to another issue, hoping in the process to have generated more support for his bandwagon. This technique was largely dictated by his own economic position. Dependent entirely on his earnings from journalism, Yexley needed a large readership, and to attract this he had to project himself and his paper as the main spokesman for reform. Having achieved some prominence as a result of his early *Bluejacket* and *Fleet* campaigns he was able to extend his influence through freelance writing in a number of journals and newspapers up to 1914.

The tone was a judicious blend of angry protest over injustices and soothing sentiments of cameraderie between officers and men. In producing a purely lower-deck paper Yexley was venturing on to virgin territory: there was considerable opposition in the higher echelons of the Navy, and he had to guard against the possibility of reprisals. The needs of survival dictated a certain moderation, especially in the early years. But in any case Yexley was no wild-eyed radical: he saw solutions to the men's problems within the existing structure of the service. But it is arguable that he became even more restrained when he had established contact with Fisher and, through him, with McKenna, Macnamara and Churchill. It is hard to see how associates like these could have done other than colour his outlook. At the very least they must have confirmed his belief that change could be effected from within simply by cultivating the right people.

From 1907 onwards the lower-deck societies were producing an annual loyal appeal for reforms through their port joint committees. The petitions were of uneven quality, they suffered from a lack of continuity and were open to the criticism that they were the work of an elite group of ratings who ignored important general complaints while at times seeking to shore up the privileges of a few. Nevertheless the benefit societies and the petitioning remained the one possible means of combining to present a collective appeal. If the rather vague requests for direct representation were ever granted the lower deck would have had immediate access to the authorities. Boosted by the public attention being given to lower-deck affairs in the immediate pre-war years, the societies proliferated and their membership began to extend to junior ratings.

However, the main achievements of the pre-war years were all due at least in part to Yexley. His marshalling of support in Parliament and the press had led to a public airing of the enormously complex problem of naval victualling. It led to changes that went a long way towards allaying the complaints. Together with the benefit societies he had helped bring about reforms in clothing regulations. With their assistance he had submitted detailed proposals for a pay rise which provided the basis of the modest increase awarded by Churchill in 1912. He had won the confidence of Jacky Fisher and through him had managed to persuade Churchill of the need to democratise the service by opening up a channel of promotion to commissioned rank. His single-handed exposé of the archaic system of discipline and punishment had produced major reforms.

At every turn he had defended the rights and civil liberties of ratings, pressing for their acceptance as responsible and respectable members of society. Much of the work he was engaged in did not come to fruition until the inter-war years, but in helping to raise the consciousness of the lower deck over discrimination in these matters he was laying the all-important groundwork.

On the other hand there were a number of important weaknesses in the reform movement. Firstly, heavy reliance on the intervention of one individual in the person of Yexley left it without permanent machinery for negotiating improvements. What was equal to the occasion for a single campaign was far from adequate when the question at issue was a permanent voice in the councils of the Navy on matters of service conditions and personnel. And by this stage some ratings were concerned about more than achieving immediate substantive reforms: they wanted a continuing influence. If the societies and the joint committees were to be the means, their structure left a lot to be desired. Even though junior ratings were being recruited to membership, their numbers were still very small. By and large the societies were the creation of the petty officers and reflected the concerns of men with long years of service.

The fragmentation of the lower deck into numerous different branch organisations was another problem, and attempts at co-ordination and co-operation through the joint committees never really solved it. Some of the small but better organised societies such as the writers wielded disproportionate influence on the joint committees, and the policies the committees adopted were not always representative of the interests of the lower deck as a whole.

Finally a most important feature of the movement was the combination of active-service ratings and pensioners among the benefit societies' and joint committees' membership. This was not necessarily a weakness but it was a complicating factor where policy-making was concerned. Pensioned ratings had a vested interest in deliberations over death benefits and in representations to the Admiralty on matters such as pensions, employment opportunities for ex-servicemen and conditions relating to reservists. In the main issue – conditions of service for active servicemen – however, they had no direct interest. Yet their influence was powerful and sometimes dominant. They held office frequently, and their ability to attend meetings regularly gave them an advantage over ratings who might at any time be at sea or on a foreign station. And the fact that pensioners – with a civilian outlook – were so influential was a strong factor in the Admiralty's refusal to recognise or do business with the societies as representatives of the lower deck. To have done so would have meant treating with people over whom it had no disciplinary control.

Experience of war and contact with Hostilities Only ratings had had a radicalising influence. The success of the 1918 police strike in winning a substantial wage increase and the promise of some form of recognition for a policemen's representative organisation left important sections of the lower deck keen to improve their own material conditions and to establish a mechanism for collective representation at the Admiralty.[6] Additional impetus came from the success of another uniformed service, the fire brigades, in achieving the right to collective organisation after they had held a strike ballot in 1918. Of extra significance here was the firemen's traditionally close connection with the Navy: many were recruited from ratings who then continued as naval reservists.[7] The climate of industrial militancy in 1918–19 attracted many men strongly to the idea of collective organisation and representation. Workers in a variety of trades that had not hitherto been unionised were organising, and the government was assisting the process with its own policy of introducing Whitley Councils.

Sensing a danger to the service from the support for union-style organisation, Yexley worked hard to obtain from the Admiralty immediate substantive concessions so as to cool the situation. He stood as an independent at the 1918 general election to draw off any support from the lower deck for the Labour Party. The Admiralty's own prime concern at this stage was to forestall any form of autonomous collective organisation of ratings with outside affiliations. It had been compelled by a wave of militancy to make some concessions in 1919 and the aim now was to conduct a holding operation until things had quietened down or the time seemed ripe to counter-attack. In this it was following the strategy of the coalition government in its dealings with other groups of militant workers.[8]

Just as the police authorities, despite concessions, had no intention of sanctioning trade unionism in the force, so the Admiralty was not prepared to allow an organisation of ratings any real influence on pay and conditions of service.[9] Its position was that a disciplined service could not countenance allegiance to an external organisation which might compete with the command structure of the Navy. It was the traditional, conservative view that effective discipline meant unquestioning obedience. There was no suspicion that a complex, modern service required intelligent men in whom a tendency to question orders might be a positive virtue. If they were entitled to dissent from or query policy, even on minor issues, the whole edifice would crumble. The idea of autonomous organisation and independent representation was nothing less than creeping socialism. As such it had to be stopped at all cost.

Only as the 1920s wore on did it become clear to ratings that the welfare committees devised by the Admiralty gave them no real say. The hierarchy was able to keep their representatives at arm's length and was under no pressure to treat their requests seriously. In 1920 when some leaders of the lower deck were becoming aware of this and supporting affiliation to the trade union movement, the Admiralty ordered the societies to confine their activities to death benefit work. The militant phase was passing, authority had reasserted control of the situation, and, with the societies restricted in their operations, a process of slow strangulation began which gradually killed them off as vigorous representative organisations.

What was it that made the welfare system of the 1920s and early 1930s so unsatisfactory? From the men's point of view representation through the welfare conferences lacked a democratic infrastructure by which policies and requests could be forwarded; nor was there any continuity in the system. Their representatives were elected in officially supervised ballots where the vote was usually very low. They then went off to the annual or biennial conference to draw up a programme of requests. No general meetings of ratings were permitted, there was no system of reporting back and there was no means of holding the representatives accountable. The lower deck were without a permanent secretariat to sift and process their views and co-ordinate a coherent programme. The joint committees did attempt to perform this role unofficially from outside the service, but it could never be a satisfactory arrangement, and as we have seen the lower-deck societies were specifically barred from involving themselves in welfare work.

As time went on the number of issues that could be raised at the welfare conferences was whittled down until most subjects of any importance were barred. The Admiralty took the line that government economies in defence spending left it without the means to meet lower-deck proposals and that it would be a waste of time to allow costly requests to be submitted. There was some truth in this, but of course the weakness of the representative structure of the welfare system and the ban on certain issues simply denied the men the chance of ever campaigning openly and generating support for a reallocation of scarce resources. In effect they were being asked to trust the 'Fathers of the Fleet' to look after their best interests. Many would have much preferred the right to state their case in public through their own organisation and press the Admiralty – perhaps more vigorously than it would have liked – to fight for their interests in Whitehall.

The Admiralty might have argued in return that on many issues it was not possible to deal effectively with an organisation representing only naval ratings. Questions of pay and some conditions of service concerned the army and the Air Force too, and the government dealt with all three forces as a body. The Board argued consistently in the 1920s and '30s that improvements could not be granted in one service alone; the fact that soldiers and airmen were unorganised left ratings in a weak position and likely at times to be outmanoeuvred. The 1925 pay cuts, for example, had been bid up by the War Office over the muted protests of the Admiralty and finally imposed on sailors as well as soldiers. Similarly the ratings' persistent attempts to get the qualifying age for marriage allowances reduced to twenty-one were always met with the rebuttal that they were already entitled to them a year earlier than their army counterparts and so no change was possible.

However, the argument that the services could not treat with their own men independently ought not perhaps to be oversold. When rank-and-file pressure was strong enough in 1918–19 the Admiralty insisted in Cabinet that the Jerram committee should be a purely naval inquiry and allowed to judge the facts as they appeared in that service, unimpeded by War Office obstructionism over pay and conditions.[10] The question of whether or not to deal with an independent lower-deck organisation hinged on pragmatic considerations to do with the amount of pressure being exerted from below as much as on arguments about administrative principles and practice. The simple fact was that in the 1920s the Admiralty judged itself strong enough to resist the pressure.

Consequently the naval authorities paid less attention to personnel in the 1920s and early '30s than was prudent. This is reflected, among other things, in the downgrading of the status of the Naval Personnel Committee, the body through which welfare requests were officially processed. After the departure of its first president, Rear-Admiral Jerram, subsequent chairmen were of the rank only of captain and had to combine their personnel functions with other responsibilities. By the crucial year of 1931 the Personnel Committee was but an adjunct of the Admiralty's Department of Physical Training and Sports.

How did the inter-war welfare arrangements compare with what preceded it? The main difference was that after 1919 the system was official; previously there had been no formal arrangements at all. On that count alone it might be thought that the welfare conferences had something to offer. That was how most ratings saw it in 1919: the main advantage seemed to be that there would be no more need of anonymous petitioning and hole-in-the-corner meetings. But by the mid-1920s few were prepared to argue that there had been any advance.

Until the system was amended in 1921 the welfare delegates had been able to meet the Naval Personnel Committee and explain the reasoning behind their requests, but from 1922 that feature was dropped, and with it the essence of direct representation. Thereafter the preparation of a list of written requests for mailing to the Admiralty with no follow-up contact differed little in practice from the old method of petitioning. It was also evident that, whereas before the war the men had regarded the anonymity of petitioning as a handicap, after it, when such activities were officially permitted, there was no great willingness to become involved. Fear of being branded a sea lawyer was deeply ingrained. Many officers, especially junior ones, never really accepted the welfare system. They regarded it as a threat to discipline and morale, and ratings were justifiably wary of being identified as activists. Deprived of the protection that anonymity conferred, fewer were willing to engage in reform campaigns after the war. In this respect the psychology of the serviceman was all-important. Years of bitter experience of complaints being followed by punishment would have to be overcome before a system of open collective representation was likely to flourish.

From the Admiralty point of view also the pre-war system had much to commend it. Though officially unrecognised the lower-deck societies were tolerated, and their petitions conveyed a reasonably accurate impression of the men's thinking. More important still, Yexley's presence as a highly informed intermediary supplied an informal contact with the lower deck through which it could take detailed soundings of their mood. The fact that Yexley had the ear of people at the highest level in the Admiralty meant that policy-makers could know at once what the reaction of the lower deck would be to any of their decisions. That was no longer the case after the war. Yexley lost close touch with the men, and equally there was no Fisher, Churchill or Macnamara to intercept rumbles of discontent.

Why then did the lower-deck movement collapse? In the first place, many of the glaring disabilities under which ratings had laboured for so long had been put right by the early 1920s. The Jerram committee's inquiry resulted in a relatively large pay increase in 1919, and if this did not give immediate satisfaction all round it appreciated in value as the cost of living began to fall in the 1920s. Together with the fact that certain monetary allowances were indexed to the cost of living, it served to take the edge off demands for better remuneration. In addition a number of wartime concessions on matters such as uniform and marriage allowances were made permanent. There were to be no further milestones, but occasional improvements eliminated minor grievances and helped to make life more tolerable. In general the old pressing call for reform was absent.

In any event, circumstances were scarcely favourable. Post-war retrenchment, cuts in all forms of military spending, reductions in the size of the service, together with the swelling ranks of the unemployed outside the dockyard gates, made ratings appreciate simply having employment. The main function of an organised lower-deck movement in this situation was to defend existing benefits. And it was hard to generate enthusiasm for a mere defence of the *status quo*.

If the example of civilian unionisation had once been influential, such examples were no longer in evidence. From 1922 even well organised industrial workers with a tradition of unionism were hard put to keep their organisations intact. During the next ten years membership fell by half, and in many cases they were forced into a collaborative relationship with employers merely to survive. It was hardly an atmosphere in which notions of vigorous democracy and ideals of collective organisation were likely to flourish. With this situation confronting civilian labour, how much more unlikely was it that servicemen, in their exposed position, would be able to maintain a thriving, independent organisation.

The position of the benefit societies changed, and with this went their capacity for acting as the organisational base of the lower-deck movement. Before the war they had organised the petitioning while the Admiralty turned a blind eye. After the war the authorities took a much firmer line, and the December 1920 Fleet Order confining the societies to their benefit functions left no room for doubt about their legal position. Henceforth they were granted official recognition for their benefit work, but their scope for wider agitation was considerably reduced. The lower-deck press and the benefit societies were kept under surveillance. The Admiralty took steps to prevent ratings raising grievances through their Members of Parliament, while at the same time men experienced difficulty in exercising their general political rights.

From 1920 onwards the movement was on a downward path, and the process was difficult to reverse. What had been its pre-war strength – the dominant influence of Yexley – had become a weakness. Yexley was a sick man. From 1918 until his death in 1933 he was subject to bouts of serious ill health. Consequently he was much less mobile than before, and unable to keep in touch with developments in the ports. The age gap between him and the new generation of ratings became more and more obvious. He was no longer fully in tune with the mood of the men, and the quality of *The Fleet* as a campaigning journal declined accordingly.

Writing about the welfare conference system in 1929, he observed that as long as it remained in being then at least it provided a safety valve and made a repetition of the 1918 strike threat impossible.[11] Yet that was precisely where it failed, and it has been one of the arguments of this book that the structural weaknesses of the welfare system, together with the other factors which in the 1920s undermined the lower-deck movement, prepared the way for mutiny in 1931. The immediate cause of the mutiny was, of course, the substantive grievance over pay and pensions. But Admiralty policy in the years before had effectively closed off such outlets as might have prevented it.

It is, perhaps, significant that among the police there were no breaches of discipline in 1931, though the economy measures affected them too and their mood was just as militant. An important difference was that the police had an advisory and consultative body, the Police Council, which included elected policemen, and this body was able to exert some influence on the government when the package of economies was being prepared. In contrast the lower deck were voiceless. Policemen were represented on the Police Council through the Police Federation, the in-house union created after the strike of 1919 as an alternative to the Police and Prison Officers' Union, membership of which then became illegal. It fell far short of what the 1918 agitation had demanded and remained a rather tame organisation, largely under official control[12] But it did have its own elected officers, a regular income, a permanent presence and a degree of continuity which the Navy's welfare delegates never enjoyed, and this may have been just enough to make it that much more effective in 1931 than anything the lower deck had access to.

Ultimately, therefore, we are forced to consider the relevance of the concept of collective organisation in a uniformed service and to ask whether the Admiralty acted against its own interests in resisting the idea of combination so vigorously. Its opposition contained two elements. Firstly, as has been suggested, the military mind recoiled from anything that affected the likelihood of commands being obeyed instantly. A permanent organisation of lower-deck ratings, perhaps competing with the naval authorities for the loyalty of the men, appeared to threaten this principle. The second point was a development of the first. One of the armed services' key roles was to act as the last line of defence against a threat to society from what were regarded as subversive movements. In the final analysis ratings had to be prepared to move against strikers in an industrial crisis, and if by any chance their own organisation were linked with the trade unions they might fail in this duty.

Yet was the movement likely to be such a threat to the establishment? The benefit societies' members and the leading activists were moderate men with a stake in society. It seems at the least unlikely that petty officers, who made up the core of this group, would have engaged in anything subversive unless positively driven to it. Certainly they were conspicuous by their absence from the war councils at Invergordon. And was it a foregone conclusion that a lower-deck organisation would affiliate to the TUC and fully identify with the aspirations of Labour? In 1918–19 contacts with the Workers' Union and the Labour movement proper never got beyond the exploratory stage and it was by no means certain that ratings would have welcomed the TUC's embrace. They were workers too and had interests in common with civilian labour, it is true, but the factors determining their economic situation were not the same. As members of the security forces, servicemen were at a premium when government resistance to the demands of militant civilians was greatest. At such times they could expect more in the way of sympathetic treatment – the reforms won in 1911–12 and 1919–20 were not unrelated to events in the industrial world – and this would tend to drive a wedge between them.

There is another way of assessing the threat to the establishment from lower-deck unionism. The case for organisation in the armed services can be argued in terms of the defence of civil liberties and as part of an active strategy of democratising society. The civil liberties argument holds that service personnel do not forego their rights as citizens; they simply take on additional responsibilities. The argument for union organisation as a means of spreading democratic ideals holds that no society with undemocratic armed forces can itself be democratic, that thoroughgoing democracy requires a restructuring of relations between leaders and rank and file in the services. The two arguments complement one another, but they can be advanced separately, and clearly the second implies a much more radical challenge to the *status quo*. Yet the self-justification of the reform movement, to the extent that such a defence was ever put forward in philosophical terms, was always along the lines of the civil liberties argument and hence capable of accommodation without restructuring the hierarchy of service relationships wholesale. Of course, had the Admiralty allowed some form of collective organisation in recognition of sailors' civil liberties it may be that their appetite for democracy would only have been whetted, and a process started that the authorities could not then stop. But on the face of it the challenge to the existing order was not as profound as it might have been.

Sophisticated arguments about democratisation for its own sake were hardly ever heard. No one in the reform movement claimed that a democratic service was a necessary support for a democratic society, or that an authoritarian structure of command represented a threat to it. This is hardly surprising. The movement was uninfluenced by the kind of radical political thought which might have favoured, for example, a citizen army or navy.

Even at the time when the lower deck were most under the influence of the Labour movement, in 1918–20, neither the trade unions nor the Labour Party had any policies for adapting the armed services to the needs of an educated democracy. The two minority Labour governments of the inter-war years left the internal organisation of the services much as they found it. Not until the late 1930s did Labour express some interest in this subject. In a preface to a book dealing with structural reform of the armed forces in 1938 the party leader, Clement Attlee, argued that citizens had a right to expect that the service ' [. . .] will be used for the defence of democracy at home and abroad and that it will be so organised that self-respecting and intelligent men will be able to find satisfaction in that service'.[13] In the following year the party's policy document on defence argued:

[. . .] the Armed Forces should not become separated from the people they serve, [. . .]. A democratic state must have democratic forces to serve it. [. . .]

A democratic force is one which will, as far as possible, reproduce in its own organisation and conditions of life the democracy of the nation it serves, [. . .] .

And went on to observe:

[. . .] undemocratic organisation, and unsatisfactory conditions of life have nevertheless continued, as in pre-war days, to a greater extent than is generally realised.

[. . .] there should be full freedom for members of the Armed Forces to join Trade Unions and professional associations [. . .] . A Labour Government would make arrangements for the ranker to have some say in the determination of his pay, and conditions of service. These should be negotiable by suitable machinery on the lines of the original Admiralty Welfare Committees. The ranker should have the right to choose and instruct his representatives.[14]

But this line of thinking emerged only late in the period under review, and barely survived in a very diluted form in the programme of the 1945 Labour government.[15]

In the absence of this sort of argument inspired by consciously democratic notions it seems not unreasonable to suggest that a measure of independent collective organisation could have been allowed without the authorities having to fear a collapse of the system of command. The point cannot, of course, be proved, but this conclusion would seem to be supported by recent experiments in armed service unionism in Western Europe. These indicate that such a development is quite compatible with military efficiency. They also demonstrate that a liberal extension of civil liberties to service personnel does not necessarily result in an uncontrollable radicalisation of the rank and file. Service unions tend to limit their interests to the professional concerns of the men, and if anything they operate as a lobby in support of national defence while displaying a moderately conservative, pro-military stance.[16] The same general point holds for the modern Police Federation, which stands as a major defender of traditional authority and law and order, despite acquiring more power and independence in the post-war years. A lower-deck union dominated by petty officers might have been expected to display a broadly similar orientation.

Only from the class-ridden perspective of the naval hierarchy could the demands of the lower deck be seen as particularly radical. The interesting thing is that, after Invergordon when the welfare machinery had been seen so obviously ineffective, the Admiralty chose not to try and reopen the safety valve by making genuine collective representation work. Instead it sought to reduce further the degree of organisation among ratings and, as an alternative, to foster the individual relationship between a rating and his officer.

In this the Admiralty appeared to be reacting to the 1931 experience in much the same way as the Metropolitan Police. The mass meetings and agitation conducted by constables against the threat of pay cuts in 1931 were regarded by the Commissioner, Lord Trenchard, as detrimental to discipline and reflecting a lingering vestige of Bolshevism. He therefore set about curbing yet further the powers of the Police Federation. Mass meetings were prohibited and the allowable number of branch meetings was reduced.[17] Likewise in the Navy there was a deliberate attempt to fragment the lower deck in the Review of Service Conditions under which all manner of meetings to discuss requests and grievances were prohibited and the whole idea of the lower deck as a collectivity was denied. Taken in conjunction with the stiffening of discipline for those suspected of agitation, and the passing of the Incitement to Disaffection Act, restricting the literature that could be brought to the men's attention, it amounted to a much more authoritarian regime than under the welfare conference system.

From the point of view of substantive conditions of service the Navy was much improved over what it had been at the turn of the century. But in terms of their scope for acting in combination and pressing a collective viewpoint ratings were severely disadvantaged, and the slow progress in achieving further amelioration must, in large measure, be attributed to this. Writing in 1975 about the post-second world war

Navy, a former First Sea Lord, Admiral of the Fleet Sir Peter Norton-Hill reflected:

[. . .] it seems inconceivable that long overdue reforms in conditions of service should have taken so long to set in motion. Not until ten years after the end of the Second World War was the two or three year commission away from families reduced to twelve months and then, much later, to nine months. Married Quarters, tolerable living conditions ashore and afloat, and many other amenities long and properly taken for granted by the other two Services, took many years to become a reality.[18]

Even after 1945, then, the Navy lagged behind social changes already normal elsewhere. But such a state of affairs is 'inconceivable' only if no regard is paid to the history of the service. The foregoing chapters are testimony to the causes of the tardiness of reform of ratings' conditions in the pre-war years. Whether or not adequate machinery exists even now to ensure that service personnel can be represented collectively is for them alone to decide.

Appendix

INSTANCES OF COLLECTIVE INDISCIPLINE/MUTINOUS
BEHAVIOUR IN SHIPS AND ESTABLISHMENTS

Year	Unit	Circumstance	Source
1899	HMS *Majestic*	Widespread disaffection – gun sights thrown overboard.	*The Bluejacket*, January 1899
1900	HMS *Barfleur*	Protest over lack of leave – gun sights thrown overboard – six men court-martialled, sentenced to ninety days' to one year's hard labour.	Court Martial Returns, 1901
1900	HMS *Alexandra*	Protest over too much cleaning work – gun sights thrown overboard.	*Naval Chronicle*, 1 February 1901
1901	HMS *Magnificent*	Ill feeling towards an officer following excessive punishment – gun parts thrown overboard – four men discharged to barracks for punishment.	*Naval Chronicle* 26 October 1901
1903	HMS *Ramillies*	Gun sights thrown overboard – four men court-martialled, sentenced to two years' hard labour and dismissal.	Court Martial Returns, 1903
1904	HMS *Cornwallis*	Gun sights and gun locks thrown overboard – four men court-	Court Martial Returns, 1904

Year	Unit	Circumstance	Source
		martialled, sentenced to two years' hard labour and dismissal.	
1904	HMS *Astraea*	Gun sights thrown overboard – one man court-martialled, sentenced to two years' hard labour and dismissal.	Court Martial Returns, 1904
1905	HMS *Hyacinth*	Collective refusal to work – five men court-martialled, sentenced to six to twelve months' hard labour and dismissal.	Court Martial Returns, 1905
1906	HMS *Fox*	'Government property' thrown overboard – four men court-martialled, sentenced to ninety days' to fifteen months' hard labour and dismissal.	Court Martial Returns, 1906
1906	Portsmouth Barracks	Disturbances following unauthorised order – thirteen men court-martialled, sentenced to forty-two days' to five years' hard labour and dismissal.	Court Martial Returns, 1906
1906	HMS *Carnarvon*	Gun sights thrown overboard – two men court-martialled, sentenced to two years' hard labour and dismissal.	Court Martial Returns, 1906
1907	HMS *Highflyer*	Pinnace falls cut, gun sights thrown overboard and abusive letter written about captain – two men court-martialled, sentenced to twelve and twenty-four months' hard labour and dismissal.	Court Martial Returns, 1907

Year	Unit	Circumstance	Source
1908	HMS *Gibraltar*	Gun parts thrown overboard – one man court-martialled, sentenced to two years' hard labour and dismissal.	Court Martial Returns, 1908
1908	HMS *Amethyst*	Gun part thrown overboard – two men court-martialled, sentenced to twelve and twenty-four months' hard labour and dismissal.	Court Martial Returns, 1908
1909	HMS *Hannibal*	Unrest over general stoppage of leave, gun parts thrown overboard.	*Naval Chronicle*, 19 June 1909
1909	HMS *Furious*	Excessive summary punishments provoke mass refusal of duty.	*The Fleet*, November 1909. Log of HMS *Furious*, Adm 53/21136
1910	HMS *Leviathan*	Lack of leave and overwork provoke large-scale refusal of duty and refusal to clear lower deck. Sixty to seventy men arrested and four men court-martialled, charged with making mutinous assembly; sentenced to two years' hard labour and dismissal.	*Naval Chronicle*, 25 December 1909. Court Martial Returns, 1909
1910	HMS *Irresistible*	Lack of leave and system of punishment led to lower-deck demonstration of disapproval and gun sights thrown overboard.	*Naval Chronicle*, 19, 26 March 1910
1910	HMS *Mars*	Lack of leave provokes collective refusal of duty and attempts to break out of ship.	*Naval Chronicle*, 25 November 1910, 3 February 1911; *The Fleet*, February 1911
1911	Home Fleet (First and Second	Mass leave-breaking in protest at general	*The Fleet*, August 1911

Year	Unit	Circumstance	Source
	Divisions)	restriction of leave.	
1911	HMS *Natal*	Stokers refuse duty – seven men court-martialled, sentenced to six to nine months' hard labour and dismissal.	Court Martial Returns, 1911
1911	HMS *Lord Nelson*	Collective disobedience of a lawful command – three men court-martialled, sentenced to four months' hard labour and dismissal.	Court Martial Returns, 1911
1913	HMS *Chatham*	Overwork and excessive punishments provoke mass leave-breaking.	*Daily News*, 29 December 1913. *Naval Chronicle*, 2 January 1914
1914	HMS *Newcastle*	Collective insubordination, Marines called out to protect officers – five stokers court-martialled and sentenced to detention (sentence later quashed).	*The Fleet*, April–May 1914. Log of HMS *Newcastle*, Adm 53/52527
1914	HMS *Zealandia*	Excessive punishments lead to mass refusal of duty – twelve stokers court-martialled on charge of mutinous assembly and wilful disobedience, eight men sentenced to two years' hard labour and dismissal (later quashed).	Court Martial Returns, 1914
1916	HMS *Psyche*	Collective refusal of duty – seven stokers court-martialled, sentenced to twelve to twenty-four months' hard labour and dismissal.	Court Martial Returns, 1916
1916	*Teutonic* (auxiliary ship)	Discontent over pay – eight men court-martialled on charge of	Court Martial Returns, 1916

Year	Unit	Circumstance	Source
		non-violent mutiny, sentenced to two years' hard labour and dismissal.	
1916	HMS *Dartmouth*	Refusal to carry out punishment – four men court-martialled for disobedience of a command, sentenced to twelve months' hard labour.	Court Martial Returns, 1916
1917	HMS *Fantome*	Collective disobedience – seven men court-martialled, sentenced to twelve months' detention.	Court Martial Returns, 1917
1917	HMS *Fantome*	Twelve stokers court-martialled on charge of non-violent mutiny, sentenced to twelve months' hard labour and dismissal.	Court Martial Returns, 1917
1917	HMS *Amphitrite*	Excessive punishments cause sixty-two men to refuse duty – eight men court-martialled on charges of non-violent mutiny, sentenced to eighteen to twenty-four months' hard labour (subsequently reduced).	Court Martial Returns, 1917
1917	HMS *Resolution*	Grand Fleet unrest – two men court-martialled on charges of combining to write letters referring to an anonymous petition – sentenced to loss of good-conduct medals and badges.	Court Martial Returns, 1917
1919	Grand Fleet (minesweepers)	Refusal to put to sea in protest over low pay – £2 per week bonus conceded to auxiliary crews.	*Naval Chronicle*, 10 January 1919

Year	Unit	Circumstance	Source
1919	HMS *Kilbride*	Refusal of duty and red flag hoisted – eight men court-martialled on charges of non-violent mutiny, sentenced to ninety days and two years' hard labour and dismissal.	Court Martial Returns, 1919
1919	Sixth Battalion Royal Marines	General dissaffection in north Russia results in wholesale refusal of duty – eighty-seven men court-martialled on charges of insubordination and refusal of duty, thirteen sentenced to death, twenty to five years' penal servitude, fifty-one to two years' hard labour (all subsequently reduced).	*Naval Chronicle*, 26 December 1919
1919	HMS *Cicala*	General refusal of duty in Baltic service.	Kenneth Edwards, *The Mutiny at Invergordon*, 1937
1919	HMS *Vindictive*	Demonstration on board over lack of leave after Baltic service. Equipment sabotaged – two men court-martialled on charges of joining a mutiny accompanied by violence, sentenced to five years' penal servitude.	Court Martial Returns, 1919
1919	HMS *Delhi*	Refusal of duty as a result of general grievance over food and conditions in Baltic service – one man court-martialled on charge of joining a mutinous assembly and uttering words of sedition,	W. N. Basford, Acc 00669/19, Imperial War Museum

Year	Unit	Circumstance	Source
		sentenced to eighteen months' hard labour and dismissed.	
1919	First Destroyer Flotilla	Baltic service – mass refusal to sail – ten men court-martialled, charged with desertion and non-violent mutiny, sentenced to twelve to twenty-four months' hard labour and dismissal.	Court Martial Returns, 1919
1920	HMS *Pembroke*	Mutinous assembly – one stoker court-martialled on a charge of leading this, sentenced to two years' hard labour and dismissal.	Court Martial Returns, 1920
1921	HMS *Hood*	Suspicion of mutiny in preparation, two men court-martialled on charge of mutinous practice, one man charged with concealing a mutinous practice and one man charged with inciting men to commit an act of mutiny – last sentenced to three years' penal servitude.	Court Martial Returns, 1921
1931	HMS *Lucia*	Collective refusal of duty – twenty-seven men arrested – four men court-martialled, sentenced up to six months' hard labour (later commuted).	Court Martial Returns, 1931
1931	Atlantic Fleet	Mutiny over reduction in pay by upwards of 12,000 ratings – no courts martial – over twenty-four ratings subsequently dismissed.	Adm 178/110–14

Year	Unit	Circumstance	Source
1931	HMS *Delhi*	Refusal of duty by afternoon watch in sympathy with action of men at Invergordon.	Adm 178/73
1931	HMS *Durban*	Collective insubordination – some ratings dismissed SNLR.	Adm 12/1710
1936	HMS *Guardian*	Refusal of duty by twenty men in protest over excessive work, poor food and cramped living conditions – one man court-martialled for endeavouring to incite mutiny, sentenced to twelve months' hard labour and dismissal.	Court Martial Returns, 1936
1937	HMS *Warspite*	Protest over lack of leave leads to disturbance on board, Marines called out against ratings – three men dismissed without court martial, nine men posted overseas.	Adm 178/190–91

Notes

INTRODUCTION

1   Norman E. Saul, *Sailors in Revolt* (Lawrence, Kansas, The Regents Press of Kansas, 1978); Daniel Horn, *The German Naval Mutinies of World War I* (New Brunswick, N.J., Rutgers University Press, 1969).
2   In 1885 the basic period of engagement was extended to twelve years, meaning a full naval career of twenty-two years.
3   Eugene L. Rasor, *Reform in the Royal Navy* (Hamden, Conn., Archon Books, 1976). This book overstates the degree of *real* change in conditions between 1850 and 1880.
4   E. C. Millington, *Seamen in the Making* (Potter, 1935), pp. 14–15.
5   Sir W. Laird Clowes, *The Royal Navy*, vol. VII (Sampson Low, 1903), pp. 72–4.
6   Peter Kemp, 'The Royal Navy', in S. Nowell-Smith (ed.), *Edwardian England, 1901–14* (Oxford University Press, 1964), p. 490.
7   Commander Harry Pursey, 'From lower deck to quarter deck, 1818–1937', *Brassey's Naval Annual*, 1938, p. 87.
8   Lord Charles Beresford, *The Memoirs of Lord Charles Beresford* (Methuen, 1914), pp. 120–1.
9   Lionel Yexley, *The Inner Life of the Navy* (Pitman, 1908), p. 178.
10 *Ibid.*, p. 38.
11 Millington, *Seamen in the Making, op. cit.*, p. 79; Arnold White, *The Navy and its Story* (Macdonald & Evans, 1911), p. 101; Admiral Sir John Fisher, 'State education in the Navy', March 1906, quoted in R. F. Mackay, *Fisher of Kilverstone* (Oxford, Clarendon Press, 1973), p. 427.
12 Commander C. N. Robinson, *The British Fleet* (Bell, 1894), p. 143.
13 E. H. Phelps Brown, *The Growth of British Industrial Relations* (Macmillan, 1965), pp. 44–55; 334.
14 *The Fleet*, May 1913, p. 141.
15 Adm. 116/1893, Public Record Office, London.
16 Sidney Knock, *Clear Lower Deck* (Allan, 1933), p. 24.
17 *Ibid.*, pp. 25–6; Sir Sydney Fremantle, *My Naval Career* (Hutchinson, 1949), p. 77.

18   Fisher to Lord Selborne, 5 August 1902, Fisher Papers, National Library of Scotland; Assistant Secretary to the Board of Admiralty, minute, 17 May 1923, Adm. 167/68.
19   *The Fleet*, August 1909, p. 175.
20   *Ibid.*, June 1915, p. 164; October 1916, p. 307; December 1916, p. 367.
21   George Crowe, *The Commission of HMS Terrible* (Newnes, 1903), pp. xv–xvi.
22   *The Fleet*, September 1912, p. 591.

ONE
The origins of the reform movement

1   *Naval Warrant Officers' Journal*, May 1910, p. 58; October 1926, pp. 183–4. Its name was subsequently changed to the Naval Warrant Officers' Death Benefit Association.
2   Lewis Hanbidge, *W. Stoddard: a Biographical Sketch* (Westminster Press, 1930), p. 16.
3   *Register of Friendly Societies*; *The Fleet*, August 1914, p. 231; March 1906, p. 85; October 1920, p. 174; *The Bluejacket*, September 1900, p. 578; *Naval Chronicle*, 20 April 1902.
4   *Naval Chronicle*, 15 December 1900; 12 January 1901; 11 January 1902.
5   In the 1890s there was a Painters' Society in existence at Portsmouth, but no trace of it occurs after the turn of the century. *Reports, 1893*, in H. D. Capper, *Devonport Record*, 1889–94, Pursey Collection. This is a collection of newspaper cuttings and reports to the Warrant Officers' Society by Capper in his capacity as General Secretary.
6   Harry Pursey, 'From petitions to reviews: the presentation of lower-deck grievances', *Brassey's Naval Annual*, 1937, p. 97.
7   *Ibid.*, p. 99.
8   C. N. Robinson, *The British Fleet*, *op. cit.*, p. 363.
9   Pursey, 'From petitions to reviews', *op. cit.*, p. 98.
10   Later to become Article 11.
11   Pursey, 'From petitions to reviews', *op. cit.*, p. 99.
12   *Ibid.*, p. 100.
13   *Naval Chronicle*, 11 April 1903; *The Fleet*, November 1913, p. 338.
14   *Naval Chronicle*, 26 October 1901; interview with Pursey, 5 May 1972; David Dougan, *The Shipwrights* (Newcastle upon Tyne, Graham, 1975), pp. 36–7, 95–6, 106.
15   Fisher to Churchill, 11 November 1911, Churchill Papers, Churchill College, Cambridge.
16   See in particular *The Admiralty and Horse Guards Gazette*, April–December, 1890. Always a self-seeker, Capper later offered to retire from the service and become full-time agent for the Warrant Officers' Society at a guaranteed salary of £100 p.a. for ten years and additional payment at the rate of 5s for each article he got published and 10s for articles published in London dailies. Capper to W. Bacon

(chairman of the Warrant Officers' Society), 21 October 1893, Pursey Collection.

17   *Parliamentary Debates*, 3, vol. CCCL, 2 March 1891, cols. 1978–81.
18   *Naval and Military Record*, 13 March 1891.
19   Capper, Reports, 1891, *Devonport Record, op. cit.*
20   Capper, Reports, 25 January 1892, *Devonport Record, op. cit.* With evident satisfaction Capper wrote in his cutting book, 'Kearley and Morton were put in for Devonport (1892). Consequence of this Captain Price, who sold us, never again sat in Parliament.'
21   *Federation of all Ranker Societies RN*, in Capper, Reports, 1893, *Devonport Record, op. cit.*
22   Capper, Reports, 16 November 1893, *Devonport Record, op. cit.*
23   Capper, Reports, April 1894, *Devonport Record, op. cit.*
24   Pursey, 'From petitions to reviews', *op. cit.*, pp. 99–100; *The Bluejacket*, May 1899, p. 186; September 1900, p. 578. Many of the claims made by Capper in his book *Aft – from the Hawsehole* (Faber & Gwyer, 1927) about reforms achieved in this period are exaggerated.
25   *The Fleet*, February 1923, p. 20; Capper, *Aft – from the Hawsehole, op. cit.*, p. 131; *Naval Warrant Officers' Journal*, December 1934, p. 179.
26   V. L. Allen, 'The National Union of Police and Prison Officers', *Economic History Review*, vol. XI, No. 1, 1958, pp. 133–4.
27   *The Bluejacket*, February 1900, pp. 403–4.
28   *Ibid.*, July 1899, p. 222.
29   *Ibid.*, February 1900, p. 395.
30   *Ibid.*, September 1900, p. 559.
31   *Ibid.*, July 1899, p. 222.
32   *The Fleet*, December 1931, p. 224.
33   *The Bluejacket*, April 1900, p. 447.
34   *Ibid.*, July 1900, p. 511; *The Fleet*, March 1906, p. 68; November 1910, p. 262; August 1928, p. 143.
35   *Masters Ltd, Annual Report*, 1899, Pursey Collection.
36   *The Bluejacket*, November 1899, p. 317.
37   *Ibid.*, August 1900, p. 546.
38   *The Fleet*, October 1929, p. 174.
39   *Ibid.*, September 1910, p. 196; December 1931, p. 225.
40   *Ibid.*, April 1928, p. 71.
41   *Ibid.*, September 1912, p. 590.
42   Fisher to Yexley, 30 July 1912, Fisher Papers, 2199, National Library of Scotland.
43   *The Fleet*, May 1905, p. 10; Charles Walker, *Thirty-four Years at the Admiralty* (Lincoln Williams, 1933), p. 13.
44   *The Fleet*, March 1906, p. 82.
45   *The Bluejacket*, November 1900, p. 608.
46   *Naval Warrant Officers' Journal*, February 1900, pp. 22–3; September 1903, p. 105; *The Bluejacket*, March 1900, pp. 425–6.
47   *Naval Chronicle*, 28 April 1900.

48   *The Fleet*, September 1905, p. 155; May 1912, p. 458; *History of the Ships' Stewards' Society*, (RN Stores Branch Benevolent Society, 1972), mimeographed.
49   *Register of Friendly Societies*.
50   *Jubilee History* (Portsmouth, Writers' Society, 1937).
51   *Naval Chronicle*, 11 January 1902, 16 January 1904.
52   *The Fleet*, March 1906, p. 85.
53   *Ibid.*, May 1921, p. 74.
54   *Ibid.*, September 1906, p. 265.
55   *Naval Chronicle*, April 1906, p. 121.
56   *Naval Chronicle*, 31 March 1906.
57   *The Fleet*, May 1908, pp. 140–2.
58   *Naval and Military Record*, 10 November 1904.
59   *Naval Chronicle*, 19 November 1904.
60   *The Fleet*, February 1906, pp. 36–7; March 1906, p. 82.
61   *Ibid.*, February 1907, p. 62; December 1916, p. 360.
62   *Ibid.*, February 1913, p. 53; *Naval Chronicle*, 8 August 1908.
63   *The Fleet*, March 1912, p. 393.
64   *Ibid.*, November 1912, p. 666.
65   *Ibid.*, April 1909, p. 86.
66   *Ibid.*, September 1926, p. 176.
67   *Ibid.*, March 1906, p. 85.
68   *Ibid.*, June 1931, p. 107.
69   *Ibid.*, April 1909, pp. 82, 86. The man lost one badge and was threatened with dismissal from the service; when Yexley proposed to have the matter raised in Parliament the man was drafted to the East Indies at twenty-four hours' notice to get him away from any possible inquiry. Lionel Yexley, *Our Fighting Sea Men* (Paul, 1911), pp. 248–50.
70   *The Fleet*, December 1905, p. 248.
71   *Naval Chronicle*, 16 February 1907.
72   *The Fleet*, December 1906, p. 369; March 1907, p. 77.
73   *Ibid.*, December 1907, p. 388; May 1908, p. 146.
74   Fisher to Yexley, 1 August, 11 December 1909, Fisher Papers, 1954, 2004; Yexley to McKenna, 4 September 1911, Yexley Papers, Pursey Collection.
75   *The Fleet*, January 1923, p. 2.
76   *Ibid.*, June 1928, p. 101.

TWO

The Yexley–Fisher reforms

1   In 1870 an Admiralty Committee on Victualling had failed to agree on a general assessment of the system, but one committee member's report pointed to the fact that the feeding arrangements encouraged the men to smoke in order to allay hunger. That system remained unchanged in 1900. W. E. Clayton, 'Victualling the Navy – as it was

and as it is', *Brassey's Naval Annual*, 1936, p. 94.

2   *Report of the Committee on Navy Rations*, 1901, *op. cit.*, p. 35.

3   See the letter from a ship's cook, *Naval Chronicle*, 14 December 1901.

4   *Report of the Committee on Naval Cookery*, 1905, pp. 6, 11–12, Pursey Collection. The 1870 Committee on Victualling reported: 'The Ship's Cooks generally know nothing about cooking in the proper acceptation of the term.' Following the inquiry a School of Cookery was established at Portsmouth in 1873. But it was another thirty years before similar schools were opened at Chatham and Devonport. Cited in *Report of the Committee on Naval Cookery, op. cit.*, pp. 3, 8.

5   Yexley, *The Inner Life of the Navy, op. cit.*, p. 222; *Report of the Committee on Navy Rations*, 1901, *op. cit.*, p. 38. *The Bluejacket*, August 1899, p. 245; *The Fleet*, August 1907, p. 244; September 1907, p. 278.

6   *The Bluejacket*, September 1899, p. 270.

7   *Ibid.*, November 1899, pp. 318–19.

8   *Ibid.*, October 1899, p. 295.

9   *Ibid.*, August 1900, p. 548.

10 *The Fleet*, November 1909, pp. 252–4. One witness before the Committee on Canteen and Victualling Arrangements claimed that Maltese bumboatmen went as far as to furnish naval officers' houses free of charge. Minutes of evidence, *op. cit.*, p. 76.

11 *The Bluejacket*, August 1900, p. 534. In evidence to the Login Committee on Naval Victualling in 1906 ex-master-at-arms George Crowe was to relate how he had seen thirty petty officers from a ship taking bribes from a bumboatman's agent in the Prince of Wales Hotel, Chatham. On one occasion he himself had been offered £500 to use his influence to get rid of one canteen operator and have him replaced by another. See also Commodore Stopford, evidence to the Committee on Canteen and Victualling Arrangements (the Login Committee), 1907, pp. 90–2, Adm. 1/7880.

12 *The Fleet*, March 1906, p. 70.

13 *The Bluejacket*, September 1899, p. 271.

14 *Ibid.*, May 1900, p. 462.

15 *Ibid.*, June 1899, p. 197.

16 *Ibid.*

17 *Parliamentary Debates*, 4, vol. LXVIII, 16 March 1899, col. 1105; *United Service Gazette*, 3 June 1899, p. 431; *Clarion*, 23 September, 7, 14, 28 October 1899; *Truth*, 8 February 1900, pp. 304–5; 15 February, p. 368.

18 *Parliamentary Debates*, 4, vol. LXXIX, 2 March 1900, col. 1519; vol. LXXX, 9 March 1900, cols. 514–15.

19 Hudson Kearley, 1856–1934. Director of the grocery firm of Kearley & Tonge. Elected to Parliament with the support of the Warrant Officers' Society. Made Parliamentary Secretary to the Board of Trade in 1905 and created Viscount Devonport in 1917.

20 *Parliamentary Debates*, 4, vol. LXXX, 8 March 1900, cols. 412–13.

21 *Naval Chronicle*, 17 March 1900.
22 *Daily Leader*, 18, 20–25, 27–31 August 1900.
23 *Report of the Committee on Navy Rations*, 1901, *op. cit.*, pp. 3–4; *The Fleet*, June 1905, p. 45.
24 *The Bluejacket*, October 1900, pp. 581–2.
25 *Report of the Committee on Navy Rations*, 1901, *op. cit.*, pp. 17, 22, 35.
26 *Ibid.*, p. 16, pp. 50–1.
27 *Ibid.*, p. 32.
28 *Naval Chronicle*, 2 January 1904.
29 *Parliamentary Debates*, 4, vol. CLXII, 2 August 1906, cols. 1341–2.
30 *Report of the Committee on Naval Cookery*, *op. cit.*, pp. 5–6.
31 *The Fleet*, May 1911, p. 116.
32 *Ibid.*, June 1906, p. 163.
33 Yexley, *Inner Life of the Navy*, *op. cit.*, p. 251.
34 *The Fleet*, January 1907, p. 23.
35 *Ibid.*, September 1906, p. 273.
36 *Ibid.*, June 1906, p. 167; August 1906, p. 242.
37 *Ibid.*, January 1906, p. 12.
38 *Naval Warrant Officers' Journal*, September 1903, p. 105.
39 *Parliamentary Debates*, 4, vol. CLVI, 30 April 1906, col. 228.
40 Murray to Yexley, 5 May 1906, Yexley Papers, Pursey Collection.
41 *Parliamentary Debates*, 4, vol. CLVII, 24 May 1906, cols. 1444–9.
42 *The Fleet*, October 1930, p. 188.
43 *The Times*, 26 June 1906.
44 No copy of this letter has survived. Yexley referred to it several times in *The Fleet*, and it seems likely that this first meeting took place in June or July 1906.
45 *The Fleet*, June 1931, p. 107.
46 *Report of the Committee on Canteen and Victualling Arrangements*, *op. cit.*, p. 1; *The Fleet*, November 1906, p. 341.
47 *Report of the Committee on Canteen and Victualling Arrangements*, *op. cit.*, p. 2.
48 *Ibid.*, pp. 8–9, 17.
49 *The Fleet*, October 1909, p. 220.
50 Admiralty circular letters, 103 V586/1907, 31 August 1907; 109 V586/1907, 4 September 1907. These are reproduced as appendices I and II of Yexley, *Inner Life of the Navy*, *op. cit.*
51 *The Fleet*, February 1908, p. 38.
52 *Ibid.*, November 1907, p. 342.
53 Yexley, *The Inner Life of the Navy*, *op. cit.*, p. 163.
54 *Ibid.*, p. 320.
55 *Naval and Military Record*, 10 March 1904; *Illustrated Daily Mirror*, 21 March 1904.
56 'Blacksheesh in the Navy', *Truth*, 14 April 1904, pp. 918–19.
57 Lionel Yexley, 'The bluejackets and the tailors', *Nineteenth Century*, June 1904, p. 1034.

58 *Naval Chronicle*, 8 October 1904.
59 *The Fleet*, May 1905, p. 8.
60 *Naval Warrant Officers Journal*, August 1903, p. 89.
61 *The Fleet*, May 1905, p. 9.
62 *Ibid.*, July 1905, pp. 89–90.
63 *Ibid.*, June 1906, p. 163; March 1907, p. 80; April 1907, pp. 111–12.
64 *Ibid.*, May 1907, p. 150.
65 *Parliamentary Debates*, 4, vol. CLXXI, 14 March 1907, col. 269; vol. CLXXIV, 27 May 1907, col. 1305; vol. CLXXV, 11 June 1907, cols. 1276–77.
66 *The Fleet*, April 1907, p. 114; February 1908, p. 57.
67 *Naval Chronicle*, 21 May 1910.
68 *The Fleet*, October 1910, p. 238; September 1911, p. 204.
69 *Ibid.*, October 1913, p. 304; *Report of the Committee on Naval Discipline*, 1912, p. 3, Admiralty Library.
70 *Report of the Select Committee on the Naval Discipline Act*, HC 421 (HMSO, 1956), p. 8.
71 *The Naval Discipline Act and its Application*, lecture by the Deputy Judge Advocate of the Fleet, 1929, p. 1, Pursey Collection.
72 *King's Regulations and Admiralty Instructions*, vol. 1, 1939, Article 543.
73 *Parliamentary Debates*, 4, vol. CXXXVIII, 19 July 1904, col. 412; Alan Skelley, *The Victorian Army at Home* (Croom Helm, 1977), pp. 150–1.
74 *The Bluejacket*, December 1899, p. 343; *Parliamentary Debates*, 4, vol. LXXXI, 2 April 1900, col. 943.
75 *Parliamentary Debates*, 4 vol. CXLII, 7 March 1905, col. 605.
76 *Ibid.*, 4, vol. CXLII, 7 March 1905, col. 527.
77 *Ibid.*, 4, vol. CIV, 28 February 1902, col. 8; *The Fleet*, May 1905, pp. 23–4.
78 *The Fleet*, July 1905, p. 77.
79 Adm. 12/1356; *Naval Chronicle*, 18 October 1902.
80 *Naval Chronicle*, 31 May 1902.
81 *Reynolds's Newspaper*, 2 October 1904.
82 *Naval Chronicle*, 23 April 1904.
83 *Parliamentary Debates*, 4, vol. CXXXVII, 5 July 1904, col. 636.
84 *Ibid.*, 4, vol. 138, 26 July 1904, cols. 1202–3.
85 *Naval Chronicle*, 14 October 1905.
86 *Parliamentary Debates*, 4, vol. CLII, 21 February 1906, col. 363.
87 *Ibid.*, 4, vol. CLXV, 20 November 1906, col. 604.
88 *Truth*, 11 December 1902, pp. 1449–50; *The Bluejacket*, September 1900, p. 560.
89 *Parliamentary Debates*, 4, vol. CLVII, 24 May 1906, cols. 1456–8.
90 *Naval Chronicle*, 1 March 1902; *The Fleet*, February 1909, p. 31.
91 Yexley, *Our Fighting Sea Men*, *op. cit.*, p. 242.
92 *The Fleet*, May 1911, p. 110.
93 Yexley, *Our Fighting Sea Men*, *op. cit.*, pp. 232–3.

94   Sir Reginald Acland, 'Crime and punishment in the Royal Navy during the last fifty years', *Naval Review*, vol. XI, No. 3, August 1923, p. 480.

95   *Returns of Court Martial Punishments* (Admiralty, 1902).

96   *The Fleet*, November 1908, p. 284.

97   *Returns of Court Martial Punishments* (Admiralty, 1909).

98   *Naval Chronicle*, 4 August 1906, 25 June 1910.

99   *Crime and Punishment in the Royal Navy*, August 1920, Adm. 1/8941.

100 *Returns of Court Martial Punishments* (Admiralty, 1902, 1912).

101 Hard Labour in Naval Prisons, Adm. 116/1065A.

102 Yexley, *Inner Life of the Navy, op. cit.*, p. 98.

103 *Parliamentary Debates*, 5, vol. IV, 13 May 1909, col. 2016.

104 *Ibid.*, 5, vol. XII, 21 October 1909, col. 624.

105 Fisher to Yexley, 1 June 1909, Fisher Papers, 1939.

106 Fisher to Yexley, 13 January 1910, Fisher Papers, 2023; Fisher to McKenna, 10 December 1909, Fisher Papers, 444; *Naval Chronicle*, 27 April 1923.

THREE
The Yexley–Churchill–Fisher reforms

1   R. K. Arbuthnot, *A Battleship Commander's Order Book* (Portsmouth, Griffin, 1899).

2   Captain Stephen Roskill mistakenly refers to this as 10B, *Churchill and the Admirals* (Collins, 1977), chapter 1, ref. 17A.

3   *The Fleet*, June 1908, p. 164.

4   Judge Advocate of the Fleet, memorandum to the Committee on Naval Discipline, 5 March 1912, Adm. 116/1202; *Parliamentary Debates*, 4, vol. LXXIX, 27 February 1900, col. 1255.

5   Yexley, evidence to the Committee on Naval Discipline, *op. cit.*

6   *The Fleet*, November 1908, p. 286; June 1910, p. 125.

7   *The Bluejacket*, January 1899, p. 67.

8   *The Fleet*, July 1912, p. 525.

9   *Returns of Court Martial Punishments* (Admiralty, 1902–11).

10   *The Fleet*, May 1938, p. 81.

11   *Ibid.*, October 1909, p. 230.

12   *Ibid.*, December 1911, p. 299.

13   For example see Lieutenant A. C. Dewar, 'Principles of naval discipline', *United Service Magazine*, December 1907, pp. 225–38.

14   *The Bluejacket*, July 1900, p. 520: November 1900, p. 619; *The Fleet*, May 1905, p. 16; November 1906, p. 322; also Arnold White and E. Hallam Moorhouse, *Nelson and the Twentieth Century* (Cassell, 1905), p. 188. MAA Goldsack was to tell the Committee on Naval Discipline in 1912, 'There are not sufficient safeguards in making the ships' police. They do not make the best men, and by making the worst men they make most of the crime.' Written evidence to the Committee

on Naval Discipline, 1912, Adm. 116/1202.

15   Loyal Appeals, 1904, 1907, 1908 and 1909, Pursey Collection.
16   Naval Grievances of Petty Officers and Men, Adm. 1/7993.
17   *The Fleet*, June 1909, p. 124.
18   Admiralty circular letter 10741/1909, 5 April 1910, text given in *The Fleet*, June 1910, p. 140.
19   Yexley, 'Naval summary punishments and other things', *The Fleet Annual and Naval Year Book*, 1909, p. 36.
20   *Ibid.*, pp. 37–8.
21   *Ibid.*, p. 39.
22   Yexley, 'Courts martial and other things', *The Fleet Annual and Naval Year Book*, 1911, p. 29.
23   Yexley, *Our Fighting Sea Men*, op. cit., p. 185.
24   *Ibid.*, p. 246.
25   This point was corroborated by the Judge Advocate of the Fleet, minute, 28 June 1912, Adm. 116/3154.
26   In 1913, after seeing some cells in the Mediterranean Fleet, Winston Churchill was to remark that they '[. . .] were without exception the most disgraceful place of confinement I have ever seen in a very varied and wide experience in such matters'. Memorandum, 6 January 1913, Adm. 116/3154; Yexley, *Our Fighting Sea Men*, op. cit., pp. 187–9.
27   Yexley, *Our Fighting Sea Men*, op. cit., pp. 183, 254.
28   *The Fleet*, December 1929, p. 214.
29   *The Observer*, 1 October 1911; *Vanity Fair*, 30 August, 6, 13 September 1911; *Pall Mall Gazette*, 28 October 1911; *Army and Navy Gazette*, 23 September 1911.
30   Stephen Reynolds, 'Navy discontents', *English Review*, October 1911, pp. 513–24.
31   *Naval and Military Record*, 11 October 1911.
32   *Ibid.*, 8 November 1911.
33   *Parliamentary Debates*, 5, vol. XIX, 20 July 1910, col. 1354.
34   Arthur Marder (ed.), *Fear God and Dread Nought*, vol. II (Cape, 1956), p. 401.
35   Masterton-Smith to Yexley, 27 November 1911, Yexley Papers, Pursey Collection.
36   Yexley, evidence to the Committee on Naval Discipline, 1912, op. cit.
37   Churchill memorandum, 15 November 1911, Adm. 116/3154.
38   Prince Louis of Battenberg, minute, 9 February 1912, Adm. 116/3154.
39   Captain Fremantle, written evidence to the Committee on Naval Discipline, 18 May 1912, Adm. 116/1202.
40   Captain Leveson, evidence to the Committee on Naval Discipline, 1912, op. cit.
41   Captains Vaughan Lee and Leveson, evidence to the Committee on Naval Discipline, op. cit.
42   Leveson, evidence to the Committee on Naval discipline, 1912, op. cit.
43   PO Bellerby, CPO Elkins, LS Maitland, Chief MAA Blow and

Signalman Butler, evidence to the Committee on Naval Discipline, 1912, *op. cit.*

44   *The Fleet*, December 1929, p. 213.
45   Yexley, evidence to the Committee on Naval Discipline, 1912, *op. cit.*
46   In fact the recommendation was not followed up. Not until 1938 did ships' libraries begin to carry copies of King's Regulations. *The Fleet*, May 1938, p. 81.
47   Report of the Committee on Naval Discipline, *op. cit.*, p. 19.
48   Churchill, minute, 27 July 1912, Adm. 116/3154.
49   Admiralty circular letter 32, 7 September 1912, text given in *The Fleet Annual and Naval Year Book*, 1913, pp. 13–19.
50   *Daily Express*, 9 September 1912.
51   Head of Naval Law Branch, minute, 30 December 1912, Adm. 116/3154.
52   Admiralty circular letter 35, 27 September 1912, text given in *The Fleet Annual and Naval Year Book*, 1913, pp. 20–6. Roskill states that no concession was granted on the question of disrating. *Churchill and the Admirals*, *op. cit.*, chapter 1, ref. 17A. He is, of course, quite wrong. Before this circular letter was issued Yexley was called back off holiday to check its wording. Yexley to Stephen Reynolds, 8 October 1912, Pursey Collection. Churchill's letter of 6 September 1912 to his secretary, Masterton-Smith, indicates that he was prepared to hold up the issuing of this regulation in order to be assured by outside experts of its acceptability. Churchill Papers, Churchill College, Cambridge.
53   Admiralty circular letter 41, 18 November 1912, text given in *The Fleet Annual and Naval Year Book*, 1913, p. 21.
54   *The Fleet*, February 1914, p. 48.
55   Pursey, 'Lower deck to quarter deck', *op. cit.*, p. 87; *Naval Chronicle*, 5 April 1902.
56   Capper, *Aft – from the Hawsehole*, *op. cit.*, p. 173.
57   Fisher to Yexley, 1 August 1909, Fisher Papers, 1954; *Naval Chronicle*, 29 July 1910; *The Fleet*, December 1910, p. 276.
58   *The Fleet*, June 1905, p. 48; May 1907, p. 160; June 1907, p. 192.
59   *Parliamentary Debates*, 5, vol. XVII, 9 June 1910, cols. 896–7, 903.
60   *Daily News*, 11 June 1910.
61   *Naval and Military Record*, 22 June 1910.
62   *Ibid.*, 9 November 1910.
63   *The Fleet*, August 1910, p. 179.
64   Fisher to Yexley, 3 August 1910, Fisher Papers, 2075.
65   *The Fleet*, May 1928, p. 83.
66   *Naval Chronicle*, 23 September 1910; *The Fleet*, October 1910, pp. 224–5; 'Lower-deck promotion', *The Fleet Annual and Naval Year Book*, 1911, pp. 10–28.
67   Fisher to Yexley, 5 October 1911, Fisher Papers, 2151.
68   Fisher to Yexley, 12 October 1911, Fisher Papers, 2153.
69   Fisher to Churchill, undated (October 1911?), Churchill Papers.
70   *The Fleet*, February 1910, p. 30; *Naval Chronicle*, 27 April, 1923.

71 Harry Pursey to author, 3 May 1976. Pursey was given a first-hand account of these developments when he visited Yexley at his home at Easter 1913 to discuss the re-formation of the Seamen's Society.

72 Commissioned Rank for Warrant Officers: Precis of Case, 12 March 1912, Battenberg Papers.

73 *Parliamentary Debates*, 5, vol. XXXV, 18 March 1912, cols. 1569–70.

74 Admiralty Weekly Order 672, 9 August 1912, Adm. 182/3.

75 Mountbatten interview, 18 April 1974; Richard Hough, *Louis and Victoria* (Hutchinson, 1974), p. 256.

76 Commissioned Rank for Warrant Officers: Precis of Case, *op. cit.* Altogether there is no evidence from the previous twenty years of Battenberg's career to indicate that he ever had any interest in lower-deck commissions.

77 Walker, *Thirty-four Years at the Admiralty, op. cit.*, p. 69; *The Fleet*, September 1912, p. 584.

78 *Parliamentary Debates*, 5, vol. LI, 7 April 1913, col. 826; Battenberg speech to the boys on the TS *Warspite*, *Naval Chronicle*, 25 October 1912.

79 Harry Pursey, 'Lower deck to quarter deck', *op. cit.*, p. 91.

80 *Ibid.*, p. 96. At the outbreak of World War II three of the early mates – Figgins, Martin and Enright – were in command of cruisers. Martin served as a rear-admiral and Enright as a vice-admiral. They retired as vice-admiral and admiral respectively.

81 Winston Churchill memorandum to Cabinet, 17 October 1912, Adm. 116/1661.

82 *The Bluejacket*, June 1900, p. 495.

83 Stephen Reynolds, *Daily Chronicle*, 29 August 1912; Knock, *Clear Lower Deck, op. cit.*, p. 184.

84 *The Bluejacket*, April 1900, p. 450; September 1900, p. 573.

85 Admiralty circular letter 96, 16 August 1907, Yexley Papers; Yexley, *The British Navy from Within* (Hodder & Stoughton, 1914), p. 85; *The Fleet*, November 1907, pp. 352, 354, 359.

86 *The Fleet*, October 1914, p. 380.

87 Churchill memorandum, *op. cit.*

88 In October 1912 an Admiralty investigation into the comparative cost of living in various parts of the United Kingdom showed that Portsmouth, Sheerness, Chatham and Plymouth were the second, fourth, seventh and sixteenth most expensive towns out of some seventy surveyed. Churchill memorandum to Cabinet, 23 November 1912, Churchill Papers.

89 Churchill memorandum, 17 October 1912, *op. cit.*

90 Naval Grievances of Petty Officers and Men, Adm. 1/7993.

91 *The Fleet*, September 1910, p. 201.

92 Department of Employment, *British Labour Statistics, Historical Abstract, 1886–1968* (HMSO, 1971), table 197.

93 Rodger Charles, *The Development of Industrial Relations in Britain, 1911–39* (Hutchinson, 1973), p. 44.

94   Loyal Appeal, 1912, Yexley Papers.
95   Vice-Admiral Sir Peter Gretton, *Former Naval Person* (Cassell, 1968), p. 97.
96   *Parliamentary Debates*, 5, vol. XXXV, 18 March 1912, col. 1618.
97   *Parliamentary Debates*, 5, vol. XXXVII, 15 April, 1912, cols. 30–1; vol. XXXVIII, 15 May, cols. 1106–7; 20 May, col. 1561; *Daily Chronicle*, 4 May 1912; *Daily Mail*, 20 May 1912; *Truth*, 29 May 1912, p. 1337; *Pall Mall Gazette*, 3 June 1912; *Weekly Dispatch*, 16 June 1912; *Naval Chronicle*, 7, 28 June 1912.
98   Masterton-Smith to Yexley, 13 May 1912, Yexley Papers; Yexley to Churchill, 18 May 1912, Churchill Papers; *The Fleet*, July 1914, p. 198.
99   Fisher to Yexley, 20 May 1912, Fisher Papers, 2187.
100 Fisher to Yexley, 4 June 1912, Fisher Papers, 2189.
101 Fisher to Churchill, 7 July 1912, Churchill Papers. See also Fisher to Churchill, 21 June 1912, and to Marsh, 14 July 1912, Churchill Papers. To the latter he wrote, 'You will see the enclosed letter from Mr Yexley the Editor of *The Fleet* is very secret and very important. Ask him [Churchill] to read it and show it to the Prime Minister and Lloyd George in strict confidence [. . .] I spoke again to the Prime Minister on July 11, as to seeing Mr Yexley on increasing the pay of the Navy. He said he would.'
102 Churchill, memorandum to Head of Naval Branch, 24 July 1912, Adm. 116/1661.
103 Masterton-Smith to Yexley, 26 July 1912, Yexley Papers.
104 *The Fleet*, December 1929, p. 214.
105 Yexley to Churchill, 14 August 1912, Yexley Papers.
106 Churchill memorandum, 17 October 1912, *op. cit.*
107 Churchill memorandum, undated 1912, Churchill Papers.
108 *Daily Mail*, 1, 2 November 1912; *Pall Mall Gazette*, 11 November 1912; *Naval Chronicle*, 1 November 1912; *Parliamentary Debates*, 5, vol. LXIII, 30 October 1912, cols. 418–19; 13 November 1912, col. 1963; vol. XLIV, 18 November 1912, col. 28.
109 Churchill to Lloyd George, 3 November 1912 (not sent), Churchill Papers.
110 Churchill memorandum to Cabinet, 17 November 1912, Adm. 116/1661.
111 Gretton, *Former Naval Person*, *op. cit.*, p. 103.
112 *Naval Chronicle*, 6 December 1912; *Naval and Military Record*, 11 December 1912.
113 *The Bluejacket*, May 1900, p. 475.
114 *Ibid.*, September 1912, p. 591. There were no official Admiralty figures for the number of married men in the service, and this in itself was evidence of the Admiralty's indifference to the subject.
115 *Parliamentary Debates*, 5, vol. XLI, 22 July 1912, col. 851.
116 Yexley to Churchill, 14 August 1912, *op. cit.*
117 Head of Naval Branch, memorandum, 1 August 1912, Adm.

116/1661; *Naval Chronicle*, 6 December 1912.

118 *Parliamentary Debates*, 5, vol. VLVIII, 12 February 1913, col. 973.
119 Churchill, minute, 26 March 1913, Adm. 116/1661.
120 Yexley to secretary of Chatham joint committee, 6 May 1914, Pursey
     Collection; *The Fleet*, July 1915, p. 192.
121 Yexley to secretary of Chatham joint committee, *op. cit.*
122 Churchill, minute, 4 September 1914, Adm. 116/1661.
123 *The Fleet*, December 1914, p. 422.
124 *Daily Chronicle*, 10 July 1912.
125 Fisher to Yexley, 1 August 1909, Fisher Papers, 1954.
126 Yexley to Fisher, 12 January 1910, Yexley Papers.
127 Fisher to Yexley, 30 November 1909, 13 January 1910, Fisher Papers,
     2000, 2023.
128 Esther (Hallam Moorhouse) Meynell to Fisher, 17 January 1911;
     Fisher to Yexley, 27 June 1913, Fisher Papers, 2101, 2243.
129 Fisher to Yexley, 30 July 1912, Fisher Papers, 2199; *Parliamentary
     Debates*, 5, vol. LXIV, 30 June 1914, col. 199.

FOUR
Naval unrest and lower-deck organisation

1 *Parliamentary Debates*, 5, vol. L, 18 March 1913, cols. 862–3. This
   was about the same rate of desertion as in the army, where, at the turn
   of the century, 1·9 per cent of the men were deserting annually. Alan
   Skelley, *The Victorian Army at Home, op. cit.*, p. 134. In the middle of
   the nineteenth century desertion rates in the Royal Navy ranged from 1
   per cent on the West Africa station to nearly 10 per cent on the
   Australian and Pacific stations (figures for 1862). John Winton,
   Hurrah for the Life of a Sailor (Michael Joseph, 1977), p. 173.
2 *Parliamentary Debates*, 5, vol. CCVIII, 30 June 1927, col. 576.
3 *The Fleet*, April 1907, p. 134.
4 *Ibid.*, January 1906, p. 5.
5 *Ibid.*, September 1907, p. 276.
6 *Parliamentary Debates*, 4, vol. LXXIX, 2 March 1900, cols. 1524–5.
7 *Ibid.*, 5, vol. CCVIII, 30 June 1927, col. 576.
8 Admiral Bridgeman, memorandum to Prince Louis of Battenberg, 28
   April 1912, Battenberg Papers.
9 *The Fleet*, August 1914, p. 228.
10 Yexley, evidence to the Committee on Naval Discipline, 1912, *op. cit.*,
   p. 111.
11 *Parliamentary Debates*, 5, vol. LI, 31 March 1913, col. 90.
12 For an account of an earlier, unrecorded mutiny which Yexley
   witnessed see *The Fleet*, April 1925, p. 57.
13 *The Fleet*, December 1906, p. 368.
14 CPO J. Taylor and CPO T. Baldwin, evidence to the Cross court of
   inquiry, Adm. 116/1022.
15 *The Fleet*, August 1906, pp. 223–4; December 1906, pp. 368–9;

Parliamentary Debates, 4, vol. CLXII, 1 August 1906, col. 1038.

16   Report of Commodore Stopford, Adm. 116/1022; Yexley, *Inner Life of the Navy, op. cit.*, p. 333; Lieutenant D. J. Dwyer, *A History of the Royal Naval Barracks Portsmouth, op. cit.*, p. 28; Commander Drury-Lowe, evidence to the Cross court of inquiry, *op. cit.*; C-in-C Portsmouth, telegram to Admiralty, 6 November 1906, Adm. 116/1022.

17   *Returns of Court Martial Punishments* (Admiralty, 1906); Dwyer, *A History of the Royal Naval Barracks Portsmouth, op. cit.*, p. 28.

18   Stopford to Sir Charles Drury, Second Sea Lord, 17 November 1906, Adm. 116/1022.

19   Yexley, evidence to the Committee on Naval Discipline, 1912, *op. cit.*, p. 124. Lieutenant Dwyer, the historian of Portsmouth barracks, has also concluded that the causes of the mutiny had been building up for several months before. *Op. cit.*, p. 28.

20   *The Fleet*, July 1907, p. 220.

21   See Appendix 1.

22   *The Fleet*, November 1909, p. 244.

23   *Ibid.*, January 1913, p. 5; March 1912, p. 399; December 1912, p. 700; May 1913, p. 136; January 1914, p. 6; *Naval Chronicle*, 22 August 1913.

24   *The Fleet*, May 1913, pp. 137, 148; January 1914, p. 30; interview with Harry Pursey, 5 May 1972. Pursey was the first chairman of this society.

25   *The Fleet*, June 1914, p. 188.

26   *Ibid.*, January 1913, p. 5; March 1914, p. 69.

27   Commodore Seymour Erskine, evidence to the Committee on Naval Discipline, 1912, *op. cit.*

28   Bridgeman to McKenna, 7 January 1910, McKenna Papers, 8, 3/5, Churchill College, Cambridge.

29   *Naval Chronicle*, 1 July 1910, 16 June 1911; *Naval and Military Record*, 27 September 1911.

30   *Daily Chronicle*, 4, 14, 16 May 1912.

31   *Daily Citizen*, 16 April 1913.

32   *Daily Chronicle*, 24 August 1912.

33   *Ibid.*, 19 August 1910.

34   *Portsmouth Evening News*, 29 June 1912.

35   *Weekly Dispatch*, 16 June 1912; *Daily Graphic*, 18 July 1912; *Army and Navy Gazette*, 20 July 1912; Stephen Reynolds, 'Ships versus men in the Navy', *English Review*, September 1912, p. 287.

36   *Parliamentary Debates*, 5, vol. XXXIX, 5 June 1912, col. 120.

37   *Naval Chronicle*, 12 December 1913; *The Fleet*, June 1914, pp. 166–9.

38   *Portsmouth Evening News*, 18 May 1914.

39   *Morning Post*, 26 May, 16 June 1914.

40   *Naval Chronicle*, 13, 20 March, 3 April 1914; *Naval and Military Record*, 18 March 1914; *The Fleet*, May 1914, p. 138; *Returns of Court Martial Punishments, Quarter ending March 31, 1914* (Admiralty); Log of HMS *Zealandia*, Adm. 53/69291; 'Naval Mutiny in 1914', *Naval Review*, vol. 60, July 1972, pp. 250–3.

41   'Discipline in the Navy and the Ulster pogrom', *United Service Magazine*, July 1914, pp. 337–42; *Naval and Military Record*, 20 May 1914; see also the *Record* for 1, 8, 29 April 1914.

42   *Morning Post*, 17 June 1914.

43   Yexley, 'Our naval personnel', *The Fleet Annual and Naval Year Book*, 1914, pp. 2–7; *The Fleet*, April 1914, p. 101.

44   *The Fleet*, January 1913, p. 5; April 1914, p. 126.

45   *Ibid.*, May 1914, p. 137; February 1915, p. 36.

46   *Ibid.*, April 1914, p. 101.

47   *Ibid.*, July 1914, p. 201.

48   *Ibid.*, August 1914, p. 261; January 1915, p. 18.

49   *Special Report from the Select Committee on Naval and Military Services (Pensions and Grants)* (HMSO, 14 April 1915).

50   Captain of HMS *Resolution* to Admiral Madden, 14 September 1917, Adm. 1/8498/201.

51   *Naval Chronicle*, 2 April 1915; *The Fleet*, January 1915, p. 18, April, p. 102.

52   *The Fleet*, November 1915, pp. 339–40.

53   *Ibid.*, January 1917, p. 6; Lionel Yexley, 'The pay of the Navy', *English Review*, March 1917, pp. 243–50; Captain of HMS *Resolution* to Admiral Madden, 14 September 1917, *op. cit.*; *The Fleet*, April 1917, pp. 114–15; July, pp. 180–4; 'Naval hospital stoppages', *New Statesman*, 26 May 1917.

54   *The Fleet*, January 1917, p. 4.

55   *Ibid.*, August 1917, p. 202; June p. 158.

56   *Parliamentary Debates*, 5, vol. XCII, 4 April 1917, cols. 1328–39; *The Fleet*, May 1917, p. 140; July, p. 190.

57   Harry Pursey, 'From petitions to reviews: the presentation of lower-deck grievances', *op. cit.*, p. 105.

58   *Disabilities which require Redressing in H.M. Navy*, Pursey Collection.

59   *Weekly Dispatch*, 29 July 1917; *Parliamentary Debates*, 5, vol. XCVI, 30 July 1917, cols. 1747–78.

60   *Parliamentary Debates*, 5, vol. LXXXVII, 14 November 1916, col. 688; Vice-Admiral de Robeck to Admiral Beatty, 22 September 1917, Adm. 1/8498/201.

61   *Daily Express*, 23, 30 August; 6, 13, 20, 27 September; 4 October 1917.

62   Fisher to Yexley, 25, 29 August 1917, Fisher Papers, 3030, 3034; Fisher to Lambert, 25 August 1917; Lambert to Fisher, 27 August 1917, Fisher Papers, 3031, 3032.

63   Cabinet Minutes, 31 July 1917, Cab. 23/3.

64   *Naval Chronicle*, 3 August 1917.

65   Cabinet Minutes, 31 July 1917, *op. cit.*

66   *The Fleet*, October 1917, p. 238.

67   Pursey, 'From petitions to reviews: the presentation of lower-deck grievances', *op. cit.*, p. 105; Admiral Madden to Admiral Beatty, 21 September 1917, Adm. 1/8498/201; Len Fagg, 'A man of Kent', unpublished MS, pp. 93–4.

68   A copy of the petition is to be found in Adm. 1/8498/201.

69   The first official information on the concessions was a Fleet Order of 26 October 1917, and that only dealt with free kit.

70   Adm. 1/8498/201.

71   Admiral Madden to Admiral Beatty (enclosure), 21 September 1917, Adm. 1/8498/201.

72   *The Fleet*, August 1917, p. 204.

73   Financial Secretary to the Admiralty, minute, 27 November 1917, Adm. 1/8501/229.

74   *The Fleet*, February 1918, p. 24.

75   John Bush, 'Big ship Navy', unpublished MS, p. 20.

76   *The Fleet*, April 1918, p. 52.

77   Admiral Madden to Admiral Beatty, 21 September 1917, *op. cit.*

78   Vale had been a leading figure in the lower-deck societies at Devonport before the war, and was to play an equally important role in that position after the war.

79   *The Fleet*, November 1917, pp. 249–50; December, pp. 269–70; Second Sea Lord, memorandum to First Sea Lord, 19 October 1917, Adm. 1/8501/229.

80   *The Fleet*, November 1917, p. 251; Cabinet Minutes, 22 November 1917, Cab. 23/4; Financial Secretary to the Admiralty, minute, 22 October 1917, Adm. 1/8501/229.

81   Second Sea Lord, memorandum to First Sea Lord, 19 October 1917, *op. cit.*

82   Yexley to Macnamara, 1 November 1917, Adm. 1/8511/18.

83   *The Times*, 3 November 1917.

84   Cabinet Minutes, 22 November 1917, *op. cit.*

85   *Parliamentary Debates*, 5, vol. XCIX, 26 November 1917, col. 1634.

86   Admiral Madden to Admiral Beatty, 21 September 1917, *op. cit.*

FIVE
'Direct representation'

1 Admiral Beatty to Flag Officers, Grand Fleet, 29 September 1917,
   Adm. 178/157; *id.* to Vice-Admiral de Robeck, 4 November 1917,
   Adm. 116/1728.
2 *The Fleet*, October 1918, p. 152.
3 *Pall Mall Gazette*, 3 February 1908.
4 *The Fleet*, October 1927, p. 180; Beresford's success in combining his
   naval, political and court interests can be seen from his career path:
   MP for Waterford 1874–80 and aide-de-camp to Prince of Wales
   1875–76; active service 1880–85; MP for East Marylebone 1885–89
   and Commissioner of the Admiralty 1886–88; active service 1889–97;
   MP for York 1897–1900 and aide-de-camp to Queen Victoria 1897.
   Second-in-command, Mediterranean Fleet, 1900–02; MP for
   Woolwich 1902–03; Commander-in-Chief, Channel Fleet, 1903–05;
   Commander-in-Chief, Mediterranean Fleet, 1905–07; Commander-
   in-Chief, Channel Fleet, 1907–09; MP for Portsmouth 1910. *Royal
   Navy List* (Witherby, 1915).
5 Head of Naval Law Branch, minute, 15 March 1922, Adm.
   1/8622/46.
6 *The Fleet*, April 1906, p. 107.
7 *Ibid.*, July 1906, p. 198.
8 *Ibid.*, July 1907, p. 220.
9 *Ibid.*, December 1910, p. 270.
10 *Ibid.*, March 1910, p. 66; November 1910, p. 256; Fisher to Yexley, 9
   November 1909, Fisher Papers, 1973.
11 *The Fleet*, February 1910, p. 30; January 1911, p. 7; July 1912 p. 540;
   July 1913, p. 204; July 1914, p. 199; April 1928, p. 71.
12 Churchill to Albert Illingworth and Fisher, 1 September 1912, in
   Randolph Churchill, *Winston S. Churchill*, vol. II Companion, part 3,
   1911–14 (Heinemann, 1969), pp. 1645, 1932; Fisher to Yexley, 19
   June, 25 October 1913, Fisher Papers, 2240, 2257; *The Fleet*, March
   1913, p. 68.
13 Interview with Commander Pursey, 30 May 1975.
14 Adm. 1/7993; *The Fleet*, September 1909, p. 208.
15 Pursey, 'From petitions to reviews: the presentation of lower-deck
   grievances', *op. cit.*, pp. 101–12.
16 *Naval and Military Record*, 15, 22 April 1914.
17 *The Fleet*, June 1907, p. 196.
18 *Ibid.*, August 1906, p. 239; 'Lower deck societies', *The Fleet Annual
   and Naval Year Book*, 1913, pp. 51–2.
19 *The Bluejacket*, November 1900, p. 606; *The Fleet*, July 1913, pp.
   202–4; December 1913, p. 359; *Naval Chronicle*, July 19, 1918.

20 *The Fleet*, September 1913, p. 266.
21 *Ibid.*, October 1912, p. 624.
22 *Naval and Military Record*, 4 September 1912.
23 *The Fleet*, May 1912, p. 457.
24 *Naval Chronicle*, 24 August 1917.
25 *Ibid.*, 15 March 1918; *Parliamentary Debates*, 5, vol. CIII, 6 March 1918, col. 1982; *The People*, 26 May 1918.
26 *Naval Chronicle*, 23 November 1917; *The Fleet*, February 1918, p. 20.
27 *Naval Warrant Officers' Journal*, April 1918, p. 31.
28 Draft Loyal Appeal, Portsmouth, March 1918, Pursey Collection.
29 N.L. 81079/17, Yexley Papers.
30 Draft Loyal Appeal, March 1918; Portsmouth Joint Committee Minutes, 9 October 1918, Yexley Papers.
31 There were ten societies affiliated to the Portsmouth joint committee at this time.
32 Tewkesbury to Yexley, 7 June 1918, Yexley Papers.
33 Albert Hickey (president, Portsmouth joint committee) to Yexley, 23 September 1918; Tewkesbury to Yexley, 13 September 1918, Yexley Papers. Protesting over the victimisation of the president of the Writers' Society, David Thomson, in 1918, Yexley wrote to Macnamara: 'That particular man is one of the greatest assets for "law and order" you have; drive such men out and the wilder spirits will assume control and you will bring about the very thing we are trying to avoid.' Letter to Macnamara, 10 September 1918, Adm. 116/1603.
34 *The Fleet*, June 1918, pp. 81–4; *Naval Chronicle*, 16 January 1920; *Naval and Military Record*, 27 November 1918.
35 *Naval Chronicle*, 24 October 1919.
36 *The Fleet*, March 1929, p. 43.
37 Financial Secretary to the Admiralty, minute, undated, 1918, Adm. 167/55.
38 Cummins to Yexley, 7 July 1918, Yexley Papers.
39 Simmonds to Yexley, 8 July 1918, Yexley Papers.
40 *The Fleet*, February 1929, p. 23.
41 *Naval and Military Record*, 27 November 1918; Portsmouth Joint Committee Minutes, 9 October 1918, *op. cit.*
42 He later admitted that in working with the joint committee in Portsmouth he was trying to drive a wedge between the lower deck and the Labour movement. Yexley to Secretary to the Board of Admiralty, 29 January 1919, Yexley Papers.
43 *The Fleet*, July 1918, p. 104. This policy was adopted at a joint committee meeting on 14 August 1918 and conveyed to the Admiralty by Yexley, letter of 30 August.

44 Second Sea Lord, memorandum, 27 September 1918, Adm. 1/8539/250.
45 V. L. Allen, 'The National Union of Police and Prison Officers', *op. cit.*, pp. 135–6.
46 John Horner, *Studies in Industrial Democracy* (Gollancz, 1974), pp. 163–4.
47 Director of Naval Intelligence, minute, undated 1918, Adm. 167/55.
48 *Naval Chronicle*, 17 October 1919.
49 Yexley, confidential memorandum to the King and Cabinet, 4 September 1918, Pursey Collection.
50 It was reproduced in *The Fleet*, February 1927.
51 War Cabinet Minutes, 27 September 1918, Cab. 23/7. See also his letter to Lloyd George, 26 September 1918, which was in the same vein. The draft of this letter refers twice to 'unrest', but the word was deleted in the final version, Adm. 116/1603.
52 Geddes to Bonar Law, 3 September, 1918, Adm. 116/1603.
53 Horatio Bottomley to Geddes, 13 September 1918, Adm. 116/1603.
54 Second Sea Lord, minute, 15 September 1918, Adm. 116/1603.
55 Fisher to Lambert, 6 September 1918, Fisher Papers, 3278.
56 Board of Admiralty Minutes, 405, 20 September 1918; 414, 26 September; 502, 28 November, Adm. 167/53.
57 *The Fleet*, May 1928, p. 83; August 1931, p. 142.
58 Financial Secretary to the Admiralty, memorandum, 14 September 1918; Financial Secretary, memorandum to Second Sea Lord, 17 September 1918, Adm. 116/1603; *The Fleet*, May 1928, p. 83; June 1919, p. 90; *Naval Chronicle*, 16 January 1920.
59 Tewkesbury to Yexley, 7, 15 June 1918, Yexley Papers.
60 Tewkesbury to Yexley, 7 June 1918; Portsmouth Joint Committee Minutes, June 1918, Yexley Papers.
61 *The Fleet*, July 1918, p. 104; *Naval Chronicle*, 17 October 1919.
62 Yexley to Churchill, 1 December 1917, Churchill Papers.
63 Yexley to Tewkesbury, 3 July 1918; Portsmouth Joint Committee Minutes, 10 July 1918, Yexley Papers. The approach was evidently unsuccessful.
64 Portsmouth Joint Committee Minutes, 14 August 1918, Yexley Papers.
65 *The Fleet*, February 1929, p. 23.
66 Hollamby to Yexley, 21 September 1918, Yexley Papers.
67 Tewkesbury to Yexley, 26 September 1918, Yexley Papers.
68 Yexley to Fisher and Churchill, 2 October 1918, Yexley Papers.
69 George Norton, (secretary, Sick Berth Stewards' Society) to Yexley, 1 October 1918, Yexley Papers.
70 *The Fleet*, November 1918, p. 161.
71 *Ibid.*, p. 163.

72   *Ibid.*, January 1919, p. 4.

73   A deputation of ASE, Boilermakers' Society and ERA officials went to the Admiralty on 19 September 1918 to put the case for a pay increase. *ASE Journal and Monthly Report*, October 1918, pp. 8–9; L. Hanbidge, *W. Stoddard: a Biographical Sketch*, op. cit., p. 15.

74   *The Fleet*, November 1918, p. 162; January 1919, p. 1.

75   *Ibid.*, November 1918, p. 162. Yexley had to provide most of the funds himself in the first instance, merely hoping that collections and levies among the lower-deck societies at the three ports would reimburse him. In the event he recouped £139 out of the £350 he laid out from his own pocket. There were difficulties in raising the money within the service and at Devonport an officer challenged the men's right to launch a public appeal for donations. Tewkesbury to Yexley, 4 March 1919, Yexley Papers.

76   Adm. 1/8541/279. One of the officers in question was the Director of Naval Intelligence, Sir Reginald Hall. The Admiralty even appears to have considered the possibility of Hall retaining his post in the Intelligence Department while sitting in Parliament. Two years earlier when Admiral Meux, C-in-C at Portsmouth, successfully stood as Tory candidate for Portsmouth he did not even ask for Admiralty permission but merely announced his candidature as a *fait accompli* and the Admiralty took no action against him. Head of Naval Law Branch, minute, 15 March 1922, Adm. 1/8622/46.

77   Rear-Admiral Jerram, memorandum to Fourth Sea Lord, 22 October 1918, Adm. 1/8538/244.

78   Second Sea Lord, minute, 5 November 1918, Adm. 1/8538/244.

79   Admiralty Weekly Order 3571 a/18, 13 November 1918, Adm. 182/13.

80   Admiralty Weekly Order 3676, 21 November 1918, Adm. 182/13. Even so, the insistence on men wearing civilian clothing was likely to hurt the lower deck more than officers, since many ratings would have no suit of clothing other than their uniform. Recognising that servicemen were still at a disadvantage, Cronin's election committee wrote to the War Cabinet on 27 November demanding the abolition of all regulations restricting sailors and soldiers during the election campaign, but to no avail. Cab. 24/71.

81   Adm. 1/8538/244.

82   *Naval Chronicle*, 18 October, 6 December 1918.

83   *The Fleet*, January 1919, pp. 1–4; *Portsmouth Evening News*, 28 November, 2 December 1918.

84   These errors in the distribution of ballot papers were well known to the Cabinet a week before the election, but nothing appears to have been done about it. Minutes of Cabinet Meeting, 10 December 1918, Cab. 23/8.

85   *The Fleet*, March 1921, p. 41.

86   Six months later he committed suicide. Portsmouth Joint Committee Minutes, 11 June 1919; Yexley Papers.

87   *The Fleet*, January 1919, pp. 10, 14.

88   Dave Lamb, *Mutinies, 1917–1920* (Solidarity, 1977), p. 17. Willie Gallacher is said to have branded him as an Admiralty agent. Stanley Bonnett, *The Price of Admiralty* (Robert Hale, 1968), p. 208.

89   *The Fleet*, August 1930, p. 143.

90   Admiral Colville to Geddes, 29 September 1918, Adm. 116/1603.

91   Geddes to Colville, 19 September 1918, Adm. 116/1603.

92   *Naval Chronicle*, 7 September 1918.

93   *The Fleet*, March 1929, pp. 45–6.

94   Second Sea Lord, minute, 15 September 1918, *op. cit.*

95   First Lord, minute, 11 September 1918, Adm. 116/1603.

96   See chapter 6.

97   Secretary to Board of Admiralty to Yexley, 27 January 1919, Yexley Papers.

98   Yexley to Secretary to Board of Admiralty, 29 January 1919, Yexley Papers.

SIX
The militant years

1   Adm. 1/8566/235; Fourth Sea Lord, minute, 7 October 1918, Adm. 1/8539/250.

2   War Cabinet Minutes, 24, 27 September, Cab. 23/7, 6 November 1918, Cab. 23/8, Adm. 116/1728.

3   Financial Secretary, memorandum, 28 January 1919, Cab. 23/9.

4   *The Observer*, 22 December 1918.

5   Financial Secretary, minute, 23 December 1918, Adm. 116/1728.

6   Admiralty memorandum to War Cabinet, 23 December 1918, Adm. 116/1772.

7   Adm. 116/1728.

8   Cabinet Minutes, 1 May 1919, Cab. 23/10.

9   Board of Admiralty minute 565, 2 January 1919, Adm. 167/56.

10 *Jerram Report*, 1919, Cmd. 149.

11 *Naval Chronicle*, 10 January 1919; Board of Admiralty minute 596, 16 January 1919, Adm. 167/56.

12 Rear-Admiral Jerram, minute, 6 December 1918, Adm. 116/1728.

13 Adm. 116/1728; Portsmouth Joint Committee Minutes, 8 January 1919.

14 Portsmouth Joint Committee Minutes, 8 January 1919.

15 *Naval Chronicle*, 24 January 1919.

16 *Portsmouth Evening News*, 20 January 1919; Tewkesbury to Yexley, 21 January 1919, Yexley Papers; *Naval and Military Record*, 22 January 1919.

17 Porstmouth Joint Committee Minutes, 8 January 1919, Yexley

Papers.

18 Tewkesbury to Yexley, 21 January 1919, Yexley Papers; Adm. 116/1728.

19 *Jerram Report, op. cit.*

20 Charles, *The Development of Industrial Relations in Britain, 1911–39, op. cit.*, pp. 229–30.

21 Board of Admiralty meeting, 17 February 1919, Adm. 167/57.

22 *Naval Chronicle*, 10 January 1919.

23 *The Times*, 30 January 1919.

24 *Returns of Court Martial Punishments, First Quarter, 1919*, (Admiralty).

25 Cabinet Minutes, 8 January 1919, Cab. 23/9; *Daily Herald*, 11 January 1919; *Naval Chronicle*, 10 January 1919.

26 First Lord of the Admiralty, memorandum to Cabinet, 16 January 1919, Adm. 116/1772.

27 Cab. 23/9; *The Fleet*, December 1919, pp. 196–7; Board of Admiralty minute 605, 23 January 1919, Adm. 167/56. There was also a suggestion that the increase be paid only to active-service ratings and not Hostilities Only men, a proposal which, said the Admiralty, would lead to two men of the same rating getting different pay, 'would be quite intolerable and [. . .] would lead to a situation for which the Board could not be responsible'. Board of Admiralty memorandum, 28 January 1919, Cab. 24/75. This reaction is interesting, considering that six years later the Admiralty accepted just such a two-rate scheme.

28 *Jerram Report, op. cit.*

29 Portsmouth Joint Committee Minutes, 12 March 1919, Yexley Papers.

30 *Naval Chronicle*, 3, 17 January 1919.

31 *Naval and Military Record*, 22 January 1919; *Parliamentary Debates*, 5, vol. CXII, 20 February 1919, col. 1166.

32 Second Sea Lord, minute, 14 February 1919, Adm. 1/8566/235. Roskill incorrectly attributes this statement to Admiral Oliver, who only later became Second Sea Lord. Heath was consistently hawkish on matters to do with the lower-deck societies. Roskill also refers to welfare societies, apparently confusing two separate bodies. See *Naval Policy between the Wars*, vol. 1 (Collins, 1968), pp. 119, 402.

33 *The Fleet*, April 1919, p. 55.

34 *Ibid.*, February 1919, p. 32.

35 Portsmouth Joint Committee Minutes, 11 December 1918, Yexley Papers; *The Fleet*, March 1919, p. 39.

36 *Naval Chronicle*, 15 August 1919.

37 Ministry of Labour, *Twenty-second Abstract of Labour Statistics* (HMSO, 1937), p. 137.

38 *The Fleet*, March 1920, p. 47.

39 Browett to Yexley, 30 April 1919, Yexley Papers; *The Fleet*, July 1920, pp. 135–6; *Naval Chronicle*, 30 July 1920.

40 *The Fleet*, July 1919, p. 103.

41 *The Bluejacket and Soldier*, March–April 1919.

42 Portsmouth Joint Committee Minutes, 11 December 1918, *op. cit.* Duncan was already the honorary secretary of the Police and Prison Officers' Union, and between the police and servicemen there were obvious affinities.

43 Browett to Yexley, 29 December 1918, *op. cit.*

44 Browett to Yexley, 4 February 1919, Yexley Papers.

45 Tewkesbury to Yexley, 28 February 1919, Yexley Papers.

46 Home Office Directorate of Intelligence, Report of Revolutionary Organisation in the United Kingdom, 2 December 1918, Cab. 24/71; 10 March 1919, Cab. 24/76; *Daily Herald*, 11 January 1919.

47 *Daily Herald*, 18 January 1919.

48 Report of Revolutionary Organisation, 28 January 1919, Cab. 24/75.

49 SSAU recruiting leaflet.

50 Report of Revolutionary Organisation, 10 March 1919, Cab. 24/76; 30 April 1919, Cab. 24/78. A Petty Officer Tebbenham was thought to have organised the Harwich and Devonport branches of the union.

51 Cabinet Minutes, 10 February 1919, Cab. 23/9.

52 Sir Basil Thompson, *The Scene Changes* (Collins, 1939), p. 382. The possibility that DORA officials were behind the cancellation was entertained by Yexley, who had agreed to be on the platform at the rally. A few days before it was due to take place he had met a DORA officer who warned him off, telling him that the SSAU was a Bolshevik organisation. Yexley had been invited to become a vice-president of the union but declined. *Naval Chronicle*, 8 February 1924.

53 Report of Revolutionary Organisation, 30 April 1919, Cab. 24/78. At this time Kenworthy was kept under constant surveillance.

54 *Naval Chronicle*, 23 May 1919.

55 Report of Revolutionary Organisation, 30 April 1919, *op. cit.*; 21 May Cab. 24/80; 10 June, Cab. 24/83; 23 October 1919, Cab. 24/90; Basil Thompson, *Queer People* (Hodder & Stoughton, 1922), p. 277.

56 John Norton, (secretary, Portsmouth joint committee) to Yexley, 19 June 1919; Portsmouth Joint Committee Minutes, 11 July 1919, Yexley Papers; *Naval Chronicle*, 11 July 1919; *Parliamentary Debates*, 5, vol. CXV, 8 May 1919, col. 1123.

57 Minutes of Quarterly Conference of Joint Committees, 21 June 1919; Portsmouth Joint Committee Minutes, 12 March 1919, Yexley Papers.

58 Browett to Yexley, 30 April 1919, Yexley Papers; *The Fleet*, July 1919, p. 103; November 1919, pp. 180, 187.

59 *Naval Chronicle*, 18 April 1919.

60 *Jerram Report*, *op. cit.*

61 Financial Secretary, minute, 1 April 1919, Adm. 116/1728.

62 Walter Long to Austen Chamberlain, 22 April 1919, Adm. 116/1728; Cabinet Minutes, 29 April 1919, Cab. 23/10.

63   Cabinet Minutes, 1, 8, 9 May 1919, Cab. 23/10; Lady Wester
     Wemyss, *The Life and Letters of Lord Wester Wemyss* (Eyre &
     Spottiswoode, 1935), pp. 428–9.
64   *Naval and Military Record*, 28 May 1919.
65   *Naval Chronicle*, 30 May 1919.
66   Admiralty Memorandum to Cabinet, 1 August 1919, Cab. 24/85.
67   Adm. 116/1772.
68   Lieutenant-Commander C. Drage, 'Some modern naval mutinies',
     lecture given at the Royal Naval Staff College, 1928, Drage Papers,
69   *Naval Chronicle*, 26 December 1919. The death sentences were later
     commuted to five years' penal servitude and the prison sentences
     reduced to six months.
70   *Naval Chronicle*, 31 January 1919.
71   Rear-Admiral Cowan to Admiralty, 10 November 1919, Adm.
     1/8570/291.
72   Kenneth Edwards, *The Mutiny at Invergordon* (Putnam, 1937), pp.
     52–3. Cowan, of course, had been captain of the *Zealandia* when her
     crew mutinied in 1914.
73   *Ibid.*, pp. 56–8; *Returns of Court Martial Punishments, Fourth
     Quarter, 1919* (Admiralty).
74   Interview with W. N. Basford, Acc. 00669/19, Sound Archives,
     Imperial War Museum.
75   Adm. 1/8570/291.
76   Director of Intelligence, Special Branch, Report of Inquiry, 29
     October 1919, Adm. 1/8570/291.
77   Adm. 1/8570/291; Admiral Sir Hugh Tweedie, *The Story of a Naval
     Life* (Rich & Cowan, 1939), pp. 201–3.
78   *Naval Chronicle*, 17 October 1919.
79   *Ibid.*
80   First Lord, minute, 20 October 1919, Adm. 1/8570/291.
81   Memorandum to Fourth Sea Lord, 10 November 1919, Adm.
     1/8570/291.
82   Altogether one submarine, two minesweeping sloops and two
     destroyers were lost in this campaign. Stephen Roskill, *British Naval
     Policy between the War, op. cit.*, pp. 153–4.
83   Rear-Admiral Clinton-Baker, Report of Inquiry, 20–21 October
     1919; Financial Secretary, minute 15 November 1919, Adm.
     1/8570/291.
84   First Sea Lord, minute, 12 November 1919, Adm. 1/8570/291.
85   Admiralty telegram to SNO, Baltic, 10 November 1919, Adm.
     1/8570/291.
86   *The Fleet*, October 1919, p. 155; Board of Admiralty Minutes, 19
     August 1919, Adm. 1/8566/235.
87   *Naval Chronicle*, 14 February, 7 March 1919.
88   Report of meeting of First Sea Lord with three commanders-in-chief,

12 June 1919, Adm. 116/1893; Admiralty Monthly Order 2903, October 1919, Adm. 182/26.

89   *The Fleet*, April 1919, p. 55; *Naval Chronicle*, 14 February 1919.
90   *The Bluejacket and Soldier*, November–December 1919.
91   Admiralty Monthly Order 2903, October 1919, Adm. 182–26.
92   Second Sea Lord, minute, 21 December 1918, Adm. 116/1728.
93   This point was made very clear at the Board of Admiralty meeting of 13 December 1934, when a replacement for the welfare conferences was under discussion. Adm. 116/3748.
94   *The Fleet*, February 1938, p. 25.
95   *Ibid.*, November 1919, p. 177.
96   Adm. 116/1893.
97   *The Fleet*, August 1923, p. 113.
98   Report of Welfare Committee, February 1920, Adm. 167/61.
99   *The Fleet*, August 1919, p. 130.
100 *Ibid.*, March 1920, p. 53.
101 *Naval Chronicle*, 2 July 1920.
102 Secretary to the Board of Admiralty, memorandum, 29 September 1920, Adm. 167/62. The level of membership in each branch was given as follows: Regulating (police), 87 per cent; Sick Berth, 68 per cent; Seamen, 37 per cent; Artisans, 64 per cent; Shipwrights and Joiners, 81 per cent; Marines, 13 per cent; Writers, 100 per cent; Victualling, 90 per cent; Stokers and Mechanicians, 33 per cent; Electrical Artificers, 73 per cent; Officers' Stewards and Cooks, 34 per cent; ERAs, 100 per cent; Cooks, 87 per cent; CPOs, 77 per cent.
103 Cabinet Paper 1129, 22 April 1920, Cab. 24/104; Cabinet Paper 1707, 29 July 1920, Cab. 24/110.
     April 1920, Cab. 24/104; Cabinet Paper 1707, 29 July 1920, Cab. 24/110.
104 *Naval and Military Record*, 14 July 1920; *Naval Chronicle*, 1 April 1921.
105 Admiralty Weekly Order 2359, 5 August 1920, Adm. 182/19.
106 *Naval and Military Record*, 28 July 1920.
107 *Ibid.*, 4 August 1920; *Naval Chronicle*, 22, 27 April 1921.
108 *Naval Chronicle*, 6 May 1921; Board of Admiralty minute 1247, 29 July 1920, Adm. 167/60.
109 *Naval Chronicle*, 6 August 1920, 3 June 1921.
110 *Naval and Military Record*, 11 August 1920.
111 *The Fleet*, December 1920, pp. 208–9; *Naval Chronicle*, 24 September 1920.
112 *The Fleet*, September 1920, p. 161.
113 Cabinet Paper 1793, 19 August 1920, Cab. 24/110.
114 Daniel F. Calhoun, *The United Front* (Cambridge University Press, 1976), p. 35.
115 Cabinet Paper 1830, 2 September 1920, Cab. 24/111.

240

The lower deck

116 *Naval Chronicle*, 10 September 1920; Cabinet Paper 1848, 9 September 1920, Cab. 24/111.

117 *The People*, 24 October 1920.

118 *Naval and Military Record*, 27 October 1920; Cabinet Paper 2027, 28 October 1920, Cab. 24/114. Malone had earlier tried to recruit Yexley to the revolutionary wing of the ex-service movement. He had been under suspicion at the Admiralty for some time, having made an unauthorised visit to Russia in 1919 while still on the active-service list as a Royal Marine officer. The Admiralty considered prosecuting him for treason but decided against it and settled for striking him off the active list. In 1920 he formally resigned the Liberal whip and declared himself a Communist. Adm. 12/1634; Cabinet Paper 1589, 8 July 1920, Cab. 24/108.

119 *Naval and Military Record*, 3 November 1920; Cabinet Paper 2169, 25 November 1920, Cab. 24/115.

120 At this juncture Beatty, apparently quite out of touch with developments on the question of welfare during the previous two years, complained to his staff that there was no naval department in close contact with the lower deck. Believing that healthy minds went hand in hand with healthy bodies, he recommended that responsibility for welfare be given to the Physical Training Department. It was a bizzare idea, given the seriousness of the problem posed by lower-deck organisation, and the Secretary to the Board, who had been closely involved in devising the welfare scheme, was clearly exasperated. However, Beatty's idea came to fruition later in the 1920s. The Naval Personnel Committee was downgraded in status, and one result was that before the Invergordon mutiny of 1931 little serious attention was being paid to the condition of the lower deck. First Sea Lord, minute, 7 October 1920; Secretary to the Board of Admiralty, minute, 30 October 1920, Adm. 116/1893.

121 *The Fleet*, December 1920, p. 209; *Naval Chronicle*, 31 December 1920; 8 February 1924.

122 Adm. 12/1635. Dave Springhall later became the British representative at the Comintern. Fred Copeman, *Reason in Revolt* (Blandford Press, 1948), p. 177.

123 Admiralty Fleet Order 3657, 22 December 1920. This was adopted at the Board of Admiralty meeting of 9 December 1920. Adm. 167/60.

124 *Naval Chronicle*, 23 September 1921.

125 Paymaster Captain Hall to Commodore, Portsmouth Barracks, 12 April 1923; Admiral Calthorpe to Admiralty, 6 April 1923, Adm. 1/8666/159.

126 *The Fleet*, October 1920, p. 177; 'Welfare Committee representation', *Naval Review*, vol. IX, No. 1, February 1921, pp. 168–9; *Naval Chronicle*, 2 April 1920.

127 *The Fleet*, May 1921, p. 76.

128   *Ibid.*, July 1922, p. 98.
129   *Ibid.*, June 1922, pp. 82–3.
130   Admiral Sturdee to Admiralty, 16 February 1921, Adm. 116/1893.
131   Admiral Browning to Admiralty, 16 February 1921, Adm. 116/1893.
132   Admiralty Fleet Order 3604, 4 November 1921, Adm. 182/31; Board of Admiralty minute 1318, 16 March 1921, Adm. 167/63.
133   *The Fleet*, July 1922, pp. 107–8; *Naval Chronicle*, 28 October 1921.
134   Admiralty Fleet Order 1703, 26 June 1923, Adm. 182/36.
135   *Committee on Pay etc. of State Servants*, 1923, paragraph 13.
136   *Naval Chronicle*, 9 February 1923. Lane was now contributing a regular weekly column to the *Naval Chronicle*. These had begun before he left the service and appeared under various pseudonyms, most commonly 'C. Boot' or 'Scribe'.
137   *Naval Chronicle*, 22 June 1923.
138   *The Fleet*, September 1923; p. 129; April 1924, p. 62.
139   *Ibid.*, August 1923, p. 126.
140   Chairman of Naval Personnel Committee, minute, 22 November 1923, Adm. 1/8666/159.
141   *Naval and Military Record*, 31 October 1923.
142   *Naval Chronicle*, 3 August 1923.
143   *Ibid.*, 26 October 1923.
144   Admiralty to commanders-in-chief, 4 August 1923, Adm. 1/8666/159.
145   Letters from C-in-C, Devonport, to Admiralty, 7 August 1923; C-in-C, Portsmouth, to Admiralty, 10 August 1923; C-in-C, Nore, 21 August 1923, Adm. 1/8666/159.
146   Admiralty to commanders-in-chief, 24 October 1923, Adm. 1/8666/159.
147   Head of Naval Law Branch, minute, 12 November 1923, Adm. 1/8666/159.
148   Admiral Fremantle to Admiralty, 1 November 1923, Adm. 1/8666/159.
149   *Id.* to *id.*, 9 November 1923, Adm. 1/8666/159.
150   *The Fleet*, March 1924, p. 47.
151   *Ibid.*, March 1924, p. 45.
152   Commodore, Devonport barracks, memorandum to Admiralty, 20 February 1924, Adm. 1/8666/159.
153   Robert Young to First Lord, 6 February 1924, Adm. 1/8666/159.
154   First Lord to Young, 3 March 1924, Adm. 1/8666/159.

SEVEN

The movement in abeyance

1   *Returns of Court Martial Punishments* (Admiralty, 1921).
2   In order to win approval for the expenditure the commander of the *Dragon* had to disband the committee and hold new elections. Len

Fagg, 'Man of Kent', *op. cit.*, pp. 106–8. The *Dragon* was not the only ship whose canteen committee opposed any expenditure over this wedding. The canteen representatives on the *Ajax* voted against a suggestion to pay for a tea and dance to celebrate the event. John Bush, *Diary*, 28 February 1922. In January 1922 Beatty wired all commanders-in-chief that soundings had indicated that the vast majority of ratings in the service were in favour of buying the princess a present, although in Devonport it was with the *caveat* that only a small sum should be spent on a gift and the balance of the money collected given to charity. Altogether £2,684 was extracted from the lower deck in contributions, and the small present Princess Mary bought herself was a diamond and emerald pendant. Such money as remained was handed over to the Seamen's and Marines' Orphan Home. Adm. 1/8618/14.

3   Admiralty to Fagg, 30 November 1923, Fagg Correspondence.
4   *Parliamentary Debates*, 5, vol. CCXIV, 14 March 1928, col. 1934.
5   John Bush, 'Big ship Navy', *op. cit.*, p. 356; ex-Writer Percy Mabb, interview, 8 November 1973.
6   *The Fleet*, June 1922, p. 83.
7   Yexley's interpretation of the episode was that the engineer whose signature appeared on the letter had probably not written it and that the real author was an ERA in the engineer's office who was paying off a political score against the mechanician. Whatever the truth, the incident demonstrates the scope there was for men to be victimised.
8   Rear-Admiral Cowan, Memorandum on Discipline, 6 June 1921, Cowan Papers, COW/13/2, National Maritime Museum.
9   Cabinet Papers 399(23), 6 September 1923, Cab. 24/161; 402(23), 20 September 1923, Cab. 24/162; Adm. 1/8657/48. On the question of the Admiralty receiving early warning of Communist Party plans see Naval Intelligence Department, minute 29 October 1926, Adm. 1/8695/36.
10 *Workers' Weekly*, 6 March 1925; 'The Navy and Communism', *Naval Review*, vol. XIV, No. 1, February 1926, pp. 124–38.
11 Adm. 1/8675/34.
12 *Naval Chronicle*, 25 September 1925.
13 *The Admiralty's New Swindle*, 1925.
14 *Naval Chronicle*, 3 April 1925.
15 *Ibid.*, 19 March 1926.
16 *Parliamentary Debates*, 5, vol. CLXXXVI, 15 July 1925, cols. 1265–6; 16 July, cols. 1638–40.
17 *Naval Chronicle*, 27 November 1925.
18 Adm. 1/8695/36.
19 *Sailors' and Marines' Programme*, 1928; *Naval Chronicle*, 30 March 1928; *Parliamentary Debates*, 5, vol. CCXXXVI, 5 March 1930, col. 416.
20 Chaplain of the Fleet, minute, undated 1925, Adm. 167/72; Knock, *Clear Lower Deck, op. cit.*, p. 176. The political role of chaplains was at times obvious for all to see. Marine Private George Davies recorded in

his diary the Sunday service aboard his ship just after the 1918 general election had been announced. The Chaplain talked about the election: 'He said that most of us had been in foreign countries during the war and that the majority of us had never been out of England before. We'd seen different people with different ideas and customs. The consequence was our English minds had been reformed. He mentioned about the men using their vote. He said he, himself, seeing that he had been away from civil life for four years, it would not be right for him to vote since he would not know who he was voting for. Therefore he said he would not vote. And he advised us not to. I thought he was going beyond his limit for a sermon. I wonder what authority he had to talk of politics to his congregation. I know this much, that 99 out of every 100 men on this ship are for Labour and if they do not vote the Tories, profiteers and pompuritarians would certainly get the old government back to prepare for another of their wars. Oh, no, reverend gentleman. It is time that the working man was represented by a working man and not governed by a man that was born in luxury [. . .]. After the Chaplain finished the Captain said a few words. He said the Chaplain had said practically all that he had intended to say and he hoped that the men had listened to him and that they would try to carry out the chaplain's wishes.' George Davies, *Diary, op. cit.*, 17 November 1918.

21   Adm. 178/66.
22   *Naval Chronicle*, 1 December 1922; *The Fleet*, December 1922, p. 174; *Parliamentary Debates*, 5, vol. CLXII, 28 March 1923, col. 533. Bramsdon polled 537 votes less than the winning candidate.
23   *The Fleet*, July 1929, p. 122.
24   *Naval Chronicle*, 2 May 1924.
25   Secretary to the Board of Admiralty, memorandum, 1 May 1924, Adm. 167/70; Admiralty Fleet Order 2813a, 24 October 1924, Adm. 182/40.
26   *Naval Chronicle*, 24 October 1924, 16 January 1925, 16 September 1927; *Parliamentary Debates*, 5 vol. CLXXXI, 19 March 1925, col. 2561; vol. CCX, 23 November 1927, col. 1770; vol. CCXXXII, 20 November 1929, col. 469.
27   *The Fleet*, January 1928, p. 15. This question of the servicemen's right to attend political meetings was still a contentious one during World War II. Public protests were raised in 1940 after servicemen had been ordered away by military police from open-air political meetings in Hyde Park, and again the following year after soldiers had been refused admittance to a public meeting addressed by an MP in South Wales. *Civil Liberty*, March 1940, June 1941.
28   *Naval Chronicle*, 16 September 1927; *Parliamentary Debates*, 5, vol. CCX, 16 November 1927, cols. 1017–18.
29   *The Fleet*, October 1927, p. 190.
30   *Parliamentary Debates*, 5, vol. CCXXIX, 10 July, 1929, cols. 855–6. During World War II the serviceman's right to stand for Parliament was still being tampered with. There were two instances in the early years of the war where servicemen were illegally prevented from

standing in by-elections. Arising from these, the Secretary of State for War had to apologise for 'misunderstandings and mistakes' and 'misinterpretation of the regulations' by the commanding officer. *Civil Liberty*, June 1941.

31 Secretary to the Board of Admiralty, memorandum for Board meeting, 13 December 1934; Adm. 116/3748.
32 *The Fleet*, July 1925, p. 105.
33 Head of Naval Law Branch, minute, undated 1922, Adm. 1/8666/159.
34 Head of Naval Law Branch, minute, 12 December 1934, Adm. 178/90.
35 Head of Naval Law Branch, minute, 7 August 1929, Adm. 178/90.
36 Financial Secretary, minute, 20 September 1929, Adm. 178/90; *Parliamentary Debates*, 5, vol. CCXXX, 24 July 1929, col. 1314.
37 The strict legal position about ratings contacting MPs was not altogether clear even during World War II. While not treating such behaviour as an automatic breach of discipline, the Admiralty forbade any method of obtaining redress of a complaint other than through the established service channels. As late as 1940 a government Minister denied that servicemen had a right to complain to MPs, and a suggestion that King's Regulations should be amended to include this positive right was flatly refused. *Parliamentary Debates*, 5, vol. CXV, 6 May 1919, col. 747; *Civil Liberty*, June 1941. The matter surfaced again in Parliament in 1945 after complaints had been made that a notice displayed on all ships appeared to debar men from communicating with their MPs on service matters. This time the First Lord denied that was the intent of the notice. *Parliamentary Debates*, 5, vol. CDVIII, 21 February 1945, cols. 789–90.
38 *The Fleet*, February 1924, p. 33.
39 *Ibid.*, July 1924, p. 108.
40 *Parliamentary Debates*, 5, vol. CLXXXI, 19 March 1925, col. 2561.
41 *The Fleet*, July 1927, p. 124.
42 *Ibid.*, March 1930, p. 43.
43 Head of Naval Branch, memorandum, 1925, N727/25, Adm. 167/72.
44 *The Fleet*, October 1929, p. 178.
45 The RNBT was viewed by the Admiralty as a bulwark against radical tendencies in the lower-deck societies. In this respect it was intended to play much the same role as the British Legion *vis à vis* the more militant organisations of ex-servicemen. For a more detailed discussion of this see A. B. Carew, 'The Royal Naval lower-deck reform movement, 1900–39', unpublished D.Phil. thesis, Sussex University, 1980.
46 Second Sea Lord, minute, 29 February 1925, Adm. 1/8689/194.
47 *The Fleet*, December 1926, p. 220; *Naval Chronicle*, 6 December 1929.
48 *The Fleet*, April 1926, p. 72.
49 *Ibid.*, December 1926, p. 220; January 1929, p. 15; August 1930, p. 144; *Naval Chronicle*, 24 September 1926, 15 June, 21 September 1928.
50 Commander-in-Chief, Portsmouth, memorandum, 4 February 1925, Adm. 1/8957.

51   Vice-Admiral K. G. B. Dewar, *The Navy from Within, op. cit.*, chapters XXIII and XXIV. The admiral in question was Collard, who as a lieutenant, had been responsible for the mutiny at Portsmouth barracks in 1906.
52   *The Fleet*, May 1929, p. 77.
53   Vice-Admiral Dewar, 'Make it safe to complain in the Navy', *Daily Herald*, 24 January 1931. By this time Dewar had joined the Labour Party.
54   *Naval Chronicle*, 3 April 1925.
55   A. L. Colton to author, 23 March 1978; G. Sellick to author, 12 May 1978; J. Malyon to author, 22 March 1978.
56   Adm. 12/1706.
57   *Naval Chronicle*, 23 January 1931; *Parliamentary Debates*, 5, vol. CCXLVII, 28 January 1931, cols. 949–50.
58   HMS *Lucia*, Insubordination, Adm. 178/109.
59   *Parliamentary Debates*, 5, vol. CCXLVII, 28 January 1931, cols. 949–50.

EIGHT
The road to Invergordon

1   *Parliamentary Debates*, 5, vol. CCVIII, 30 June 1927, col. 576.
2   *Ibid.*, 5, vol. CLXX, 12 March 1924, col. 2370.
3   *Naval Chronicle*, 20 December 1912; *The Fleet*, October 1934, p. 178.
4   *Parliamentary Debates*, 5, vol. CXCIX, 14 March 1935, col. 596; Sir Reginald Acland (Judge Advocate of the Fleet), 'Crime and punishment in the Royal Navy during the last fifty years', *Naval Review*, vol. XI, No. 3, p. 483.
5   *Brassey's Naval Annual*, 1923, p. 29; Board of Admiralty minute 1516, 5 October 1922; minute 1520, 12 October 1922, Adm. 167/65.
6   *The Fleet*, June 1925, pp. 91, 93.
7   *Naval Chronicle*, 28 August 1925.
8   *Workers' Life*, 16 March 1928.
9   Medical Director General, minute, 23 April 1937, Adm. 1/9160.
10   *The Fleet*, July 1925, pp. 97–98; August 1929, p. 142; Unnatural Vice, 20 August 1917, Adm. 167/54. In 1929, with 4,426 boys in the service, no fewer than 4,747 punishments of various kinds were awarded. Naval Law Branch memorandum on the Caning of Boys, 10 July 1931, Adm. 167/84; Board of Admiralty minute 2835, 6 July 1931, Adm. 167/83.
11   Ex-Chief Yeoman of Signals R. Purvis to author, 8 May 1973; *The Fleet*, April 1925, p. 49; Lewis Clive, *The People's Army* (Gollancz, 1938), p. 173.
12   Jerram committee, vol. 1, Adm. 116/1728.
13   Second Sea Lord, minute 16 January 1918, Adm. 116/1734.
14   *The Fleet*, November 1934, p. 184; Commander-in-Chief,

Portsmouth, to Second Sea Lord, 17 November 1937, Adm. 116/3989.

15 1922 Welfare Conference, Adm. 167/68; *Parliamentary Debates*, 5, vol. CXXXIX, 23 March 1921, col. 2557; vol. CLXIII, 2 May 1923, col. 1352; vol. CLXXIII, 21 May 1924, col. 2215; vol. CCIV, 30 January 1929, col. 922; vol. CCXXVI, 19 March 1929, cols. 1672–3.

16 Head of Naval Personnel Committee, quoted in Head of Naval Branch memorandum on Welfare Conference, undated 1924, Adm. 167/72.

17 *The Fleet*, November 1920, p. 189; October, p. 173; V. L. Allen, 'The National Union of Police and Prison Officers', *op. cit.*, pp. 141–2.

18 *The Fleet*, June 1920, p. 117.

19 Admiralty Weekly Order 2359, 5 August 1920, Adm. 182/19.

20 *Parliamentary Debates*, 5, vol. CXXXIII, 27 October 1920, col. 1758; *The Fleet*, November 1920, p. 189.

21 *Ibid.*, January 1921, p. 6.

22 *Ibid.*, August 1923, p. 120.

23 Assistant Secretary to Board of Admiralty, minute, 15 May 1923, Adm. 1/8643/154.

24 Board of Admiralty memorandum, 29 November 1923, Adm. 1/8637/63.

25 Admiralty memorandum to Anderson committee, 19 March 1923, Adm. 1/8637/52.

26 Secretary to Board of Admiralty, minute, 3 November 1923, Adm. 1/8643/154.

27 Admiralty memorandum to Anderson committee, *op. cit.*

28 Board of Admiralty minute 1845, 24 March 1924, Adm. 167/69.

29 *The Fleet*, March 1924, pp. 40–2.

30 *Ibid.*, October 1923, p. 159.

31 *Western Morning News*, 27 October 1923.

32 *The Fleet*, March 1924, p. 42.

33 The First Lord, Viscount Chelmsford, was not a Labour Party member and in accepting office had made it clear that he had no political affiliations.

34 Board of Admiralty minute 1845, 24 March 1924, *op. cit.* The First Lord of the Admiralty was never likely to support Hodges and Ammon on an issue which appeared to contain a strong element of party politics.

35 *Parliamentary Debates*, 5, vol. CLXXI, 18 March 1924, col. 293.

36 Secretary to the Board of Admiralty, minute, 14 March 1934, Adm. 116/2891.

37 *Naval Chronicle*, 31 July 1925.

38 Secretary to the Board of Admiralty, minute, 14 March 1934, *op. cit.*

39 Head of Naval Personnel Committee, quoted in Head of Naval Branch memorandum on Welfare Conference, undated 1924, Adm. 167/72.

40 Admiralty Fleet Order 2858/59, 3 October 1925, Adm. 182/42.

41 R. R. James (ed.), *Memoirs of a Conservative: J. C. C. Davidson's Memoirs and Papers, 1910–37* (Weidenfeld & Nicolson, 1969), pp.

206/15; *The Times*, 22 July 1925; Hankey to Beatty, 30 April 1927, Beatty Papers, Chicheley Hall.

42 Admiralty Weekly Order 2359, 5 August 1920, Adm. 182/19.

43 Admiralty Fleet Order 2858/59, 3 October 1925, Adm. 182/42.

44 Head of Naval Branch memorandum on Welfare Conference, undated 1924, Adm. 167/72.

45 *The Fleet*, October 1925, p. 148.

46 Head of Naval Branch memorandum on Welfare Conference, undated 1924, *op. cit.*

47 Secretary to the Board of Admiralty, minute, 14 March 1934, *op. cit.*

48 *The Fleet*, February 1930, p. 21.

49 *Ibid.*, August 1929, p. 134; June 1934, p. 92.

50 *Ibid.*, August 1929, p. 134; *Naval Chronicle*, 14 December 1928.

51 Assuming the seaman had served three years' man's time – i.e. from the age of eighteen.

52 Report of Committee of Enquiry into Hardships, Portsmouth, 22 September 1931, Adm. 116/2891.

53 *Ibid.*

54 Lieutenant-Commander J. H. Owen, *Insubordination and Mutiny in the Navy*, chapter 3, p. 8, Adm. 178/133.

55 *The Fleet*, October 1925, p. 159; November 1928, p. 217.

56 *Ibid.*, May 1932, p. 84.

57 Adm. 1/8600/31.

58 *Naval Chronicle*, 31 March 1922.

59 Admiralty Fleet Order 3119, 23 November 1923, Adm. 167/68; *Parliamentary Debates*, 5, vol. CLI, 16 March 1922, cols. 2503–4; vol. CLIII, 10 April 1922, cols. 16–17; 12 April 1922, col. 391.

60 *Parliamentary Debates*, 5, vol. CLXXX, 18 February 1925, cols. 1062–3; 25 February 1925, cols. 1918–19.

61 Report of Committee of Enquiry into Hardships, Plymouth, 22 September 1931, Adm. 116/2891.

62 Report of Commodore, Portsmouth barracks, July 1934, Adm. 116/2891.

63 *The Fleet*, February 1930, p. 21.

64 *Ibid.*, April 1930, p. 63.

65 *Ibid.*, September 1930, p. 169.

66 *Naval Chronicle*, 28 December 1928.

67 *Parliamentary Debates*, 5, vol. CCXLIX, 11 March 1931, col. 1347.

68 *The Fleet*, March 1924, p. 40.

69 Viscount Cunningham of Hyndhope, *A Sailor's Odyssey*, (Hutchinson, 1951), p. 152.

70 Owen, *Insubordination and Mutiny in the Navy*, *op. cit.*, chapter 3, p. 9.

71 *The Fleet*, August 1929, p. 134.

72 Report of Admiral Kelley, 9 November 1931, Adm. 1/8761/240.

73 *Journal of the Royal United Service Institute*, vol. LXXV, No. 498, May 1930, pp. 419–20.

74   Noreen Branson and Margot Heinemann, *Britain in the Nineteen Thirties* (Panther, 1973), p. 19.

75   *Committee on Finance and Industry Report*, Cmd. 3897 (HMSO, 1931).

76   *Committee on National Expenditure Report*, Cmd. 3920 (HMSO, 1931).

77   David Marquand, *Ramsay MacDonald* (Jonathan Cape, 1977), p. 610.

78   *Committee on National Expenditure Report, op. cit.*, p. 39.

79   *Portsmouth Evening News*, 31 July; *Western Morning News*, 1 August; *Daily Worker*, 6 August 1931.

80   *Portsmouth Evening News*, 26 August; *Daily Worker*, 7, 19 August; *Naval Chronicle*, 21, 28 August 1931.

81   *Daily Worker*, 6, 7 August 1931.

82   Admiral Kelly, Report, 9 November 1931, Adm. 1/8761/240.

83   This same point is made in an undated draft of a lecture contained in the Kelly papers. The author is unknown. Kelly Papers, National Maritime Museum; Lieutenant-Commander J. H. Owen, *Insubordination and Mutiny in the Navy, op. cit.*, chapter iv, p. 1, Adm. 178/133.

84   C. R. Benstead, *HMS 'Rodney' at Sea* (Methuen, 1932), p. 169.

85   *The Fleet*, September 1931, p. 169. The letter was signed 'Neutralis' and was apparently written by a seaman in the destroyer HMS *Acasta*.

86   Ernie Trory, *Between the Wars* (Brighton, Crabtree Press, 1974), p. 26; Barry Duncan, *Invergordon '31* (Southampton, Duncan, 1976), p. 13.

87   Director of Naval Intelligence, Final Report, May 1932, Adm. 178/110. This interpretation is supported by Commander Harry Pursey, who was the commander's assistant on the flagship *Hood* at Invergordon. Interview with Pursey, 23 January 1974. See also his chronological account of events at Invergordon, 'Invergordon, first hand – last word?', *Naval Review*, vol. 64, April 1976, pp. 157–64.

88   *Naval Chronicle*, 10 July, 21 August 1931.

89   *Western Morning News*, 27 October 1923, 21 September 1931.

90   Pursey was told this by Hall. Letter to author, 14 August 1973. That Falle was oblivious to the danger (apparently he did not expect any action on the May proposals) was indicated by his agent, Jimmy Lane, to Stephen Hill at a meeting on 10 September 1931, Interview with ex-CPO Hill, 9 August 1973.

91   Director of Naval Intelligence, Final Report, May 1932, *op. cit.*

92   *Ibid.* Later, under questioning by Naval Intelligence, he did not disclose his source of information, and Intelligence concluded that he was working from a hunch.

93   *Daily Express*, 5 September 1931.

94   Benstead, *HMS 'Rodney' at Sea, op. cit.*, p. 168; see also report of Captain R. M. Bellairs, 12–16, 18 September 1931, Kelly Papers, National Maritime Museum. All the captains' reports covering the

mutiny are contained in the Kelly papers.

95   *Reductions in National Expenditure*, Cmd. 3952 (HMSO, 1931).

96   Report of Captain A. J. Power, 18 September 1931, Kelly Papers.

97   *Daily Express*, 11 September 1931.

98   *Scottish Daily Record*, 11 September 1931.

99   *Daily Mirror*, 11 September 1931.

100 The English and Scottish Police Councils on which the policemen
     were represented had prevailed on the government to modify the May
     proposals. *Reductions in National Expenditure, op. cit.*, p. 7. Ratings
     were later to contrast the impotence of the Admiralty in resisting the
     committee's recommendations with the police's rather more effective
     safeguarding of their own self interest.

101 *The Fleet*, October 1931, p. 197.

102 Owen, *Insubordination and Mutiny in the Navy, op. cit.*, chapter iv, p.
     3.

103 Ex-Chief Yeoman of Signals Roland Purvis, then eighteen years of
     age, recalls that he could not count the number of times he was told,
     'Push off, sonny – this is nothing to do with you!' Letter of 8 May
     1973; C-in-C, Mediterranean Fleet, to Admiralty, 8 February 1933,
     Adm. 1/8769/127.

104 Barry Duncan, letter to *Tribune*, 30 August 1974; Len Wincott, *The
     Spirit of Invergordon* (International Labour Defence, 1931). Wincott
     now admits that he did not write the pamphlet and may not have read
     it before it was published. Interview, 24 July 1974.

105 Henry Pelling, *The British Communist Party* (A. & C. Black, 1958),
     p. 67.

106 Letter to author, 14 August 1974. The same point is made by George
     Day, who was prominent among the mutineers in the *Valiant*.
     Interview, August 1976. Many of the men who played a leading role in
     the mutiny on other ships had never heard of Wincott, and even in his
     own ship he was not universally known. For a more detailed account
     of the mutiny as it affected the lower deck and of the different claims
     to leadership see Anthony Carew, 'The Invergordon mutiny: long-
     term causes, organisation and leadership', *International Review of
     Social History*, vol. XXIII, 1979, part 2, pp. 157–88.

107 The following section dealing with events on board ship is based on the
     reports of the various ships' captains except where stated.

108 Director of Naval Intelligence, Final Report, May 1932, *op. cit.*

109 Interview with Commander Rodger, November 1974.

110 Interview with Copeman, 25 January 1974.

111 Admiralty telephone message to the King, 2.25 p.m., 16 September
     1931, Geo. V K 2330(3)/6.

122 Drage, *Diary*, 16 September 1931.

113 *Parliamentary Debates*, 5, vol. CCLVI, 17 September 1931, col. 1120.

114 C-in-C, Portsmouth, memorandum to Admiralty, 21 August 1931,
     Adm. 178/113; MI5, memorandum to Director of Naval Intelligence,
     6 November 1931, Adm. 178/80.

115   Sam Bassett, *Royal Marine* (Peter Davies, 1962), p. 101.

116   Director of Naval Intelligence, Final Report, May 1932, *op. cit.*, enclosure 3. There were twelve intelligence agents operating in Plymouth, and in addition the Chief Constable at Plymouth put 'practically his entire detective staff at our [i.e. MI5's] disposal from 18 September–9 October from 6 a.m.–midnight'. Head of MI5, minute, 9 November 1931, Adm. 178/111.

117   Bassett, *Royal Marine, op. cit.*, p. 111.

118   C-in-C, Devonport, telegram to Admiralty, 19 September 1931, Adm. 178/129.

119   It was not disclosed whether the signal was visual or made by wireless or who intercepted it. It is perhaps significant too that among the Admiralty's list of principal agitators there were no communications ratings from *Rodney* or *Nelson*. Presumably none of them was under suspicion.

120   Bassett, *Royal Marine, op. cit.*, p. 111.

121   Minutes of Cabinet Meeting, 21 September 1931, Cab. 23/68; Sir Maurice Hankey's notes of the Cabinet discussion, Cab. 23/90B; Draft of Admiralty Narrative of Events, October 1931, Adm. 178/110. In the final version of the narrative, which was sent to the King, the speculation as to what might have happened if the cuts remained unchanged was omitted.

122   C-in-C, Devonport, telegram to Admiralty, 20 September 1931, Adm. 178/129.

123   *Portsmouth Evening News, Western Morning News,* 21 September 1931. However, the nervousness of the authorities seems to have extended throughout the service during that weekend. At Portsmouth barracks, where rumours of unrest had been heard all week, the chaplain, the Rev. Fulljames, was told at the last minute to change the subject of his sermon for the Sunday service when the commodore heard that it was to be on the theme of 'sacrifice'. Gordon Taylor, *The Sea Chaplains* (Oxford, Oxford Illustrated Press, 1978), pp. 370–1.

124   Deputy Chief of Naval Staff, memorandum, 30 September 1931, *op. cit.*

125   Interviews with Copeman, 25 January 1974; Wincott, 24 July 1974. Copeman later became a member of the national executive of the Communist Party, and Wincott was sent by the Comintern to help run a seamen's mission in Leningrad.

126   Admiralty Fleet Order 2737, 20 November 1931, Adm. 182/61. There were many RAOB lodges in ships at this time, and meetings on board were routine. Ex-Chief Telegraphist C. Beecroft, who was a regular attender at lodge meetings in *Valiant*, and who was at Invergordon, is quite certain that nothing other than RAOB business was ever discussed at these meetings and that there were no effective links between lodge members in different ships. Letter to author, 11 July 1976. The RAOB remains a proscribed organisation aboard HM ships despite numerous attempts by the Order to have the ban lifted. Grand

Secretary, RAOB, to author, 1 November 1973.

127   Notes of Meeting between Fourth Sea Lord, Director of Naval Intelligence and MI5 agents, 15 October 1931; Director of Naval Intelligence, minute, 13 October 1931, Adm. 178/114; Final Report, May 1932, *op. cit.*

128   *Parliamentary Debates*, 5, vol. CCLIX, 12 November 1931, col. 270. In fact dismissed SNLR does not officially rate as a punishment and does not require a court martial. As such it is a convenient means of getting rid of undesirables.

129   Admiral Field to Admiral Beatty, 28 September 1931, Beatty Papers.

130   Notes of Meeting, 15 October 1931, *op. cit.*

131   Two of the most voluble and widely known activists at Invergordon, George Day and Fred Copeman, could not identify any of the supposed leaders on other ships. Interviews with Copeman, 25 January 1974; Day, August 1976.

132   Invergordon Incident, September 1931, Adm. 178/112.

133   Director of Naval Intelligence, minute, 29 September 1931, Adm. 178/80.

134   Secretary to the Board of Admiralty to First Lord, 15 October 1931, Adm. 178/114; Notes of Meeting, 15 October 1931, *op. cit.*

135   First Lord of the Admiralty, memorandum to First Sea Lord, 13 October 1931, Adm. 178/114; Board of Admiralty Minute 2860, 17 October 1931, Adm. 167/83.

136   Kelly, Report, 9 November 1931; Geo. V K 2330(3)/43.

137   Director of Naval Intelligence, minute, 11 November 1931, Adm. 178/112.

138   *Naval Chronicle*, 9, 23 October, 27 November 1931; *Portsmouth Evening News*, 24 October, 2 November 1931. For a more detailed analysis of this case see F. W. Chandler, *Political Spies and Provocative Agents* (Sheffield, Chandler, second edition, 1936), pp. 120–7.

139   Director of Naval Intelligence, Final Report, May 1932, *op. cit.*; Board of Admiralty Minute 2974, 30 June 1932, Adm. 167/85. Captain S. Roskill, who was later to become Depty Director of Naval Intelligence, maintains that agents were employed in the Navy at the time of Invergordon and after. Letter to author, 12 August 1976.

140   Director of Naval Intelligence, minute, 10 May 1932, Adm. 1/8757/181.

141   Director of Naval Intelligence, minute, 11 November 1931, Adm. 178/112; also Adm. 178/151.

142   NL 4085/31, 8 December 1931, Adm. 178/112.

143   Undated memorandum, Insubordination of Ships of Atlantic Fleet, Adm. 178/149.

144   Economic League to Admiralty, 30 May 1932; Admiralty to Economic League, 7 June 1932, Adm. 178/113; interview with Copeman, 25 January 1975.

145   Secretary to the Board of Admiralty, minute, 9 May 1933, Adm.

178/133.

146   Deputy Chief of Naval Staff, minute, February 1932, Adm. 1/8747/87.

147   Secretary to the Board of Admiralty, minute, 11 February 1932, Adm. 1/8747/87.

148   Deputy Chief of Naval Staff, minute, February 1932, *op. cit.*

149   Report of Proceedings, 11–16 September 1931, Senior Officer Atlantic Fleet, 24 September 1931, Kelly Papers.

150   John Bush, 'Invergordon 1931', unpublished poems.

NINE
The end of collective representation

1   Commander-in-Chief, Mediterranean, to Admiralty, 6 February 1933; Fourth Sea Lord, memorandum to First Sea Lord, 17 February 1933, Adm. 1/8769/127.

2   Cabinet Minutes, 22 February 1933, Cab. 23/75.

3   Men who entered the service before October 1921 were paid 1919 rates less 10 per cent and 1919 pensions. Men who joined between October 1921 and October 1925 were paid 1919 rates less 10 per cent, but after re-engagement went on to 1925 rates of pay and 1930 pensions. Men who joined between October 1925 and April 1930 were paid on 1925 rates; their pension for the first period was calculated on the 1919 scale and for their second ten years on the 1930 scale. Lastly, men who joined after April 1930 were paid on the 1925 rates, with their pension calculated on the 1930 scale. Fourth Sea Lord, memorandum, 16 January 1934, Adm. 167/91.

4   Fourth Sea Lord, memorandum to First Sea Lord, 17 February 1933, *op. cit.*; Secretary to the Board of Admiralty, minute, December 1932, Adm. 1/8769/127; First Lord to Chancellor of Exchequer, 12 March 1924, Adm. 167/70.

5   Admiral Kelly to Admiralty, 14 December 1932, Adm. 1/8769/127.

6   Summary of views of commanders-in-chief, Home Ports, January 1933, Adm. 167/89.

7   Fourth Sea Lord, memorandum, 16 January 1934, *op. cit.*

8   Secretary to the Board, memorandum, 14 March 1934, Adm. 116/2891; *The Fleet*, October 1936, p. 201; April 1938, p. 68.

9   *Parliamentary Debates*, 5, vol. CCCXXIII, 28 April 1937, col. 323.

10   Estimate based on a report by Colonel Harry Day, MP, that there were then 1,700 such men. *Answers*, 3 September 1938.

11   Commander-in-Chief, Mediterranean, to Admiralty, 11 December 1931, Adm. 116/3611.

12   RNBT Central Committee Minutes, 31 May 1935.

13   Replying to a suggestion from his private secretary that such expenditure would be seriously criticised, Lord Stanhope, the First Lord, explained, 'I don't think that we can go back on this now [. . .] the King is *very* strongly in favour of it.' First Lord, minute, undated

(August) 1938, Adm. 167/105.

14 Board of Admiralty Minute 3519, 3 February 1938, Adm. 167/100;
    Board of Admiralty Minute 3620, 24 February 1939, *op. cit.*

15 Sea Lords' memorandum, 8 May 1939, Adm. 167/104.

16 Lieutenant J. D. Dwyer, *A History of the Royal Naval Barracks
    Portsmouth, op. cit.*, pp. 50–1; *The Fleet*, March 1932, pp. 34–5;
    February 1934, p. 18; *Naval Chronicle*, 27 May 1932; Frank O'Brien
    Adams, 'A full life', MS collection of the University Library,
    Southampton, No. A233.

17 *The Fleet*, July 1933, p. 110.

18 *Daily Express*, 31 January 1933.

19 Fourth Sea Lord, memorandum to First Sea Lord, 17 February 1933,
    op. cit.

20 Secretary to the Fourth Sea Lord, minute, 2 March 1933, Adm.
    1/8769/127.

21 Commander-in-Chief, Mediterranean, to Admiralty, 6 February 1933,
    op. cit.; Bassett, *Royal Marine, op. cit.*, p. 123.

22 *The Fleet*, May 1934, p. 80; May 1935, p. 71; Admiralty Fleet Order
    1200, 9 May 1935, Adm. 182/69.

23 Roskill, *Naval Policy between the Wars*, vol. II, *op. cit.*, p. 240.

24 *The Fleet*, October 1935, p. 164.

25 Appendix E to Report on Shortage of Artificer Applicants in Glasgow
    Area, Glasgow Recruiting Staff Officer, 21 August 1936, Adm. 167/95.

26 Roskill, *Naval Policy between the Wars*, vol. II, *op. cit.*, p. 241.

27 Committee of Imperial Defence, Progress Report 21, March 1938,
    Adm. 167/102.

28 'The Admiralty Review of Service Conditions', *Naval Review*, vol.
    XXV, No. 1, February 1937, p. 93.

29 Board of Admiralty Minute 3067, 6 April 1933, Adm. 167/88; *The
    Fleet*, October 1935, p. 164.

30 Kelly Report, 9 November 1931, *op. cit.*

31 *Ibid.* Whenever lower-deck unrest surfaced the Admiralty's reaction
    was to examine the relationship between petty officers and men and to
    search for ways of distancing the two groups in the interests of stronger
    discipline. The last time the issue had arisen was after the trouble in the
    Baltic in 1919, when it was first suggested that, on promotion to petty
    officer, men should be drafted to another ship and away from their
    former messmates. Secretary to the Board of Admiralty, memorandum,
    18 June 1920, Adm. 167/62.

32 Viscount Cunningham of Hyndhope, *A Sailor's Odyssey, op. cit.*, p.
    151; Rear-Admiral Tovey, transcript of discussion following lecture on
    Mass Indiscipline to War College and Staff College, 8 February 1938,
    Staff College Pack 370/2, Roskill Papers, Churchill College,
    Cambridge.

33 Second and Fourth Sea Lord, memorandum, 26 April 1932, Adm.
    1/8766/88.

34 Adm. 1/8766/88.

35   Adm. 116/3283; Board of Admiralty Minute 2943, 26 May 1932, Adm.
     167/85; Lord Chatfield, *The Navy and Defence*, vol. II (Heinemann,
     1947), p. 54.
36   Admiral Tyrwhitt to Admiralty, 28 January 1932, Adm. 1/8761/240.
37   Board of Admiralty Minute 2834, 11 April 1932, Adm. 167/85.
38   Admiral Cowan to Sir Clive Wigram, 27 September 1931, Royal
     Archives, Geo. V K 2330(3)/17.
39   Wigram to Cowan, 2 October 1931, Royal Archives, Geo. V K
     2330(3)/26; Discipline in the Fleet (notes representing the collective
     views of the senior officers studying at the War College, winter session,
     1931), Staff College Papers, Pack 370/1, Roskill Papers.
40   Admiral Colville to Admiralty, 15 October 1931, Adm. 178/129.
41   Admiral Tyrwhitt to Admiralty, 9 January 1933, Adm. 1/8769/127.
42   HMS *Warspite*, Reports of Unrest on Board, 1937, Adm. 178/190.
43   Incitement to Disobedience in HMS *Guardian*, October 1936, Adm.
     178/180; Fourth Sea Lord, memorandum, 19 August 1937, Adm.
     178/190.
44   Communist Activities by Naval Personnel, Adm. 178/138. The
     Incitement to Mutiny Act already carried a maximum sentence of life
     imprisonment.
45   *Parliamentary Debates*, 5, vol. CCLXXXVIII, 16 April 1934, col. 743.
     If this figure is anywhere near correct it seems likely that the bulk of the
     literature was seized by the authorities. The author has met only two
     ratings who can recall seeing *Red Signal*, and an eight-year hunt has
     failed to turn up a single copy.
46   *Parliamentary Debates*, 5, vol. CCLXXXVIII, 16 April 1934, col. 744.
47   John Gibbons (Communist Party organiser) to author, 16 August
     1976. Gibbons's point is confirmed by George Aitken, the person
     responsible for co-ordinating the CP campaign against the Incitement
     to Disaffection Act. Letter to author, 9 August 1976.
48   Secretary to the Board of Admiralty, minute, 10 January 1931; Head
     of Naval Law Branch, minute, 13 January 1931, Adm. 178/109.
49   NL 1201/32, 12 August 1932; Roskill, *Naval Policy between the Wars*,
     vol. II, *op. cit.*, pp. 344–5.
50   For specimens of such forms see Adm. 178/191.
51   Communist Activities by Naval Personnel, Adm. 178/138.
52   Roskill, *Naval Policy between the Wars*, vol. II, *op. cit.*, p. 281.
53   Board of Admiralty meeting, 28 July 1932, Adm. 116/3748.
54   Admiral Kelly to Admiralty, 19 July 1933, Adm. 116/3748.
55   Second Sea Lord, minute, 23 October 1934, Adm. 116/3748.
56   Second Sea Lord, memorandum, No. 1073/1934, Adm. 167/91.
57   Director of Personal Services, minute, 17 November 1933, Adm.
     116/3748.
58   *Naval Chronicle*, 9 December 1932.
59   Secretary to Board of Admiralty, minute, 18 October 1934, Adm.
     167/91.
60   Admiral Chatfield, minute, 6 November 1934, Adm. 116/3748.

61 Admiral Kelly to Admiralty, 19 July 1933, *op. cit.*
62 Second Sea Lord, memorandum, No. 1073/1934, *op. cit.*
63 Head of Naval Law Branch, minute, 15 August 1933, Adm. 116/3748.
64 Second Sea Lord, memorandum, No. 1073/1934, *op. cit.*
65 Admiralty Fleet Order 2226, 23 September 1932, Adm. 182/63.
66 Admiralty Fleet Order 1672, 4 July 1935, Adm. 182/69.
67 Head of Naval Law Branch, minute, 19 December 1932, Adm. 116/3748.
68 Second Sea Lord, memorandum, No. 1073/1934, *op. cit.*
69 Second Sea Lord, minute, 25 January 1935, Adm. 116/3748.
70 Secretary to the Board of Admiralty, minute, 18 October 1934, Adm. 116/3748.
71 *Naval Chronicle*, 9 December 1932.
72 Minute (author unknown), 16 December 1936, Adm. 116/3748.
73 Adm. 116/3748; *The Fleet*, April 1937, pp. 67–8; August, p. 173.
74 *The Fleet*, April 1937, pp. 65–8.
75 Secretary to the Board of Admiralty, memorandum, 16 November 1938, Adm. 167/101.
76 *Ibid.*
77 *Ibid.*
78 *Naval Chronicle*, 28 January 1938.
79 *The Fleet*, July 1938, p. 124; July 1939, p. 102.
80 First Sea Lord, minute, 10 November 1938, Adm. 167/101.
81 *Ibid.*

TEN
The lower-deck movement in perspective

1 Charles Thomas did not survive the war. He was lost at sea in April 1942 when HMS *Hermes* was sunk off Ceylon.
2 *Daily Chronicle*, 7 September 1912.
3 Allen, 'The National Union of Police and Prison Officers', *op. cit.*, pp. 133–4.
4 Helger Herwig, *The German Naval Officer Corps* (London, Oxford University Press, 1975), pp. 142–67, 211, 264.
5 Frederick Harrod, *Manning the new Navy* (Westport, Conn., Greenwood Press, 1978), pp. 64, 101, 159.
6 Allen 'The National Union of Police and Prison Officers', *op. cit.*, pp. 136–7.
7 John Horner, *Studies in Industrial Democracy* (Gollancz, 1974), pp. 165–7.
8 Richard Hyman, in foreword to Carter Goodrich, *The Frontier of Control* (Pluto Press, 1975), pp. xvii–xx.
9 Allen 'The National Union of Police and Prison Officers', *op. cit.*, pp. 137–41.
10 After Invergordon the Board of Admiralty actually learned that under the Letters Patent of appointment it did have the right to fix rates of pay

and emoluments without an Order in Council, but on the advice of the Treasury Solicitor it decided not to test this right. Board of Admiralty Minute 3095, 13 July 1933; Minute 3098, 27 July 1933, Adm. 167/88.

11   *The Fleet*, March 1929, p. 45.
12   Robert Reiner, *The Blue-coated Worker* (Cambridge University Press, 1978), pp. 26–8; Anthony Judge, *The First Fifty Years* (Police Federation, 1968), pp. 29–32.
13   Lewis Clive, *The People's Army, op. cit.*, p. 10.
14   National Executive Committee, *Labour and Defence* (Labour Party, 1939), pp. 1, 9.
15   The Prime Minister, *The Government's Plans for 1946–47; the King's Speech* (Labour Party, 1945), p. 13.
16   David Cortright, *Military Unions of Europe: Report to the American Federation of Government Employees* (mimeographed), p. 5. The AFGE in 1975 was considering launching a major recruiting drive among United States servicemen. For more on armed forces unionism in Western Europe see M. Klepsch, *Conditions of Service in the Armed Forces: Report submitted on behalf of the Committee on Defence Questions and Armaments*, Assembly of Western European Union, Twentieth Ordinary Session (Second Part), Document 650; J. E. Kane *et al.*, 'Is military unionism an idea whose time has come?' *United States Naval Insitutute Proceedings*, vol. 102, November 1976, pp. 36–44.
17   Reiner, *The Blue-coated Worker, op. cit.*, p. 28.
18   Preface to A. Cecil Hampshire, *The Royal Navy since 1945* (Kimber, 1975), pp. xi–xii.

Bibliography

DOCUMENTS

Unpublished

British government archives available at the Public Record Office, London, include Cabinet papers and minutes in categories Cab. 23 and 24 and Admiralty records in categories Adm. 1, 12, 53, 116, 167, 178 and 182.
Annual returns of Friendly Societies, available at the office of the Registrar of Friendly Societies.

Admiralty reports
Report of the Committee on Naval Cookery, 1905, Pursey Collection
Report of the Committee on Naval Discipline, 1912
Returns of Court Martial Punishments, Admiralty Library

Private collections
King George V Papers, Royal Archives, Windsor
Yexley Papers, Capper Papers, Reynolds Papers, Commander Harry Pursey, RN, Collection
Fisher Papers, National Library of Scotland
Churchill Papers, McKenna Papers, Alexander Papers, Roskill Papers, Tomkinson Papers, Churchill College, Cambridge
Beatty Papers, Mrs Nutting Collection
Battenberg Papers, Mountbatten Collection
Kelly Papers, Dewar Papers, Cowan Papers, Hamilton Papers, Fremantle Papers, Chatfield Papers, National Maritime Museum
Henderson Papers, Imperial War Museum
PO Telegraphist Charles Thomas Papers, Mr Robert Thomas Collection
Commander Charles Drage, Diary, Drage Collection
Royal Marine Private George Davies, Diary, Mrs Pickering Collection

Manuscripts
John Bush, *Big Ship Navy*

Len Fagg, *A Man of Kent*
Frank O'Brien Adams, *A Full Life*, University of Southampton, Library
Rear-Admiral R. D. Oliver, *Recollections*, Oliver Papers, National Maritime
  Museum

Thesis
J. D. Osborne, *Stephen Reynolds: a biographical and critical study*
  (University of London, 1978)

Other
Transcripts of Lower-deck Oral History Programme, Sound Archives,
  Imperial War Museum
Records of the Royal Naval Benevolent Trust

Published

Report of the Committee on Navy Rations, 1901, Cd. 782
A Statement of Admiralty Policy, 1905, Cd. 2791.
Report of Committee on Civil Employment of ex-Soldiers and Sailors, 1906,
  Cd. 2991.
Report of the Committee on Canteen and Victualling Arrangements, 1907,
  Cd. 3703.
Jerram Report, 1919, Cmd. 149.
Committee on Pay, etc, of State Servants, 1923
Committee on National Expenditure Report, 1931, Cmd. 3920.
Reductions in National Expenditure, 1931, Cmd. 3952

OTHER PUBLISHED WORKS

Newspapers and periodicals

*Army and Navy Gazette, The Bluejacket, Brassey's Naval Annual, Civil
Liberty, Clarion, Daily Chronicle, Daily Express, Daily Graphic, Daily
Herald, Daily Leader, Daily Mail, Daily News, Daily Worker, The Fleet,
The Fleet Annual and Naval Year Book, Hampshire Telegraph and Naval
Chronicle, Illustrated Daily Mirror, Justice, Journal of the Royal United
Service Institute, Labour Leader, Morning Post, Naval and Military
Record, Naval Engineering Review, Naval Review, Naval Warrant Officers'
Journal, Navy and Army Illustrated, New Fabian Review Quarterly
Bulletin, New Statesman, Nineteenth Century, The Observer, Pall Mall
Gazette, The People, Portsmouth Evening News, Reynolds's Newspaper,
Sunday Times, The Times, Truth, United Service Gazette, United Service
Magazine, Vanity Fair, Weekly Dispatch, Western Daily Mercury, Western
Morning News, Workers' Weekly.*

Articles

Allen, V. L., 'The National Union of Police and Prison Officers', *Economic History Review*, vol. XI, No. 1 (1958), pp. 133–43.

Kane, J. E., *et. al.*, 'Is military unionism an idea whose time has come?' *United States Naval Institute Proceedings*, vol. 102 (November, 1976), pp. 36–44.

Pursey, H., 'From petitions to reviews: the presentation of lower-deck grievances', *Brassey's Naval Annual* (1937), pp. 97–110.

—— 'Lower deck to quarter deck, 1818–1937', *Brassey's Naval Annual* (1938), pp. 87–105.

—— 'The making of a seaman', *Brassey's Naval Annual* (1939), pp. 127–46.

Reynolds, S., 'Ships versus men in the Navy', *English Review*, vol. XII (September 1912), pp. 281–99.

Somerville, Rear-Admiral J. F., 'The lower deck, past and present', parts I and II, *Journal of the Royal United Service Institute*, vol. LXXXI, Nos. 521–2 (February–May 1936), pp. 109–25, 303–13.

Ward, S. R., 'Intelligence surveillance of British ex-servicemen, 1918–20', *Historical Journal*, vol. XVI, No. 1 (1973), pp. 179–88.

White, A., 'The food of the lower deck and a message from Kiel', *National Review*, vol. XXXIX (July 1902), pp. 720–41.

Yexley, L., 'The pay of the Navy', *English Review*, vol. XXIV (March 1917), pp. 243–50.

Books

Altham, E., *Jellicoe* (Blackie & Sons, 1938)

Arbuthnot, R. K., *A Battleship Commander's Order Book* (J. Griffin & Co., 1899)

Aspinall-Oglander, C., *Roger Keyes: the Biography of Ad. Lord Keyes of Zeebrugge and Dover* (Hogarth, 1951)

Barnett, C., *Britain and her Army, 1509–1970* (Harmondsworth, Penguin, 1974)

Bassett, S., *Royal Marine* (Peter Davies, 1962)

Baynham, H., *From the Lower Deck, 1780–1840* (Hutchinson, 1969)

—— *Men from the Dreadnoughts* (Hutchinson, 1976)

Bennett, G., *Charlie B* (Peter Dawnay, 1968)

Benstead, C. R., *HMS Rodney at Sea* (Methuen, 1932)

Beresford, Lord Charles, *Memoirs* (Methuen, 1914)

Boldero, H., *A Young Heart of Oak* (Hodder & Stoughton, 1892)

Bonnett, S., *The Price of Admiralty* (Robert Hale, 1968)

Branson, N., and Heinemann, M., *Britain in the Nineteen Thirties* (Panther, 1973)

Brown, E. H. Phelps, *The Growth of British Industrial Relations* (Macmillan, 1965)

Butler, J., *Personal Reminiscences of a Great Crusade* (Horace Marshall & Son, 1896)

Calhoun, D. F., *The United Front* (Cambridge University Press, 1976)

Capper, H. D., *Aft—from the Hawsehole* (Faber & Gwyer, 1927)

Chalmers, Rear-Admiral W. S., *The Life and Letters of David Beatty – Admiral of the Fleet* (Hodder & Stoughton, 1951)

Chandler, F. W., *Political Spies and Provocative Agents* (Sheffield, F. W. Chandler, 1936)

Charles, R., *The Development of Industrial Relations in Britain, 1911–39* (Hutchinson, 1973)

Chatfield, Lord, *The Navy and Defence*, vols. I and II (Heinemann, 1942–47)

Churchill, R., *Winston S. Churchill*, Companion Vol. II, part 3, 1911–14 (Heinemann, 1969)

Clegg, H., *The System of Industrial Relations in Great Britain* (Totowa, N.J., Rowman & Littlefield, 1972)

Clive, L., *The People's Army* (Gollancz, 1938.)

Clowes, Sir W. Laird, *The Royal Navy*, vol. VII (Sampson Low, 1903)

Cole, G. D. H., and Postgate, R., *The Common People* (Methuen, 1949)

Copeman, F., *Reason in Revolt* (Blandford Press, 1948)

Cortright, D., *Soldiers in Revolt* (Garden City, N.Y., Anchor Press/Doubleday, 1975)

—— *Military Unions of Europe: Report to the American Federation of Government Employees* (1975, mimeographed)

Cradock, G., *Whispers from the Fleet* (J. Griffin & Co., 1908)

Crowe, G., *The Commission of HMS Terrible* (George Newnes, 1903)

Cunningham of Hyndhope, Viscount, *A Sailor's Odyssey* (Hutchinson, 1951)

Dewar, K. G. B., *The Navy from Within* (Gollancz, 1939)

Divine, D., *Mutiny at Invergordon* (Macdonald, 1970)

Dougan, D., *The Shipwrights* (Newcastle upon Tyne, Frank Graham, 1975)

Duncan, B., *Invergordon '31* (Southampton, Duncan, 1976)

Dwyer, Lieutenant J. D., *A History of the Royal Naval Barracks Portsmouth* (Portsmouth, Gale & Polden, 1961)

Edwards, K., *The Mutiny at Invergordon* (Putnam, 1937)

Edwards, A. T., *British Bluejacket, 1915–1940* (Simpkin Marshall, 1940)

Fabb, J., and McGowern, A. C., *The Victorian and Edwardian Navy* (Batsford, 1976)

Fremantle, Admiral Sir Sydney, *My Naval Career, 1880–1928* (Hutchinson, 1949)

Gardiner, L., *The Royal Oak Courts Martial* (Blackwood, 1965)

Goodrich, C., *The Frontier of Control* (Pluto Press, 1975)

Grenfell, R., *The men who defend us* (Eyre & Spottiswoode, 1938)

—— *Service Pay* (Eyre & Spottiswoode, 1944)

Gretton, Vice-Admiral Sir Peter, *Former Naval Person* (Cassell & Co., 1968)

Hamer, W. S., *The British Army: Civil–Military Relations, 1885–1905* (Oxford, Clarendon Press, 1970)

Hampshire, A. C., *The Royal Navy since 1945* (William Kimber, 1975)

Hanbidge, L., *W. Stoddard: a Biographical Sketch* (Westminster Press, 1930)

Harrod, F., *Manning the new Navy* (Westport, Conn., Greenwood Press, 1978)

Herwig, H., *The German Naval Officer Corps* (Oxford University Press, 1975)

Hewitt, T., *From Dark to Dawn in the King's Navy* (Portsmouth, W. H. Barrell, 1930)

Higham, R., *A Guide to the Sources of British Military History* (Routledge & Kegan Paul, 1972)

Hislam, P., *The Navy of Today* (T. C. & E. C. Jack, 1914)

History of the Ships' Stewards' Society (RN Stores Branch Benevolent Society, 1972, mimeographed)

Horn, D. (ed.), *War, Mutiny and Revolution in the German Navy: the World War I Diary of Seaman Richard Stumpf* (New Brunswick, N.J., Rutgers University Press, 1967)

—— *The German Naval Mutinies of World War I* (New Brunswick, N.J., Rutgers University Press, 1969)

Horner, J., *Studies in Industrial Democracy* (Gollancz, 1974)

Hough, R., *Louis and Victoria* (Hutchinson, 1974)

Hyman, R., *The Workers' Union* (Oxford, Clarendon Press, 1971)

Irving, Lieutenant-Commander J., *Naval Life and Customs* (Altrincham, Sherratt & Hughes, 1946)

James, R. R., *Memoirs of a Conservative: J. C. C. Davidson's Memoirs and Papers, 1910–1937* (Weidenfeld & Nicolson, 1969)

James, Sir William, *The Sky was always Blue* (Methuen, 1951)

—— *The Eyes of the Navy: a Biographical Study of Admiral Sir Reginald Hall* (Methuen, 1955)

Jubilee History (Portsmouth, Writers' Society, 1937)

Judge, A., *The First Fifty Years* (Police Federation, 1968)

Kennedy, P. M., *The Rise and Fall of British Naval Mastery* (Allen Lane, 1976)

Keyes, Sir Roger, *Naval Memoirs, 1910–15* (Thornton Butterworth, 1935)

Klepsch, *Conditions of Service in the Armed Forces: Report submitted on behalf of the Committee on Defence Questions and Armaments* (Assembly of the Western European Union, Twentieth Ordinary Session (Second Part), Document 650)

Knock, S., *Clear Lower Deck* (Philip Allan, 1933)

Labour and Defence (Labour Party, 1939)

Lamb, D., *Mutinies: 1917–1920* (Solidarity, 1977)

Lewis, M., *The History of the British Navy* (Allen & Unwin, 1959)

—— *A Social History of the Navy, 1793–1815* (Allen & Unwin, 1960)

—— *The Navy in Transition* (Hodder & Stoughton, 1965)

Lloyd, C., *The British Seaman* (Collins, 1968)

Lyne, Rear-Admiral Sir Thomas, *Something about a Sailor* (Jarrolds, 1940)

Mackay, R. F., *Fisher of Kilverstone* (Oxford, Clarendon Press, 1973)

Manwaring, G. E., and Dobree, B., *The Floating Republic* (Penguin, 1937)

Marder, A. (ed.), *Fear God and Dread Nought: the Correspondence of Admiral of the Fleet Lord Fisher of Kilverstone* (Jonathan Cape, 1952)
—— *From Dreadnought to Scapa Flow: the Royal Navy in the Fisher Era, 1904–1919*, 5 vols. (Oxford University Press, 1961–70)
—— *Winston is back: Churchill at the Admiralty, 1939–40* (Longman, 1972)
Marquand, D., *Ramsay MacDonald* (Jonathan Cape, 1977)
Millington, E. C., *Seamen in the Making* (J. D. Potter, 1935)
Murray, Lady, *The Making of a Civil Servant: Sir Oswyn Murray*, (Methuen, 1940)
'Naval Officers', *White Ensign* (Roy & Co., 1896)
Noble, AB Sam, *An Autobiography* (Sampson Low, 1925)
Nowell-Smith, S. (ed.), *Edwardian England, 1910–1914* (Oxford University Press, 1964)
O'Connor, R., *Running a big Ship on 'Ten Commandments'* (Portsmouth, Gieves, 1937)
Patterson, A. T., *Jellicoe* (Macmillan, 1969)
Pelling, H., *The British Communist Party* (Adam & Charles Black, 1958)
Poore, Lady, *Recollections of an Admiral's Wife, 1903–1916* (Smith Elder & Co., 1916)
Rawson, G., *Beatty* (Philip Allan, 1936)
Reiner, R., *The Blue-coated Worker* (Cambridge University Press, 1978)
Reynolds, S., *The Lower Deck, the Navy and the Nation* (Dent, 1912)
Reynolds, S., and Woolley, B. and T., *Seems so!* (Macmillan, 1911)
Riley, P., *Memories of a Bluejacket* (Sampson Low, 1925)
Robinson, Commander C., *The British Fleet* (George Bell & Son, 1894)
Roskill, S., *Hankey: Man of Secrets*, vols. I and II (Collins, 1970 and 1972)
—— *Naval Policy between the Wars*, vols. I and II (Collins, 1968 and 1976)
—— *Churchill and the Admirals* (Collins, 1977)
Saul, N. E., *Sailors in Reovlt* (Lawrence, Kansas, The Regents Press of Kansas, 1978)
Scott, Sir Percy, *Fifty Years in the Royal Navy* (Robert Murray, 1919)
Skelley, A., *The Victorian Army at Home* (Croom Helm, 1977)
Taylor, G., *The Sea Chaplains* (Oxford, Oxford Illustrated Press, 1978)
Tillet, B., *Memories and Reflections* (John Long, 1931)
Thomson, B., *Queer People* (Hodder & Stoughton, 1922)
—— *The Scene Changes* (Collins, 1939)
Turnbull, A., *The Victualling of the Royal Navy: Past, Present and Future* (Elliot Stock, 1903)
Walker, Sir Charles, *Thirty-four Years in the Admiralty* (Lincoln Williams, 1934)
Warner, O., *Cunningham of Hyndhope: Admiral of the Fleet* (John Murray, 1967)
Wemyss, Lady Wester, *The Life and Letters of Lord Wester Wemyss* (Eyre & Spottiswoode, 1935)
Weston, Dame Agnes, *My Life among the Blue-jackets* (Nisbet, 1918)
Wincott, L., *Invergordon Mutineer* (Weidenfeld & Nicolson, 1974)

Winton, J., *Hurrah for the Life of a Sailor: Life on the Lower Deck of the Victorian Navy* (Michael Joseph, 1977)

Wintringham, T., *Mutiny* (Stanley Nott, 1936)

—— *Freedom is our Weapon: a Policy for Army Reform* (Kegan Paul & Co., 1941)

White, A., *The Navy and its Story* (Macdonald & Evans, 1911)

White, A., and Hallam Moorhouse, E., *Nelson and the Twentieth Century* (Cassell, 1905)

Wootton, G., *The Official History of the British Legion* (Macdonald & Evans, 1956)

—— *The Politics of Influence* (Routledge & Kegan Paul, 1963)

Yexley, L., *The Inner Life of the Navy* (Pitman, 1908)

—— *Our Fighting Sea Men* (Stanley Paul & Co., 1911)

—— *The British Navy from Within* (Hodder & Stoughton, 1914)

Index